Challenging Cosmopolitanism

Challenging Cosmopolitanism

Coercion, Mobility and Displacement in Islamic Asia

Edited by
Joshua Gedacht and R. Michael Feener

EDINBURGH
University Press

Edinburgh University Press is one of the leading university presses in the UK. We publish academic books and journals in our selected subject areas across the humanities and social sciences, combining cutting-edge scholarship with high editorial and production values to produce academic works of lasting importance. For more information visit our website: edinburghuniversitypress.com

Edinburgh University Press Ltd
The Tun – Holyrood Road
12 (2f) Jackson's Entry
Edinburgh EH8 8PJ

First published in hardback by Edinburgh University Press 2018

Typeset in 11/15 Adobe Garamond by
Servis Filmsetting Ltd, Stockport, Cheshire

A CIP record for this book is available from the British Library
ISBN 978 1 4744 3509 3 (hardback)
ISBN 978 1 4744 3510 9 (paperback)
ISBN 978 1 4744 3511 6 (webready PDF)
ISBN 978 1 4744 3512 3 (epub)

Contents

Preface

'Cosmopolitanism' has come to be an ubiquitous category of scholarly analysis in discussions of the dynamic histories and cultures of Muslim peoples in many parts of the world. In particular, the term has come to stand for a vision of community that extends beyond the particularistic limitations of kinship, ethnicity or nation to encompass an '*ummatic*' or even more 'humanistic' vision of inclusivity and acceptance. Such visions, in turn, usually encompass a vast complex of attributes: of diversity, religious pluralism, and openness to others; of mobility and travel; and of yearning for a universal community of faith that can transcend the mundane boundaries of everyday life. Many historians, anthropologists and religious studies scholars have deployed the concept of cosmopolitanism to frame discussions of topics such as the circulation of Muslim texts, trading diasporas and interactions between members of different religious traditions. Some have used the term more as an adjectival signifier for what they view as 'positive' aspects of Muslim histories, often intending this as a potential corrective to contemporary crises of community and co-existence. In this, cosmopolitanism has often been looked to as an antidote to the plagues of obscurantism, sectarianism and violence that still too often attaches to visions of Muslim societies by contemporary observers outside the tradition. Such discussions have displayed a tendency toward the abstract and the idealised. However, any full accounting of cosmopolitanism requires moving past normative visions toward understandings of the world as it actually was (and is), with all its attendant tensions, dislocations and displacements.

Recent histories have sought to move past more theoretical articulations to understanding the day-to-day struggles that mobility and the interests of state and other powers can produce. Stimulated by this emerging and thought-provoking scholarship, our aim is to challenge cosmopolitanism by focusing on various contexts of coercion across Asia. This volume provides a more complex and nuanced understanding of what cosmopolitanism might look like in historical practice. It includes contributions from historians and anthropologists exploring past dynamics and enduring legacies of coercive dynamics on the production of Muslim cosmopolitanism across diverse Asian contexts, particularly China, Southeast Asia and the Indian Ocean world. Empirical case studies will highlight the way various 'cosmopolitan' Muslims across time, whether intellectuals, artists, Sufi scholars, state officials, rebel leaders, soldiers or traders, wrestled with the challenging dynamics of coercion to forge connections and wider imaginations of communities across space and time. In doing so, this volume highlights the issues of conflict and asymmetric power dynamics involved in the interweaving of state power, Muslim mobility and religious pluralism.

This volume grew out of discussions at the workshop 'Wild Spaces and Islamic Cosmopolitanism in Asia', held at the National University of Singapore's Asia Research Institute (ARI) in January 2015, organised in conjunction with the International Centre for Muslim and Non-Muslim Understanding of the University of South Australia. We are grateful to ARI for their support of this event, without which this work would not have been possible. In putting together this volume, we have greatly benefited from the conversations during the conference with scholars who generously shared their thoughts and questions. We would thus like to extend our thanks to all those who joined the discussions in Singapore, and especially to Faisal Devji, Santhosh Abraham, Seema Alavi, Syed Muhd Khairudin Aljunied, Alexander Arifianto, Jowel Jose Canuday, Vladimir Hamed-Troyansky, Christopher Joll and Julie Nichols. We would also like to thank Valerie Yeo, Sharon Ong, Tay Minghua and Henry Kwan for their help with logistics for the event, and

Adora Elisapeta Jones for her assistance with formatting the manuscript of this volume for publication.

R. Michael Feener
Joshua Gedacht

1

Hijra, *Ḥajj* and Muslim Mobilities: Considering Coercion and Asymmetrical Power Dynamics in Histories of Islamic Cosmopolitanism

R. Michael Feener and Joshua Gedacht

In 750 CE, turmoil and violence engulfed the city of Damascus, then the seat of the Umayyad caliphate. The Arab rulers of the 'first dynasty of Islam'[1] had been challenged by various groups of 'piety-minded' Muslims who asserted that the Umayyad elite had betrayed their responsibilities as successors to the leadership of the Prophet Muḥammad over the community that he had established a century earlier – choosing, as their critics argued, to privilege Arab clan lineage over pious rectitude as the standard of legitimacy.[2] As a result, military forces under the control of the ascendant ʿAbbāsids brought together a coalition of disaffected segments from an increasingly diverse Islamic empire to overthrow the Umayyads. Political and religious authority would subsequently shift, with the ʿAbbāsid family claiming the mantle of caliphal authority and moving their capital out of Damascus to the newly constructed city of Baghdad.

Out of the destruction that befell the Umayyads in Syria, however, one member of the family, ʿAbd al-Raḥmān, managed to survive and flee west across North Africa before crossing the Straits of Gibraltar to the Iberian Peninsula, establishing a new Umayyad caliphate in al-Andalus.[3] Modern scholars have celebrated the cultural achievements of al-Andalus as a 'golden age of Islamic civilization'.[4] María Rosa Menocal, for example, has described the 'cosmopolitan' Andalusian caliphate as one of unparalleled prosperity and openness, as a place where Muslims, Christians and Jews, along with Arabs, Berbers and Europeans, all commingled under the beneficent leadership of the reconstituted Umayyad caliphate.[5] Literary Hebrew flourished anew with distinctive Arabic accents and prosody; Muslim scholars likes Ibn Rushd (d. 1198) studied side by side with legendary Jewish thinkers such as Maimonides (Ar. Mūsā b. Maymūn, d. 1204), cross-pollinating ideas, legal theories and theological precepts. This atmosphere of tolerance, in turn, contributed not only to commercial prosperity and an influx of mobile migrants, but also to an intellectual and artistic flourishing, with a proliferation of books, libraries and palaces like the ornate Alhambra in Granada, whose ruins survive to the present day.[6] Indeed, the Córdoban caliphate emerged as the richest, most powerful kingdom on the European continent and an estimable rival to the ʿAbbāsid caliphate in Baghdad at the same time that Muslims also spread east across Asia to the borderlands of China.

For many, the cultural, intellectual and economic efflorescence of al-Andalus has come to exemplify both the storied past and the potential future of Islamic cosmopolitanism, a model of religious vitality and peaceful coexistence that could perhaps provide a roadmap out of the fraught political impasses of the early twenty-first-century Middle East.[7] However, if one pushes a little beyond the halcyon image of religious learning and pluralism, it is also possible to discern a more complex story. The progenitor of the first Muslim Andalusian dynasty, ʿAbd al-Raḥmān, embodied not only the wisdom of broad-minded governance, but also the enduring impact of violent upheaval, displacement and coercive political projects – coming to Iberia as he did in flight from the ʿAbbāsid revolution. Menocal's study also reveals that the messy realities of cut-throat economic competition, political machinations and military conflict coexisted with, and arguably underpinned, the much-celebrated cultural achievements of al-Andalus. Indeed, the era's artistic and cultural florescence did not come at the apogee of the Córdoban caliphate, but rather after 1031 when the caliphate fragmented into numerous competing *ṭāʾifa* ('factions') or principalities. It was during this tumultuous period of intra-communal struggle that some of the greatest cultural achievements of al-Andalus were produced.[8]

The complex and sometimes uncomfortable entanglements of coercion, political competition and displacement with the celebrated pluralism and cultural achievements of golden age al-Andalus challenge our notions of cosmopolitanism, including assumptions about cultural openness, tolerance and mobility. One historian of the Middle East, Will Hanley, argues that the idea of cosmopolitanism 'has clouded rather than clarified' historical analysis, contributing to a misplaced 'nostalgia for a more tolerant past, along with grief over modern-day Middle Eastern states and societies', as a tendentious criticism of 'largely fantastical . . . nationalist and religious xenophobia'.[9] Indeed, without taking into account the contours of asymmetrical power relations and coercion – what Sheldon Pollock fleetingly referred to as 'coercive cosmopolitanism' – the search for diversity, mobility and religious pluralism risks becoming an excursion in nostalgia or, worse still, an apology for domination.[10]

Across complex histories of Muslim political formations, migration and interaction across religious boundaries have long comprised key arenas for negotiating difference, for determining what and whom were to be accepted or rejected, which solidarities to emphasise as universal, and which to reject as chauvinism. This volume will explore historical dimensions of Muslim mobility and diversity, placing particular emphasis on the coercive dimensions sometimes elided in modern visions of 'cosmopolitanism'. The chapters presented here will direct attention toward Muslim communities stretching from Arabia into Central Asia, China and Southeast Asia. These latter areas, while often considered marginal to the mainstream of Islamic Studies, offer considerable benefits for a study on mobility and the coercive dimensions of cosmopolitanism. Subject to large inflows and outflows of Muslim peoples, defined by heterogeneous histories and populations, and often at the periphery of strong states, the experiences of Muslim communities in these regions provide insights into contests to define what could and could not be defined as legitimate forms of difference in the formation of conceptualisations of inclusion and exclusion. Taken together, these case studies help to illuminate the fraught relationship between mobility, border-crossing and cultural openness, and thus help us to formulate more nuanced, multidimensional understandings of diverse cosmopolitan formations across Islamic history.

Nostalgia and Loss in Imaginations of al-Andalus

The long and troubled afterlife of al-Andalus in Muslim memory offers a useful place to start an inquiry on the coercive dimensions of cosmopolitanism. Ultimately, for all its accomplishments and fame, al-Andalus would not survive the repeated onslaught of Islamic and Christian invaders, culminating with the *Reconquista* and the fall of Granada in 1492. Images of decline, conquest and erasure largely shape Muslim discourses on al-Andalus today. In 2014, more than half a millennium after the Catholic monarchs of Castile and Aragon demanded that all Muslims on the Iberian Peninsula convert, flee or face execution, eventually erasing much of the Islamic presence there, a new movement claiming the mantle of the 'Islamic State' (IS) arose in the old Umayyad domains of Syria. As numerous media reports have indicated, IS embraced armed struggle as a central element of its campaign to produce a new Muslim polity, and while the centre of conflict unfolded on terrain scarred by the long American war in Iraq and the civil war in Syria, violence has also periodically spilled into Europe and the United States. On 17 August 2017, assailants claiming to fight for IS used a van to kill 14 and injure 130 people on the iconic Las Ramblas Boulevard in Barcelona, Spain. A week later, IS members released an online video with messages in both Arabic and Spanish claiming that the attack represented part of a campaign seeking to restore al-Andalus to the Muslim world.[11]

Memories of the Córdoban caliphate have clearly not yet been eclipsed, and can, it seems, be cast in terms of both a celebration of pluralism and aggressive claims to control over territory. In their rhetorical constructions of al-Andalus, the discourses of some modern Muslim visions (including that of IS) differ dramatically from the halcyon images of tolerance and openness portrayed by scholars such as Menocal. Indeed, long after the collapse of Córdoba and the Catholic *Reconquista*, a modern Arabic-language discourse has emerged in which mention of 'al-Andalus' most often evokes a very different kind of conversation – one heavily inflected with grief and anguish and loaded with the language of conquest and confrontation.

Tropes of loss and a longing for recovery characterised Arabic discourses on al-Andalus even during the Middle Ages – dating as far back as the eleventh century with literary lamentations over the loss of Córdoba and continuing over the centuries that followed in the forms of 'city elegies' (*rithāʾ al-mudun*).[12] Nostalgia for – and longings to reclaim – a lost al-Andalus evolved over subsequent centuries of Muslim history into the modern period. Yaseen Noorani has argued that images of al-Andalus came to function as foundations for new political subjectivities of anti-colonial resistance in the early twentieth-century poetic works of Aḥmad Shawqī and Muhammad Iqbal.[13]

By the late twentieth century, calls for the restoration of a lost caliphate echoing from Syria to Spain and beyond had come to be elaborated by some in the language of 'holy war' and the religious expulsion of non-Muslims, as well as of Muslims who do not share in a particular vision of Islam in the definition of society (*takfīr*).[14] One of the most important theorists of 'global *jihād*' in its contemporary form was ʿAbdallāh ʿAzzām (d. 1989). In a series of influential treatises, including *The Defence of Muslim Lands* (*Al-Difāʿ ʿan araḍī al-muslimīn*), ʿAzzām developed a trans-regional vision of Muslim solidarity that linked the struggle of his native Palestine with the fight against the Soviets in Afghanistan and other 'counter-crusades' waged by embattled Muslim communities across the world.[15] These ideas later found expression on a dramatic scale. In 1994, Osama bin Laden closed one of his first major international statements with a plea for Divine assistance 'to restore our *umma* its pride and honour, and in which the banner of God's unity is raised once again over every stolen Islamic land, from Palestine to al-Andalus and other Islamic lands that were lost ...'[16] From his base in Afghanistan, bin Laden emerged as a powerful symbol in struggles over opposing visions of universalising order in an era of globalisation.

Linkages between contemporary Afghanistan and Syria with historical al-Andalus in the imagination of 'landscapes of *jihād*'[17] significantly shaped the career of Abū Musʿab al-Sūrī (d. 2005), an influential propagandist for al-Qaeda. He was born in Syria and took Spanish citizenship in the 1980s. In his voluminous writings, he spoke of the special significance of having 'resided in the last Muslim stronghold of al-Andalus', and later met ʿAzzām in Peshawar where he scaled up his horizon of global *jihād* – eventually emerging as an influential architect of visions of trans-regional Muslim solidarity in agonistic opposition to dominant forms of globalisation in the twenty-first century.[18] Al-Andalus thus remains a potent term of reference for diverse historical imaginations with pitched political relevance today – from pluralist conceptions of cosmopolitanism to the universalising aspirations of a new caliphate expressed in movements advocating global *jihād*.

Popular media coverage of the spectacular violence of IS has, however, served to obscure other significant aspects of this contemporary form of aspirational Muslim community. One powerful echo and re-imagination of ideals well established within Islamic tradition is the emphasis on the moral imperatives of movement and mobility. In July 2014, when Abū Bakr al-Baghdādī proclaimed a new caliphate in the Islamic State of Iraq and Syria, he specifically invoked the theological paradigm of 'migration' (*hijra*): 'Whoever amongst you can migrate to the Islamic State should migrate. *Hijra* to Dar al-Islam is obligatory.'[19] In doing so, the leader of IS echoed Prophetic precedents of migration from Mecca to Medina to forge a new Islamic community.[20] Like ʿAbd al-Raḥmān's escape across North Africa to al-Andalus, this act of physical relocation and mobility could also be imagined as a migration to establish both a new era of Islamic sovereignty and territorial control, and a vision of cosmopolitanism that would transend boundaries of race, class and nationality to create a new Islamic society. As al-Baghdādī declared via his Twitter account in 2014:

> You now have a state and a caliphate that restores your honour, your might, your rights and your sovereignty. The state forms a tie of brotherhood between Arab and non-Arab, white and black, Easterner and Westerner. The caliphate brings together the Caucasian, Indian, Chinese, Shami, Iraqi, Yemeni, Egyptian, North African, American, French, German and Australian ... They are all in the same trench, defending each other, protecting each other and sacrificing for one another. Their blood mingles together under one flag.[21]

Here we are confronted with 'cosmopolitan' overtones and aspirations at work in the IS vision and its popular appeals. Elsewhere, one official media outlet (*Dābiq* magazine) proclaims *hijra* as the act of 'pack[ing] one's belongings and move[ing] to the Caliphate as a prerequisite for good standing as a Muslim'.[22] Likewise, Abū Bakr al-Baghdādī's profession of openness to 'Arab and non-Arab, white and black, Easterner and Westerner,' presents a broad and inclusive Islamic sensibility, while at the same time starkly defining and adopting a militant stance against those deemed to be outside the pale of their utopian vision of community.[23] By decamping from their current places of residence to the Islamic State, in other words, Muslims could take the opportunity to transcend the ephemeral ties of race, nation and ethnicity.

Challenging Cosmopolitanism in the Indian Ocean

Dramatic fluctuations of ideals of community and mobility along the geographic and historical arc stretching from Damascus to Córdoba and back again, from the early Middle Ages to the twenty-first century, point toward the challenges and coercive underpinnings at the heart of any scholarly inquiry into 'Islamic cosmopolitanism'. The philosopher Marianna Papastephanou notes that much of the extant academic literature adopts a utopian view of 'cosmopolitanism as mobility, border-crossing, readiness to live and work abroad, and openness to anything foreign'.[24] Yet, al-Baghdādī's invocation of *hijra* demands that historians pursue more critical investigation into the contexts, contents and ascribed meanings of specific acts of mobility, rather than understanding it as a relatively straightforward component contributing to cosmopolitan sensibilities.

Like al-Andalus, the Indian Ocean region has inspired extensive modern scholarship celebrating pre-modern models of Islamic cosmopolitanism. In much of this work, mobility across vast geographic spaces and cultural landscapes has been taken to be 'an axiomatic sign of cosmopolitanism'.[25] Recently, however, scholars working across several disciplines have begun to remind us of overlooked aspects of competition and conflict and to call for new research that could serve 'to adjust the widely held notion that the pre-Portuguese Indian Ocean world constituted a harmonious trading realm'.[26] As Sunil Amrith has noted:

> There is a clear – sometimes irresistible – tendency to romanticize the Indian Ocean's precolonial history, downplaying earlier episodes of violence and older forms of predatory behaviour in favour of a world in equilibrium.[27]

The temptation to look longingly towards idealised visions of Islamic cosmopolitanism as the antithesis to the militant communal solidarity associated with IS can be quite powerful.

The heavy burden of nostalgia, grief and utopianism thus might call into question the analytic value of cosmopolitanism as a category in the historiography of Muslim societies. While the aspirations of equality, justice and planetary peace might seem unimpeachable, recent critical scholarship has turned to consider the historical contingencies of dynamics of power that have shaped particular imaginations of cosmopolitanism. Philosophers such as Walter Mignolo have pointed out that such a cosmopolitan vision 'presupposes that it could only be thought of from one particular geopolitical location: that of the heart of Europe'.[28] Other scholars have attempted to redress this Eurocentric bias by articulating multiple frameworks of cosmopolitanism arising out of non-Western contexts, including Islam. Khairudin Aljunied, for example, writes of 'elite' and 'subaltern' as well as 'official' and 'vernacular' forms of Muslim cosmopolitanisms that 'can emerge both "bottom up" and "top down"'.[29]

Edward Simpson and Kai Kresse have recognised with even more nuances the difficulties of 'struggling' to break free from the deeply ingrained constraints of Eurocentric bias in discussions of cosmopolitanism arising out of non-Western contexts. Their work further pushes for moving beyond conventional (and, in their words, 'lazy') usage of the term 'cosmopolitanism' to consider the term's diverse valences as both a 'normative goal' and as a 'factual challenge' in the face of social diversity. Simpson and Kresse thus speak of 'Indian Ocean cosmopolitanism' rooted in histories that have 'created societies in which differences are recognised and individuals are, to a greater or lesser extent, equipped with the skill to navigate through such differences'. In Islamic terms, it is then incumbent upon us, as historians and anthropologists, to move beyond the reified imaginations of a universal *umma* transcending time and space towards an understanding of 'rival forms of cosmopolitanism' and a recognition of the ways in which visions of 'the global Muslim community of believers are pronounced, advocated and rehearsed in specific circumstances around the world'. In the light of this challenging complexification of the issue, we must re-emphasise the importance of careful empirical work on particular formations of cosmopolitan imaginations in relation to clearly defined times and places.[30]

Hijra, *Ḥajj* and the History of Sanctified Mobility

Even for studies of these eastern reaches of the global *umma,* any discussion of Muslim mobility must acknowledge the continuing resonance of specific trajectories of movement to and within the Arabian Peninsula sanctified by Prophetic precedent. Paradigms of travel were hard-wired into the origin narratives of Islam itself – with the forging of the first Muslim community by Muḥammad bookended with highly symbolic accounts of movements both out of, and back to, Mecca. The emphases on travel in these foundational Islamic narratives have provided templates for the invocation of 'migration' and practices of mobility by Muslims throughout the medieval and modern periods.

The first *hijra* was actually out of Arabia, across the Red Sea to the realm of the Negus in Ethiopia, where a group of the earliest Muslim converts sought refuge under a Christian king in what the Prophet is reported to have characterised as 'friendly country' where 'the king will not tolerate injustice'.[31] Recent historical scholarship has revealed new dimensions to our understanding of the importance of the Ethiopian context and entanglements with Christian and Jewish populations in Arabia for the formation of the first Muslim community.[32] Later Muslim communities came to view the formative experience of the first *hijra* in ways that served to shape understandings of their own historical experience. Zvi Ben-Dor Benite, for example, demonstrates in a recent article how 'narratives of the Ethiopian migration resonated with Hui Chinese Muslims in the eighteenth century, providing a prototype within Islamic salvation history in which a community of Muslims is formed in what might be called exilic conditions' under the authority of non-Muslim rulers – a story with obvious parallels to the Chinese situation.[33]

When most Muslims today speak of '*The hijra*', however, it is generally about the subsequent migration of the early Muslim community from Mecca to Yathrib (later designated as 'Medina' - city of the Prophet). This foundational event, in fact, marks the start of the Islamic *hijri* calendar and the symbolic beginning of the history of the Muslim community. From their new base in Medina, the nascent Muslim community established some of its core forms of practice and organisation and eventually consolidated its strength to the point at which it could overcome Meccan opposition. This dramatic turnaround was marked by the redefinition of another kind of movement, the *ḥajj*, as a return pilgrimage to Mecca.

While many of the ritual gestures associated with the rites of pilgrimage to Mecca have ancient, pre-Islamic origins, they were redefined and claimed as central to the definition of Islam. With emphasis on Qur'ānic iterations of Abrahamic precedent, Muḥammad himself undertook and 'reformed' the rites in relation to the revelations he received.[34] Following the Prophet's 'farewell pilgrimage' in 632 CE, the believers from across an expanding Islamic empire were induced to face demanding and sometimes perilous journeys to reach the Holy City in order to fulfil one of the 'pillars' of the faith. Mecca was thus (re)established as the centre of Islam and the Muslim community at the brink of a period of phenomenal geographic expansion.

With this new reorientation, the symbolic map of Islam's homeland was transformed with *ḥajj*, rather than *hijra*, representing a dominant vector of movement toward rather than away from Mecca. At the same time, new dynamics of outward mobility were also set in motion. During Muḥammad's lifetime, it was 'migration' – and particularly the *hijra* to Medina – that was seen as a testimony of one's commitment to the faith, with those who had first fled to Medina with the Prophet holding elevated positions within the growing Muslim community. *Ḥadīth* reports, however, signalled a shift here after the completion of the 'Farewell Pilgrimage'. A tradition related in two variants by both Muḥammad's wife ʿĀ'isha and Ibn ʿAbbās reports that: 'the Messenger of God, peace be upon him, said on the day of the conquest of Mecca: "There is no *hijra* now, but [only] *jihād* and sincerity of purpose; When you are asked to set out [on a campaign in the cause of Islam] you should do so".'[35]

Over the period that followed, the 'opening' of new spaces for Islam (*fatḥ*) took on militaristic connotations with Islam's rapid territorial expansion, as after the death of the Prophet 'success' came to be measured in terms of an ongoing conquest of adjacent non-Muslim lands.[36] While both *hijra* and *ḥajj* thus came to be generally framed as types of movement toward imaginaries of specifically 'Islamic' space, the new idioms of *fatḥ* and *jihād* came to be significantly coloured by conceptions of a progressive frontier of 'foreign' space that could, potentially, be incorporated into the expanding *umma* in territorial – even if not necessarily religious or cultural – terms.[37]

The vanguard of this expansion included members of the early community who had been in close proximity to the Prophet ('Companions'/ Ar. *al-Ṣaḥāba*) and were thus viewed as potential sources for authoritative knowledge. Itinerant Muslim scholars working across an expanding Islamic empire came to play important roles in collecting and compiling 'reports' of Muḥammad's words and deeds (*ḥadīth*) from geographically dispersed companions of the Prophet and those who knew them into collections that eventually came to serve as foundational sources of religious authority.[38] In the process, they established a paradigm of 'travel in search of knowledge' (*ṭalab al-ʿilm*). This association between geographic distance and scholarly status was to leave a lasting imprint on Islamic civilisation over more than a millennium.[39]

From its origins on the Arabian Peninsula, Islam spread first across the Middle East, then along the seas of the Indian Ocean to South and Southeast Asia, as well as overland across the vast continental routes of Central Asia.[40] In addition to the spread of Muslim communities by merchant diasporas along trans-regional trade routes, this expansion was also propelled by the forces of military conquest from the time of the ʿAbbāsid and Umayyad caliphates, through the later periods of the so-called 'gunpowder' empires of the Ottomans, Safavids and Mughals.[41] In the process, military expansion helped to create new frontier spaces – lands and territories at once at the margins of cultural imaginations of 'civilisation', but also essential to the legitimation of state power and the formation of evolving visions of trans-regional Islamic consciousness.

Cosmopolitan Conscience in the Islamic *Oikumene*?

In many discussions of the milieu of the most highly mobile scholars, one often hears echoes of a *ḥadīth* in which the Prophet is reported to have urged them to 'Seek knowledge, even unto China …'[42] The early *ḥadīth* scholars who first set these developments in motion did indeed sometimes travel to distant lands in search of authoritative sources of Islamic religious knowledge who could demonstrate their direct connection to the Prophet during his life in the Hijaz. Thus, we have a situation in which conceptions of community came to be geographically expansive, but at the same time also increasingly self-conscious of its specific religious identity rooted in the traditions of the Arabian prophet.

In the imagined geography of medieval Islam, however, another scriptural injunction also served to inform conceptions of travel and its consequences. This was the Qurʾānic trope of 'traveling through the land' (*yasirū fī'l-arḍ*) that occurs more than a dozen times in the Qur'ān – generally with reference to journeys along which travellers would glimpse the ruins of past civilisations and in the process were supposed to witness and reflect upon the ultimate fate of those who neglected God's commands.[43] Over the centuries, the idea that travel prompted reflection, and even amazement, upon ancient ruins, natural wonders and encounters with pre- or non-Islamic others was expanded and explored in contexts ranging from Egypt to the Indonesian Archipelago.[44] Muslim writers produced works in a number of genres that celebrated such 'marvels' and the wisdom they might convey in a way that Ulrich Haarmann, commenting on medieval descriptions of ancient Egyptian sites, has characterised as a type of 'travelling in search of wonders' (*ṭalab al-'ajā'ib*).[45] In a work representative of an adjacent field of medieval Muslim literary production known as *maqāmāt*, the tenth-century author Badī' al-Zamān al-Hamadhānī describes the process of attaining knowledge as a physical adventure on the road: 'I got it by tramping through muddy soil and leaning upon rocks, by rejecting annoyance and taking risks, by the assiduous spending of sleepless nights and liking to travel ...'[46]

The world to be explored by thoughtful Muslim travellers at that time seemed to be one of dynamic expansion as both the borders of the Islamic world widened and individual Muslims came to venture even further afield 'seeking knowledge, adventure, and prosperity'. The strange new worlds they encountered on their travels – and described in textual accounts of their journeys – engendered a range of responses. For example, in his encyclopaedic notes on the diverse branches of learning and literature, the tenth-century Baghdadi bibliophile Ibn Nadīm was able to relate a number of rather detailed reports in Arabic on what were at that time the un-Islamised lands of India, China and Southeast Asia – including the large and wondrous 'temples of idols' found at Qimār (Cambodia/Angkor) and al-Ṣanf (Champa).[47]

Some of the notices of these distant lands were incorporated into texts referred to as *riḥla.* Ian Richard Netton has noted that this genre of travel literature, likewise, originally grew out of primarily religious motivations (in this case, for performing the *ḥajj*) to include accounts of diverse countries both between and beyond the frontiers of an expanding medieval Muslim world.[48] The epitome of this *riḥla* tradition, the fourteenth-century traveller Ibn Baṭṭūṭa, wrote about that farthest of countries mentioned in *ḥadīth* literature, China. His account of the Celestial Empire, however, reveals that he found this far outpost of Muslim merchant settlement not a locus of *ʿilm*, but rather of threatening impiety and impurity.[49]

Travel, in and of itself, thus clearly does not guarantee a broadening of consciousness, wisdom or ethical subjectivity. In her important work on the *riḥla* tradition, Roxanne Euben both describes the generative, cosmopolitan potential of the *riḥla* travel narrative, while also highlighting the ways in which mobility was circumscribed within 'operations of power' that codified notions of 'Islamic heartland and frontier'.[50] These structures, in turn, not only established ideological distinctions between cosmopolitan cores and frontier peripheries of Asia, but also a dense network of pathways that connected them – pathways that carried unending flows of soldiers and scholars, merchants and saints, diplomats and labourers. These pathways could indeed serve as avenues towards the promotion of mutual understanding and learning as they cut across recognised boundaries. But these pathways could also morph into circulatory traps reinforcing insider–outsider distinctions and potentially extending violence and hierarchies of power across vast distances.

Despite such limits, the cosmopolitanism of medieval Muslim travellers is often seen by scholars today as marked by the ways in which individuals, communities and elements of dizzyingly diverse cultures came to be connected across broad swathes of the eastern hemisphere, an expansive zone that Marshall Hodgson refers to in terms of the Afro-Eurasian '*oikumene*'. Much of this territory, as Hodgson notes in the second volume of his magnum opus, came into the fold of Islam after the collapse of the central Muslim empires of the classical period – and increasingly this was accomplished not through conquest, but through the spread and reconfiguration of commerce. Bruce Lawrence's contribution to this volume (Chapter 2) presents broad-ranging reflections on Hodgson's conceptions of Islamicate civilisation across the Afro-Eurasian *oikumene*, specifically locating it as the wellspring of what he terms 'Islamicate cosmopolitanism'. As Muslims circulated across vast spaces and encountered varied peoples, Lawrence argues, they nonetheless carried with them a specific *conscience* – one that in some sense 'precedes Islam yet was reshaped by the Qurʾān and moral reflection within Muslim empires'. This facilitated the maintenance and transmission of specific theological and cultural imprints, but yet demanded 'moral reflection', 'self-criticism' and the ability to imagine other worlds beyond the territorial or political, social or religious legacies of their ancestors and her contemporaries. Lawrence thus argues that this conscience provided the wellspring of a more profound, reflexive cosmopolitanism, a cosmopolitanism that went beyond mere 'travel' or 'cultural tourism', 'tolerance' or 'reciprocity'.

Also important to Hodgson's model of the post-classical expansion of the Muslim world also, however, was the expansion of networks of Islamic learning and religious authority which provided mechanisms of connection between distant Muslim communities in the institutional forms of the established 'schools of law' (*madhāhib*) and trans-regional Sufi orders (*ṭuruq*, sing. *ṭarīqa*). By the sixteenth century, Ottoman officials appealed to conceptions of a 'juridically based universalism' in attempts to define Islamic imperial sovereignty over the Indian Ocean and to block the spread of Portuguese maritime interests.[51] At the same time, Sufi orders both mapped on to and re-shaped pathways of connection integrating Islamic itineraries across the region. Throughout Muslim history, moreover, the *ḥajj* was a source of centripetal power – even with the establishment of new urban centres of political power and cultural capital outside the Arabian Peninsula. As Garth Fowden notes, the *ḥajj* 'ensured that the bonds of the Muslim world never relaxed as entirely as did those between the Christianities of the Latin and Oriental . . . Churches'.[52]

Islamic Solidarity and Muslim Diversity

Many modern accounts of the *ḥajj* celebrate the annual pilgrimage as a great coming together of Muslims of diverse ethnic, linguistic and geographic origins into a harmonious congregation. Without denying the intense feelings of unity that these rituals foster, however, the experience of the *ḥajj* does not always equate to a permanent state of *communitas* across the global *umma.*[53] Scholars seeking to emphasise emic articulations of cosmopolitanism internal to Muslim societies often point, explicitly or more often implicitly, to this concept of *umma* as the community of Muslim believers as one possible referent. Recent historians, however, have problematised the conflation of *umma* with the idea of the 'Muslim World' and a sense of religious solidarity that transcends ethnic, cultural or national distinctions. Cemil Aydin's recent work, for example, contends that that even if 'notions of *umma* and Muslimness existed . . . whatever they meant' since the time of the earliest Islamic empires, it was only in the late nineteenth century that European colonial challenges and emerging conceptions of race 'inspired narratives of global Muslim unity along either geopolitical or civilizational lines'.[54] While Aydin perhaps overstates his case in overlooking different formations of Muslim solidarity present long before 1900, he rightly challenges the facile conflation of a concept of *umma* with a universalistic Islamic cosmopolitanism that could supersede the tremendous variegation in 'language, ethnicity, political ideology, nationality, culture, and wealth' within Muslim communities.[55]

Pre-modern travel narratives written by Muslims often underscore this sense of difference and tension that arose in the course of intra-religious encounters, thus complicating simplistic assumptions of the universal solidarity of the *umma*. Indo-Persian accounts of visits to Southeast Asia, for example, describe local Muslim populations there with some of the same dismissive tropes that were also often applied to the Buddhist kingdoms of the mainland. As Muzaffar Alam and Sanjay Subrahmaniam characterise such texts: 'Ironically we are left with the view that while proximity did not rule out curiosity, it certainly did not foster immediate comprehension, or even obviate the possibility of quite exacerbated forms of exoticism.'[56]

Such tensions between a cosmopolitan conscience of the Islamic *umma*, on the one hand, and more particularistic impulses of exoticism, cultural arrogance and theological intolerance, on the other, are also traceable through processes of early modern state formation across the Afro-Eurasian *oikumene*. Travelling Muslim scholars did not circulate across vast distances only in pursuit of knowledge. For all across the overland caravan and maritime routes connecting the expanding world of Islam itinerant scholars and shaykhs also came to play influential roles as cultural brokers, administrators and diplomats – as well as in the palace politics of diverse Muslim polities.[57] In the course of their careers many highly mobile Muslim elites lent legitimacy to local rulers, supported particular claimants to power at critical junctures in succession disputes and played direct roles in military campaigns. Some even came to take over the states that initially hosted them. Such, for example, was the case of Muḥammad Shams al-Dīn in the Maldives – as described by A. C. S. Peacock in this volume (Chapter 3).

The tendency to overlook such conjunctures of Muslim mobility, religious learning, devotional life and early modern state formation derives, at least in part, from prevalent assumptions about cosmopolitanism's relationship to Sufism. While scholars often look to the term *umma* as a signifier of communal solidarity within Islam, Sufism is frequently viewed as a source of emic articulations of cosmopolitanism in terms of tolerance and pluralism. One noted anthropologist and theorist of 'vernacular cosmopolitanism', Pnina Werbner, explicitly identifies Sufism, with its 'open, inclusive aspects' that are 'peace-loving and tolerant of difference', as a pathway to finding 'indigenous, vernacular terms used . . . to express . . . [Muslim] cosmopolitan ethical outlook or ideology'.[58] Werbner has examined one specific Sufi lodge in contemporary rural Pakistan and its articulations of Muslim cosmopolitanism, highlighting their usage of Urdu terms such as *insantyat* ('equality, compassion, and urbanity') and *admiyat* ('human nature, humanity, benevolence, compassion'). Werbner thus offers important empirical material to enrich discussions of emic analogues to dominant European conceptions of cosmopolitanism.[59]

By contrast, two contributors to this volume, A. C. S. Peacock and Simon Carlos Kemper (Chapters 3 and 4, respectively), further complicate the picture through careful historical work on the ways in which Sufis have also been part of political intrigues and armed conflict.[60] In his study of sixteenth- and seventeenth-century Sufi scholars circulating beyond the continental Muslim empires of the Turco-Persianate world to 'contested peripheries' of the Indian Ocean such as Java, Aceh and the Maldives, Peacock highlights the ways in which the propagation of a universalist '*sharīʿa*-minded' piety presented a particular vision of cosmopolitanism that was by no means characterised by an openness to other religious traditions. Sufi shaykhs like Muḥammad Shams al-Dīn travelled to Aceh and the Maldives not to learn from locals, to adapt regional customs to Islam or to engage in the moral introspection of conscience. Rather, Peacock argues, they travelled in a spirit of 'commanding the right and forbidding the wrong', to eradicate *bidʿa* ('blameworthy innovation') from Islam and to enforce adherence to textually defined norms of *sharīʿa*-minded piety. Their efforts inexorably intersected with issues of political authority and control as these Islamic cosmopolitan itinerants aligned with elite factions – as, for example, when Shams al-Dīn lent his support to a coterie of disgruntled aristocrats who sought to root out innovation and overthrow a succession of female rulers in Aceh. At other times, such highly mobile Muslims scholars could turn against their benefactors, as when in the next archipelago on his itinerary this same scholar condemned the sultan of the Maldives for corruption, neglect of mosques and the seizure of *waqf* lands – eventuating in the disgrace of the sultan and the elevation of Shams al-Dīn himself to the highest office in the realm.

If Peacock illustrates entanglements of state-building, coercion and a universalising ethos of Islamic cosmopolitanism grounded in normative conceptions of *sharīʿa*, Kemper provides a useful counterpoint in his chapter on wandering, itinerant warriors in the early modern Java Sea region. As with Peacock, Kemper describes a seventeenth-century world roiled by conflict, resistance and rival factions trying to establish their claims to political authority. However, Kemper crafts an illuminating portrait of complementarity and contrast between two of the most famous warriors in Javanese history from this period, Shaykh Yūsuf al-Maqassārī and Pangeran Puspa Ita of Giri. Kemper highlights the text-based, trans-regional models of networked Sufi orders as sources of Muslim solidarity motivating and structuring the *jihād* of al-Maqassārī. Kemper then contrasts this to what he characterises as the ways in which the Sufi martial prowess of Puspa Ita drew on cosmologies and shrines as centres of worship as well as military recruitment. In this he calls particular attention to the symbolic power of mystical weapons and other supernaturally potent heirlooms (*pusaka*) to demonstrate how an 'emplaced cosmopolis' centred on 'shrines, Sufis and warlords' could be viewed by seventeenth-century Southeast Asian Muslims to be just as compelling as trans-regional *ṭuruq* and normative textual authority. These insights into local shrine-based mobilisations of military power reveal that in addition to fostering tolerance and pluralism, Sufism could at times also serve as the basis for military recruitment and violent conflict.

China, Islamic Military Cosmopolitanism and the *Dār al-Islām*

Further complexities arise when considering empirical cases that demonstrate aspects of the evolving relationships between local Muslim communities living within or proximate to majority non-Muslim societies. Johan Elverskog's work on interactions along the Silk Road, for example, demonstrates important fluctuations in Muslim interest in and tolerance of Buddhism (and vice versa), reflecting recalibrations in the balance of power between adherents of the two traditions.[61] Furthermore, as Hyunhee Park has shown in her comparative study of Islamic and Chinese cartographic traditions, even in cases where sustained engagements were productive in the transfer of technical knowledge it is clear that this did not necessarily contribute to an associated sense of cultural openness.[62]

The two chapters in this volume on Chinese Muslims capture the contingent and fluctuating relationships between the Hui and non-Muslim political powers, especially during moments of crisis and conflict. Taken together, the contributions by Tatsuya Nakanishi (Chapter 5) and J. Lilu Chen (Chapter 6) both illuminate the changeable nature of Islamic visions of cosmopolitanism, showing how certain moments of conflict encouraged identification with a trans-regional Islamic *umma*, while others engendered more localised forms of solidarity within the framework of the Chinese state. In his chapter on Hui Muslim intellectuals from China, for example, Nakanishi develops the idea of an 'Islamic military cosmopolitanism'. By this, he refers to 'interconnection of Muslims with non-Muslims as a result of lawful Islamic responses to aggression or external domination'. Prefiguring aspects of contemporary Muslim discourses of migration and militancy, Nakanishi explores a selection of Hui texts in both Chinese and Arabic to present new insights into the ways in which Chinese Muslims repeatedly reinterpreted normative conceptions of *dār al-Islām* and *dār al-ḥarb* – sometimes in rather unexpected ways – to facilitate harmonious relationships with their majority non-Muslim neighbours, as well as with the Qing state.

J. Lilu Chen's chapter pushes the discussion of Chinese Muslim visions of cosmopolitanism in other revealing directions to examine conceptions of 'dual sovereignty' in relation to both Islamic normativity and the Chinese emperor. Chen demonstrates how the nineteenth-century Hui Muslim intellectual Li Huanyi elaborated a vision of dual sovereignty by conjoining Chinese and Islamic genealogies as part of one universal history – tracing and strategically deploying local narratives of the 'Qing dynasty back to Noah and Adam in Arabia'. In these Hui genealogies one of the Companions of the Prophet (Saʿd b. Abī Waqqāṣ) was sent as an emissary to China at the behest of the Prophet to provide needed technical knowledge and advice to Chinese emperors. In doing so, Chen argues that this particular view of Waqqāṣ as the progenitor of Hui lineages helps Chinese Muslims to situate themselves simultaneously between the two authoritative poles in Medina and Chang'an. Furthermore, Chen provides examples of expressions of something like Nakanishi's 'Islamic military cosmopolitanism' in China with Hui narratives of figures like Tie Xuan and Sha Chunyuan, who served the emperor with devotion through military action and martyrdom. This pride in martial heroism in Li Huanyi's telling of these stories testifies to a certain expansive, even cosmopolitan, optimism among these Hui intellectuals, linking the glorious past of Islamic empires in Arabia with the brave Muslim contributions to the Chinese imperial state of his day.

Loss, Grief and Coercive Cosmopolitanism in an Age of Empire

If Nakanishi's and Chen's chapters indicate a surprisingly confident assertiveness about the role Muslims could play in both the non-Muslim Chinese state and the wider Islamic world, the advent of European empire engendered a more defensive outlook among many Muslim communities by the dawn of the twentieth century across much of Asia. For most of Islam's first millennium, Muslims had found themselves in positions of relative power in an expanding Islamic world that came to connect countries stretching from southern Europe to Southeast Asia under a widening rubric of commerce, culture and statecraft. From such positions of confidence, many medieval Muslims could afford to be expansive in their relations with those of other cultures, and even those of other religions, in a way that facilitated some of the flourishing of constructive interactions that are often discussed today in connection with the concept of cosmopolitanism. However, this earlier glow of magnanimity dimmed considerably as increasing numbers of Muslims found themselves no longer to be the representatives of a powerful global civilisation, but rather members of a beleaguered community facing the predations of imperial Europe. This turn of the tide was not immediate or predetermined. As Cemil Aydin notes:

> Muslim leaders and thinkers of the nineteenth and early twentieth centuries were not, for the most part, anti-imperialists. Instead they sought fair treatment from the four major European empires: British, Dutch, French, and Russian. These were cosmopolitan arrangements, home to wide-ranging ethnic and religious groups. But racialized legal categorizations shared across European empires, the empowerment strategies of colonized Muslim subjects, and tactics employed in imperial rivalries confirmed rather than challenged Muslim difference, ensuring that Muslims would be a separate class within the imperial whole.[63]

Imperialism thus served, as Aydin suggests, to reinforce the sense of Islamic difference.

Nevertheless, these shifts ultimately had a profound effect on how many Muslims came to view their position in the world, as well as their formation and valuing of diverse cosmopolitan visions. The impact of European imperialism upon Muslims produced many unforeseen consequences. On the one hand, innovations in transportation and communications technologies, including railways, steamships, print and the telegraph, unleashed an unprecedented intensification of mobility and connectedness across the Islamic world.[64] Consequently, the number of Muslims able to perform the *ḥajj* expanded exponentially as they became able to board European-owned steamships starting in the later decades of the nineteenth century.[65] However, other more coercive dynamics in the movement of Muslims across the globe were also set into motion by European imperial interventions during this period, generating huge new flows of Muslims in the form of migrant labour, colonial military deployment, penal transportation and refugees. In this turbulent and rapidly transforming world, Muslim mobility engendered diverse and unpredictable outcomes. Increased opportunities and infrastructure for travel and intensified contacts with diverse others in the age of European empire could produce tolerance and cultural openness for some Muslims, while also inspiring resentment and anger among others.

As Amrita Malhi demonstrates in this volume (Chapter 8), the threat of global empire could sometimes galvanise new articulations of trans-regional Islamic identification and solidarity in resistance in places that had previously seen little in the way of such things. Malhi's discussion of developments in the Malayan province of Terengganu – a region on the borderlands between colonial Malaya and Siam in Southeast Asia – examines a string of Muslim rebellions against encroaching British authorities, starting with the Pahang War of the 1890s. She argues that this resistance comprised a form of 'counter-colonial form of world-making', a way to push back against both British and Siamese incursions.

Over time, this form of 'postcolonial politics' culminated in calls for Muslim political rebellion with the revived idea of the caliphate with Turkey as the inspiration, what Malhi elsewhere has referred to as the political lodestar for a reimagined form of global identity in the Muslim *umma*. Such efforts in this one corner of northern Malaya dovetailed with earlier Ottoman imperial efforts to enhance their global influence even as they lost physical territory by promoting the idea of a global caliphate across the newly colonised world from West Africa to Southeast Asia.

The Ottoman sultan Abdul Hamid II emphasised his caliphal status as a way to leverage universalistic Islamic tendencies and recover flagging Ottoman geopolitical stature in the late nineteenth century.[66] According to Seema Alavi, these efforts inspired many migrations and political movements, such as the circulations of various Arab and Indian Muslim rebels, refugees and émigrés from British-controlled South Asia to Ottoman Istanbul, where they forged a unique 'cosmopolitanism' that 'conceptualized the Muslim cosmopolis as an intellectual and civilizational zone that transcended political borders, territorial confines, and cultural particularities'.[67] As Muslims formed their own articulations of cosmopolitanism around a reimagined and resurgent Ottoman caliphate, however, Turkish power did not serve only to inspire anti-colonial rebellion. Indeed, somewhat surprisingly, in some cases it could also provide an exemplar or ally to non-Muslim empires expanding into new Muslim frontiers.

Joshua Gedacht's chapter (Chapter 7) describes how, in the southern region of the Philippine Islands, the United States sought to cultivate and harness ties with Istanbul in pursuit of projects for colonial 'pacification'. In particular, Gedacht presents the story of American attempts to fashion 'modern Mohammedan' subjects in their new imperial possessions. For at least for one American official, Istanbul represented an attractive model for progress, stability and 'modernity' that could serve as an antidote to the 'vicious habits' perceived to be characteristic of Muslim Filipinos. The US military thus arranged for an Ottoman Islamic scholar, Shaykh Wajīh al-Kilānī, to travel to the Philippines. Wending through Cairo, Singapore and other modern centres of Islamic printing and Islamic activism on his path, this shaykh was to take up the role of the 'Shaykh al-Islām of the Philippines'. Although the American government came to reverse course and deported this shaykh, this curious history offers a signal reminder of how Western imperial powers have at times also actively contributed to formations of 'coercive cosmopolitanism' in Muslim societies.[68]

Muslim Mobility and Islamic Cosmopolitanism

Muslim mobilities on land and at sea were shaped by diverse state structures in the form of the Muslim kingdoms of the seventeenth and eighteenth century, the various Euro-American empires of the nineteenth century and the emergent nation-states of the twentieth century – as well as by European trading companies and emerging forms of global capitalism. These forces have also served to reconfigure religious thought and practice in different ways for those who moved in various capacities, as well as those whose mobility was restricted or were left behind.[69] From the steppes of the Central Asian interior to the Indian subcontinent, from the maritime world of the Indian Ocean to the dynastic courts of China, Muslim mobilities thus entangled political and economic structures and the particular forms of coercive power on which they were dependent.

While today's fighters of the Islamic State seek to promote a brand of trans-national solidarity grounded in violent struggle and theological exclusivity, other Muslims around the world participate in forms of cosmopolitanism that embrace more flexible engagement with multiple and diverse cultural, ethnic and religious contexts. In this volume, Magnus Marsden and Diana Ibañez-Tirado (Chapter 9) present a striking example of this flexibility with a focus on Afghan traders in the Chinese commercial hub of Yiwu. They call special attention to the diverse ways in which many of the traders had been influenced by the decades of warfare and conflict in their region. Reflecting on what they refer to as the 'long-term workings of coercive cosmopolitanism', many of the traders in Marsden and Ibañez-Tirado's study had been involved in 'Soviet programmes that placed Afghan orphans in Soviet boarding schools (*internat*) in the 1980s' or served in Afghanistan's air force as pilots.

Tracing their complex trajectories allows us to see these highly mobile Muslims of the twenty-first century not simply as 'one-dimensional victims' of the instability of their home country' or as the type of rootless or deracinated persons that are easily lured to the universalising ideology of the Islamic State. Rather than fitting nearly into dominant contemporary tropes 'that would treat . . . [them] either as a potential Islamist militant or a hapless refugee', these Muslim traders navigate the complex political and economic structures of a global world in order to profit from a wide array of commercial opportunities in the 'many different settings and countries over which they operate'. In the process, they are not simply moving through some generalised framework of 'Islamic networks' to pursue straightforward goals. For their itineraries take them through complex entanglements, which might include the forging of intimate relations with Chinese wives, adopting passports from places where they acquire property such as Russia or Ukraine, and partying at nightclubs as a way of allaying the concerns of local authorities. These mobile Muslim traders emphasise qualities of practical flexibility and adaptability in their travels, rather than an exclusivist vision of *hijra* as guiding ideals.[70]

Such a vast variety of forms and meanings that Muslim mobility assumes in the contemporary era is remarkable, but it does not change the inescapable reality that its pathways remain shaped to a considerable degree by particular forms of coercion. The Afghan traders of Marsden and Ibañez-Tirado's chapter not only come from a region with a history of violent conflict, but in migrating out they must constantly negotiate their positions in relation to the political agendas of state officials in countries including Russia and China. Their experience, moreover, pales in regard to sheer scale when seen in relation to the current global refugee crisis. When discussing the movement of Muslim peoples across the borders of nation and religious affiliation, it is therefore important to not assume an inherently liberating, emancipatory potential, but to remain attentive of the various configurations of power and coercion that continue to shape diverse experiences of migration today. By reconfiguring coercion and power into the histories of Muslim mobility, the chapters in the book offer new perspective on the challenges and opportunities of Islamic cosmopolitanism in the present.

Notes

1. Hawting, G. R., *The First Dynasty of Islam: the Umayyad Caliphate, AD 661–750* (London: Croom Helm, 1986).
2. On the ʿAbbāsids' coalition between Shiʿīs, broader elements of the 'piety-minded', and other groups that came together in opposition to the Umayyads, see Hodgson, Marshall, G. S., *The Venture of Islam: Conscience and History in a World Civilization* (Chicago, IL: University of Chicago Press, 1974), I: 263ff. On the formation of a new model for defining the relationships between the political ruler of the Muslim community and the custodians of Islamic traditions of learning and devotional life after the fall of the Umayyads, see Zaman, Muhammad Qasim, *Religion and Politics under the Early ʿAbbāsids: the Rise of the Proto-Sunnī Elite* (Leiden: Brill, 1997).
3. Safran, Janina M., *The Second Umayyad Caliphate: the Articulation of Caliphal Legitimacy in al-Andalus* (Cambridge, MA: Harvard University Center for Middle Eastern Studies, 2000).
4. For lavish illustrations of this cultural production, see Dodds, Jerrilynn D. (ed.), *Al-Andalus: the Art of Islamic Spain* (New York: Metropolitan Museum of Art, 1992).
5. Menocal, María Rosa, *The Ornament of the World: How Muslims, Jews, and Christians Created a Culture of Tolerance in Medieval Spain* (New York: Back Bay Books, 2002), pp. 18–23.
6. Menocal, *The Ornament of the World*, pp. 151–8, 227–35.
7. As André Azoulay, founder of an annual festival of Andalusian music at Essaouira (Morocco), recently commented in an interview for *The Economist*, this 'is what the Middle East once was and might yet be again'. In 'Jews in Morocco: Shalom alaykum – Essouira, a Little Idyll of Jewish–Muslim Co-existence', *The Economist*, 4 November 2017, p. 50.
8. Menocal, *The Ornament of the World*, pp. 40–1.
9. Hanley, Will, 'Grieving Cosmopolitanism in Middle East Studies', *History Compass* 6(5) (2008): 1346–50.
10. Pollock, Sheldon I., 'Cosmopolitan and Vernacular in History', *Public Culture* 12(3) (2000): 599–600.
11. Onyanga-Omara, Jane, 'Islamic State Releases First Spanish-Language Video', *USA Today*, 25 August 2017, available at: https://www.usatoday.com/

story/news/world/2017/08/25/islamic-state-releases-first-spanish-language-video/600996001, last accessed 1 November 2017; McLaughlin, Karl, 'Jihadist Terrorists have Long had Spain in Their Sight – Here's Why', *The Conversation,* 18 August 2017, available at: http://theconversation.com/jihadist-terrorists-have-long-had-spain-in-their-sights-heres-why-82703, last accessed 1 November 2017.

12. Elinson, Alexander E., *Looking Back at Al-Andalus: the Poetics of Loss and Nostalgia in Medieval Arabic and Hebrew Literature* (Leiden: Brill, 2009).
13. Noorani, Yaseen, 'The Lost Garden of al-Andalus', *International Journal of Middle East Studies* 31(2) (1999): 237–54.
14. Wood, Graeme, 'What ISIS Really Wants', *The Atlantic*, March 2015, available at: https://www.theatlantic.com/magazine/archive/2015/03/what-isis-really-wants/384980, last accessed 29 September 2017.
15. Hegghammer, Thomas, ''Abdallah, 'Azzām and Palestine', *Die Welt des Islams* 53(3/4) (2013).
16. Lawrence, Bruce (ed.), *Messages to the World: the Statements of Osama bin Laden* (London: Verso, 2005), p. 91.
17. This phrasing is adapted from Faisal Devji and his stimulating work on al-Qaeda as an 'agent of globalisation'. Devji uses the phrase in ways extending conceptually beyond topography to refer to 'new patterns of belief and practice, so pregnant with possibilities, that have emerged as the global consequences of al-Qaeda's actions'. Devji, Faisal, *Landscapes of the Jihad: Militancy, Morality, Modernity* (London: Hurst, 2005), p. xvi.
18. Lia, Brynjar, *Architect of Global Jihad: the Life of al-Qaida Strategist Abu Mus'ab al-Suri* (London: Hurst, 2007).
19. *Al-I'tisam's* Twitter account, 1 July 2014, quoted in Carmon, Y., Y. Yehoshua and Y. Leone, 'Understanding Abu Bakr al-Baghdadi and the Phenomenon of the Islamic Caliphate State', *Inquiry and Analysis Series 1117,* Washington, DC: Middle East Media Research Institute, 2014), available at: http://www.memri.org/report/en/print8147.htm, last accessed 28 August 2016.
20. It should be noted, however, that this *hijra* was preceded by one (or possibly two) earlier migration(s) of followers of Muhammad from Mecca to Ethiopia *c.* 615 CE. For more on this, see Bowersock, G. W., *The Crucible of Islam* (Cambridge, MA: Harvard University Press, 2017), pp. 71ff.
21. Carmon, Yehoshua and Leone, 'Understanding Abu Bakr al-Baghdadi'.
22. *Dābiq* 3, p. 31 quoted in Carmon, Yehoshua and Leone, 'Understanding Abu Bakr al-Baghdadi'.

23. *Al-I'tisam's* Twitter account, 1 July 2014, quoted in Carmon, Yehoshua and Leone, 'Understanding Abu Bakr al-Baghdadi'.
24. Papastephanou, Marianna, *Thinking Differently about Cosmopolitanism: Theory, Eccentricity and the Globalized World* (Boulder: Paradigm, 2012), p. 2.
25. Such assumptions have been the subject of a provocative recent critique of previous literature in the field. The quotation cited here is drawn from this important intervention: Simpson, Edward and Kai Kresse, 'Cosmopolitanism Contested: Anthropology and History in the Western Indian Ocean', in Kai Kresse and Edward Simpson (eds), *Struggling with History: Islam and Cosmopolitanism in the Western Indian Ocean* (New York: Columbia University Press, 2008), p. 13.
26. Margariti, Roxani Eleni, *Aden and the Indian Ocean Trade: 150 Years in the Life of a Medieval Arabian Port* (Chapel Hill, NC: University of North Carolina Press, 2007), p. 9.
27. Amrith, Sunil S., *Crossing the Bay of Bengal: the Furies of Nature and the Fortunes of Migrants* (Cambridge, MA: Harvard University Press, 2015), p. 27
28. Mignolo, Walter, 'The Many Faces of Cosmo-polis: Border Thinking and Critical Cosmopolitanism', *Public Culture* 12(3) (2000): 735.
29. Aljunied, Khairudin, *Muslim Cosmopolitanism: Southeast Asian Islam in Comparative Perspective* (Edinburgh: Edinburgh University Press, 2017), p. xvi.
30. Simpson and Kresse, 'Cosmopolitanism Contested', pp. 1–41.
31. Guillaume, A., *The Life of Muḥammad: A Translation of Ibn Isḥāq's* Sīrat Rasūl Allāh (Karachi: Oxford University Press, 1967), p. 146; al-Faruque, Muhammad, 'Emigration', *Encyclopaedia of the Qur'ān*, ed. Jane Dammen McAuliffe (Brill Online, 2015), available at: http://referenceworks.brillonline.com/entries/encyclopaedia-of-the-Qur'ān/emigration-EQSIM_00132, last accessed 6 January 2015.
32. Bowersock, G. W., *The Throne of Adulis: Red Sea Wars on the Eve of Islam* (Oxford: Oxford University Press, 2013).
33. Benite, Zvi Ben-Dor. 'Hijra and Exile: Islam and Dual Sovereignty in Qing China', in Zvi Ben-Dor Benite, Stefanos Georulanos and Nicole Jerr (eds), *The Scaffolding of Sovereignty: Global and Aesthetic Perspectives on the History of a Concept* (New York: Columbia University Press, 2017), p. 293.
34. Peters, F. E., *The Hajj: the Muslim Pilgrimage to Mecca and the Holy Places* (Princeton, NJ: Princeton University Press, 1994), pp. 3–59.
35. The variant transmission by way of 'Ā'isha reads: ''Ā'isha reported that the Messenger of God, peace be upon him, was asked about migration, whereupon

he said: "There is no migration after the conquest [of Mecca], but *jihād* and sincere intention. When you are asked to set out, you should set out"' (*Ṣaḥīḥ Muslim*, 4599).

36. Paret, Rudi, 'Die Bedeutungsentwicklung von arabisch *fatḥ*', in J. M. Barral (ed.), *Orientalia Hispanica sive studia F. M. Pareja octogenario dicata* (Leiden: Brill, 1974), pp. 537–44.
37. Hoyland, Robert G., *In God's Path: the Arab Conquests and the Creation of an Islamic Empire* (Oxford: Oxford University Press, 2015).
38. Juynboll, G. H. A., *Muslim Tradition: Studies in Chronology, Provenance and Authorship of Early Ḥadīth* (Cambridge: Cambridge University Press, 1983).
39. Netton, Ian Richard, *Seek Knowledge: Thought and Travel in the House of Islam* (Richmond: Curzon Press, 1996).
40. For an overview of this geographic diffusion, see Lapidus, Ira, *A History of Islamic Societies*, 2nd edn (Cambridge: Cambridge University Press, 2002).
41. See Streusand, Douglas E., *Islamic Gunpowder Empires: Ottomans, Safavids, and Mughals* (Boulder, CO: Westview Press, 2010); Dale, Stephen F., *The Muslim Empires of the Ottomans, Safavids and Mughals* (Cambridge: Cambridge University Press, 2010).
42. *Misbah ush-Shariat*, quoted in Ali, Ameer, *The Spirit of Islam: a History of the Evolution and Ideals of Islâm, with a Life of the Prophet* (London: Chatto & Windus, [1922] 1978), p. 361.
43. Qur'ān: *Āl 'Imrān* (3):137, *al-An'ām* (6):11, *Yūsuf* (12):109, *al-Naḥl* (16):36, *al-Ḥajj* (22):46, *al-Naml* (27):69, *al-Rūm* (30):9, 42, *al-Malā'ika* (35):44, *al-Mū'min* (40):21, 82 and *Muḥammad* (47):10.
44. This section of the chapter draws upon material published previously in Feener, R. Michael, 'Muslim Cultures and pre-Islamic Pasts', in Trinidad Rico (ed.), *The Making of Islamic Heritage: Muslim Pasts and Heritage Presents* (New York: Palgrave Macmillan, 2017), pp. 23–45. More extended discussions of historical Muslim engagements with pre-Islamic civilizations can be found there.
45. Haarmann, Ulrich, 'In Quest of the Spectacular: Noble and Learned Visitors to the Pyramids around 1200 AD', in Wael B. Hallaq and Donald P. Little (eds), *Islamic Studies Presented to Charles J. Adams* (Leiden: Brill, 1991), p. 58.
46. Quoted in Rosenthal, Franz, *Knowledge Triumphant: the Concept of Knowledge in Medieval Islam*, with an Introduction by Dimitri Gutas (Boston, MA: Brill, 2007), p. 267.
47. Dodge, Bayard (ed. and trans.), *The Fihrist of al-Nadim* (New York: Columbia University Press, 1970), II: p. 830.

48. Netton, pp. 95ff.
49. Gibb, H. A. R. and C. F. Beckingham, *The Travels of Ibn Baṭṭūṭa,* AD *1325–1354*, vol. IV (London: Hakluyt Society, 1994), pp. 888–910.
50. Euben, Roxanne L., *Journeys to the Other Shore: Muslim and Western Travelers in Search of Knowledge* (Princeton, NJ: Princeton University Press, 2008), p. 14.
51. Casale, Giancarlo, *Ottoman Age of Exploration* (New York: Oxford University Press, 2010), p. 31.
52. Fowden, Garth, *Before and After Muhammad: the First Millennium Refocused* (Princeton, NJ: Princeton University Press, 2014), p. 115.
53. For a rich collection of the Southeast Asian writings on the *ḥajj*, revealing a wide range of experiences, interpretations and imaginations, see Chambert-Loir (ed.), *Naik Haji di Masa Silam: Kisah-kisah Orang Indonesia Naik Haji, 1482–1964*, 3 vols (Jakarta: Kepustakaan Populer Gramedia, 2013). For a sampling of historical *ḥajj* accounts in English translation, see Wolfe, Michael (ed.), *One Thousand Roads to Mecca: Ten Centuries of Travelers Writing about the Muslim Pilgrimage* (New York: Grove Press, 1997).
54. Aydin, Cemil, *The Idea of the Muslim World: a Global Intellectual History* (Cambridge, MA: Harvard University Press, 2017), pp. 3, 15.
55. Aydin, *The Idea of the Muslim World*, p. 2. For critical reflections on Aydin's argument in this book, see the review by Feener, R. Michael at: http://readingreligion.org/books/idea-muslim-world, September 2017.
56. Alam, Muzaffar and Sanjay Subrahmanyam, *Writing the Mughal World: Studies on Culture and Politics* (New York: Columbia University Press, 2011), p. 122.
57. See, for example, Wormser, Paul, *Le Bustan al-Salatin de Nuruddin ar-Raniri: Réflexions sur le rôle culturel d'un étranger dans le monde Malais au XVIIe siècle* (Paris: Cahiers d'Archipel, 2012).
58. Werbner, Pnina, 'Vernacular Cosmopolitanism as an Ethical Disposition: Sufi Networks, Hospitality, and Translocal Inclusivity', in Leon Buskins (ed.), *Islamic Studies in the Twenty-First Century: Transformations and Continuities* (Amsterdam: Amsterdam University Press, 2016), p. 224.
59. Werbner, 'Vernacular Cosmopolitanism as an Ethical Disposition', pp. 224, 236.
60. Green, Nile, *Sufism: A Global History* (Chichester: Wiley-Blackwell, 2012).
61. Elverskog, Johan, *Buddhism and Islam on the Silk Road* (Philadelphia, PA: University of Pennsylvania Press, 2010).
62. Park, Hyunhee, *Mapping the Chinese and Islamic Worlds: Cross-Cultural Exchange in Pre-Modern Asia* (Cambridge: Cambridge University Press, 2012).

63. Aydin, *The Idea of the Muslim World,* p. 7.
64. Feener, R. Michael, 'New Networks and New Knowledge: Migrations, Communications and the Refiguration of the Muslim Community in the Nineteenth and Early Twentieth Centuries', in Robert W. Hefner (ed.), *The New Cambridge History of Islam,* vol. 6 (Cambridge: Cambridge University Press, 2010), pp. 39—68.
65. Slight, John, *The British Empire and the Hajj: 1865–1956* (Cambridge, MA: Harvard University Press, 2015), p. 2.
66. Cemil Aydin narrates a history of the fluctuations of the appeal through the 'long' twentieth century – over the course of which 'the meaning of "caliphate" became globally synchronized and refashioned . . . [as] a polity representing all Muslims' – to the point that by the turn of the twenty-first century, 'mutually reinforcing cycles of Islamist and Islamophobic outburst had entrenched the illusion of the Muslim world, suffocating the diverse voices and political demands of actual Muslims in different parts of the world'. Aydin, *The Idea of the Muslim World,* pp. 67, 226.
67. Alavi, Seema, *Muslim Cosmopolitanism in the Age of Global Empire* (Cambridge, MA: Harvard University Press, 2015), p. 6.
68. Cf. Clarence-Smith, William Gervaise, 'Middle East and Philippines under American Rule', in A. C. S. Peacock and Annabel Teh Gallop (eds), *From Anatolia to Aceh: Ottomans, Turks, and Southeast Asians* (Oxford: Oxford University Press, 2015), pp. 199–219.
69. Green, Nile, *Bombay Islam: the Religious Economy of the West Indian Ocean, 1840–1915* (New York: Cambridge University Press, 2011), pp. 73–9.
70. Indeed, they might even be seen as heirs to the legacy of the 'Balkans-to-Bengal' traditions of contradictory meaning-making *as Muslims* that Shahab Ahmed extolls in his posthumous magnum opus, *What is Islam? The Importance of Being Islamic* (Princeton, NJ: Princeton University Press, 2016).

2

Islamicate Cosmopolitanism from North Africa to Southeast Asia

Bruce B. Lawrence

Who are Islamicate cosmopolitans? At once discrete and local, they are not reducible to an abstract descriptor labelled 'Islamicate Cosmopolitanism', though that category can be used as a placeholder for discrete complexities. Islamicate cosmopolitans are subjects of empires and citizens of nation-states. Both Muslim and non-Muslim, they hail from disparate parts of the known world and from distant epochs of recorded history. Above all, Islamicate cosmopolitans are freestanding agents who challenge the limits of imposed identities, whether religious or cultural, temporal or spatial.

Summary Overview

The two parts of Islamicate cosmopolitan(ism) must be parsed to grasp its full potential for redefining multiple actors in diverse contexts. Though complimentary, they are not equal. Because 'cosmopolitan' precedes and exceeds 'Islamicate', it is important to note at the outset what is not truly cosmopolitan but rather what might be regarded as counterfeit cosmopolitan. I will argue that the true cosmopolitan is focused inwardly, on conscience and moral choices. Accent on the inner gaze is a needful corrective to the discourses of self-satisfied upper-class travellers, aristocrats and state officials, which cannot, and should not, be conflated with a genuine orientation of openness to cultural and religious difference or a desire to see a world larger than oneself. The self-centred streak of such 'cosmopolitanism' remains elitist and voyeuristic. At times paternalistic or vernacular (or both), it privileges a flawed north European cosmopolitan exemplar like Richard Burton, or in the annals of Islam, the medieval Moroccan peripatetic, Ibn Baṭṭūṭa. Their engagement in travel, cultural tourism and literary exploration, notably lack moral rigour or self-criticism, in short, the inner gaze that opens the self to the world rather than simply embracing pleasure as a 'natural' pursuit, whether domestic or overseas.[1]

An Islamicate cosmopolitan refracts a Muslim experience that honours its religious antecedents while also expanding them. Just as 'Muslim' applies to actors – individual and collective – within the *umma*, 'Islamic' evokes the norms and values that project Islam as an ethical and metaphysical ideal for Muslims. In other words, both 'Islamic' and 'Muslim' have distinctly religious connotations. 'Islamicate', by contrast, projects a surplus of meaning beyond either 'Muslim' or 'Islamic'. Islamicate is at once precise and evasive. It evokes Islam – its past, present and future – yet the Islamicate influence exceeds any creedal or cultural limits. It reflects Muslim presence – often as an aesthetic taste but more often as an ethical project. Its single-line definition is best etched by Srinivas Aravamudan when he notes that Islamicate equals 'the hybrid trace rather than pure presence or absence of Islam'.[2] And while Aravamudan's translation of Islamicate relates to his own project to reconceptualise East–West relations, my own project is to understand the inherently cosmopolitan nature of the Afro-Eurasian *oikumene* (ecumene), not only prior to the rise of Europe but also after the colonial period of European rule throughout much of Africa and Asia, encompassing both majority and minority Muslim populations.

An 'Islamicate' perspective depends on and relates back to the formulation of the term by Marshall Hodgson. Locating Muslim experience across time and space, Hodgson titled his epochal work *The Venture of Islam*. That venture is collective yet also individual, both beyond time and in time, bounded by location while striving to expand boundaries, spatial as well as temporal. Islamicate cosmopolitan is the Muslim imaginary in real time in multiple places. Fungible yet durable, it occurs in multiple communities preceding and competing with pre-modern Muslim empires and now with majority Muslim nation-states.

Hodgson's neologism 'Islamicate' was introduced over a half century ago, and since then it has met numerous challenges. One deserves special note. Shahab Ahmed, in his complex revisionist engagement with Islam and Islam-related categories across numerous academic disciplines, makes much of Hodgson's distinction between 'Islamic' and 'Islamicate'. While his intent is in rebutting the latter, he continues to use Islamicate in reformulating Islam, and when he depicts Islamic cosmopolitanism, which he lauds, Ahmed underscores how it arises from, and depends on, the convergence of Muslim and non-Muslim values as well as aspirations.[3]

Ahmed, like Hodgson, wrestles at length with the categories 'religion' and 'culture', contesting the use of 'Islamic' as 'religion' and 'Islamicate' as 'culture'. But how firm are the boundaries between religion and culture? Ahmed quotes Hodgson himself urging that the two categories should be applied as fluid procedures rather than as rigid epistemes. 'In some cases,' argues Hodgson, 'the distinction [between religion and culture] is unimportant, and the choice between the terms "Islamic" and "Islamicate" may be a matter of emphasis.'[4] I side with Hodgson in averring that Islamicate adds value to both 'Islamic' and 'Muslim' as qualifiers for civilisation in general and cosmopolitan(ism) in particular. When Islamicate is embraced for the measured hope that Hodgson tried to provide in engaging Islam across time as well as space, one can then proceed to identify *what* distinguishes the Islamicate cosmopolitan.

Within the arc of Islamicate civilisation the cosmopolitan ethos has been marked by two key traits: longing and belonging. The belonging is always a reflex of power, the privilege of literacy and mobility but also the benefits of imperial patronage. There were no pre-modern Islamicate cosmopolitans who were not shaped outside hierarchical social-political structures. Their privilege did not limit their horizons, however, for allied with belonging was longing; the longing for something more, a surplus of benefit to humankind beyond their immediate time–space frame. In the Islamicate cosmopolitan belonging and longing coexist, each a catalyst coefficient to the other. Longing is always and everywhere an historical reflex. It originates in empires but persists through the era of nation-states. More than simply remembering the past, an

Islamicate cosmopolitan in the twenty-first-century projects traces of the past with new accents for change in the near and long term.

There are as many accounts of the past as there are trajectories for the future; the proliferation and diversity of such accounts is a mark of resilience not weakness. If a focal point remains (for some) the nation-state, it is because the nation-state serves as the source, rather than the endpoint of their observations. On the one hand, its resources, its imaginary and its power never cease to inform patriotism, chauvinism and parochialism writ large. Yet at the same time the embrace of humanity at large – Muslim subjective longing – persists as a salient feature for the Islamicate cosmopolitan in the twenty-first century, exceeding the instruments of loyalty to particular nation-states.

While the present encompasses hope of change, it also never escapes the frame of continuity etched by the term 'civilisation'. Embedded within the skein of empires, Islamicate civilisation exhibits a distinct conscience. It precedes Islam yet was reshaped by the Qur'ān and moral reflection within Muslim empires. Hodgson added a subtitle to his magnum opus that needs to be restated: *The Venture of Islam: Conscience and History in a World Civilization. Conscience* is the seedbed for cosmopolitan longing in Muslim empires, themselves the principal carriers of Islamicate civilisation. Cosmopolitan conscience and civilisational narrative become complementary qualifiers. They function in tandem – two sides of a single coin, each backing the other.

Yet history itself needs to be rethought if one is to grasp the depth of a cosmopolitan ethos across the centuries of Islamicate civilisation. Below we will look at Huri Islamoglu's call for a new kind of world history that is at once Islamicate and cosmopolitan, but let us first prize the value of archaeology. Revisiting history through archaeology, one can discern how the Islamicate cosmopolitan contrasts with the Philo-Hellenic cosmopolitan. At heart, there is a moral difference, and that difference has been epitomised by Sandra Scham, a Middle East archaeologist who has worked in Israel and Jordan but also in Peru and Turkey. In her essay, 'Time's Wheel Runs Back: Conversations with the Middle Eastern Past', Scham provides subtitles that etch the themes she highlights, as also the arguments she pursues. She begins with 'Hospitality and the Cosmopolitan Archaeological Project'. Specifically, she questions Jürgen Habermas' and Kwame Anthony Appiah's notion of tolerance–reciprocity as the key cosmopolitan virtue. Neither tolerance nor reciprocity, she argues, move us beyond misunderstanding the Middle Eastern past, and the accent on individual agency fails to shows how state models use classificatory templates in the service of reified religions and nationalist politics.

Indeed, patrimonial archaeology in the service of nationalism shows the moral flaws of the cosmopolitan patriot touted by Appiah as a 'rooted' cosmopolitan.[5] The final part of Scham's probing essay addresses the ancient Near East and the modern West as 'A Fallibilist Love Story' and revisits Appiah's laudatory assessment of the Victorian adventurer Richard Burton. A brutal militarist, dedicated Orientalist and lurid sexologist, Burton was also the paragon of an imperial maestro, controlling natives and women alike for his own interests. Is it possible to expand cosmopolitan to include Burton, or does Burton instead represent a category of 'counterfeit' cosmopolitan? For Scham, he is more likely the latter, an egoist at large rather than a flawed, but still viable, cosmopolitan.[6]

Individuals – and their engagements with particular 'others' – count. Neither Islamicate civilisation nor Islamicate cosmopolitan(ism) can be defined as an abstract generality, apart from people who are both morally motivated and consciously networked. Just as there were subjects of Islamicate civilisation in Muslim empires, so there are Islamicate cosmopolitan citizens in modern nation-states. In every instance, whether past empires or contemporary states, one confronts the exercise of power: political and social, local and regional, and so both subjects and citizens must be specified in their contexts, traced through their networks and their interactions with frameworks of hierarchy and powers of coercion. Not till the ninth century, at the height of the ʿAbbāsid Empire, did Muslim empires become catalysts for an Islamicate cosmopolitan ethos. It was networks of knowledge – philosophical, literary, juridical and mystical – that defined and sustained Islamicate cosmopolitans.[7] From the ninth to the twenty-first century, these nodes connected North Africa to Central, South and Southeast Asia, from the Mediterranean to the places that occupy us in this volume: China and the Indian Ocean.

As a way into our discussion of Islamicate cosmopolitans and the pattern of trans-regional Muslim networks, let us consider two exemplars. While from distant geographical and temporal locations, both were also pre-modern male elites: Bīrūnī, an Uzbek scientist, and Ibn Khaldūn, a Maghribi jurist and historian.[8]

Abū Rayḥān al-Bīrūnī and Islamicate Cosmopolitanism in Central Asia

Abū Rayḥān Muḥammad ibn Aḥmad al-Bīrūnī (d. 1048) was one of the great polymaths of the pre-modern Muslim world. A scholar trained in multiple disciplines, Bīrūnī benefited from royal patronage to pursue his research and writing. He belonged to a scientific community that shared his values and shaped his outlook. He forged a method for comparative inquiry and analysis based in Islamic epistemology, but not limited by it. Bīrūnī was a research scientist and more: a self-conscious and self-critical comparativist. For Bīrūnī, comparison provided a distinctive heuristic purpose: to eradicate common misconceptions. In his monumental work on 'India', he wrote against popular Muslim misconceptions about Hinduism, and promoted a better acquaintance between the two religious traditions. He did so as a pluralist, but not a universalist: he believed that there were multiple caches for Truth and yet maintained that these were not equivalent in value or in power. Bīrūnī argued that it was scholars – those privileged by background, training, patronage and mobility – who were properly qualified to understand the gradients of Truth. Bīrūnī saw many ways to expand human understanding of the universe and the place of religion among the scientific disciplines and yet he did not believe that all human beings, or all places, or all civilisations were equally able to grasp the subtleties of either science or God.

Bīrūnī was sympathetic to philosophy but was also its critic. A contemporary of Ibn Sīnā (Avicenna, d. 1037), Bīrūnī challenged the Aristotelian cosmology at the heart of Ibn Sīnā's worldview. He contended that a mathematical astronomer should not be bound to any prior system. The starting point for work in this field thus must be to view the evidence with as much openness to observation as his instruments and his knowledge permit. In response to Ibn Sīnā's comments on the material nature of the universe, Bīrūnī initiated a correspondence with him, in which he advanced a number of questions that critique the presuppositions of Aristotelian physics. Bluntly, but also respectfully, he asked Ibn Sīnā to respond and thus to justify his own predilection for, and reliance on, Aristotle. Well before Copernicus, Bīrūnī was trying to understand different forces in the universe that might support a heliocentric, instead of a geocentric, view of the cosmos.

Whenever possible, Bīrūnī cited his own empirical research in support of his opinions. Unlike Avicenna, he synthesised a wide swath of disciplines with an accent on observation and experimentation in all that he undertook to study, describe and publish. He underscored the need to observe broadly and to experiment with an openness to new, often unforeseen, conclusions. His many books – reputed to number up to 150 – range from astrology and astronomy to biology, geology, palaeontology, optics, cartography, geodesy, mineralogy, psychology, linguistics and mathematics. He further engaged history, religion and philosophy, with a remarkable command of languages. Though his first language was a Central Asian precursor of Uzbek, he also wrote in both Persian and Arabic and translated from Greek, Sanskrit and Syriac into Arabic.

Both culturally and linguistically Bīrūnī was not only a scientific polymath but also an Islamicate cosmopolitan. Through his persistent experiments in multiple disciplines, coupled with his moral commitment to a universal ethos, Bīrūnī secured for himself a prominent place in the pantheon of those who advanced the civilised world and gave to cosmopolitanism an Islamicate accent.[9]

Ibn Khaldūn: Assessing Islamicate Cosmopolitanism in North Africa

A Maghribi juridical philosopher turned historian, ʿAbd al-Raḥmān Ibn Khaldūn (d. 1406) came from a family that had migrated from al-Andalus to North Africa. He accepted the patronage system as readily as did Bīrūnī, but unlike Bīrūnī, Ibn Khaldūn strove to use his political wisdom to benefit the actual rulers of his day. After moving from one court to another, however, he eventually became disillusioned and retired to Mamluk Cairo as a judge. His life, like that of al-Bīrūnī, demonstrates the importance and the constraints of royal patronage as a stimulant to intellectual creativity. In *The Muqaddimah* (the 'Introduction' to his multi-volume world history), he used his double training in philosophy and law to discern patterns in history.

Like Bīrūnī, Ibn Khaldūn was pragmatic, emphasising laws of evidence to refine and theorise about observations of actual human interactions.

Whereas Muslim historians conventionally had subscribed to the view that God passed sovereignty and hegemony from one dynasty to another through divine wisdom, Ibn Khaldūn explained the fate of states in terms of a cycle of natural stages that followed an almost inevitable pattern. Observing the data of dynasties with an open mind, he ascribed the success of tribally organised migratory peoples to their stronger sense of group solidarity (*ʿaṣabiyya*). This allowed them to acquire military superiority over settled peoples, but as the tribes dispersed among sedentary peoples and ceased to live the rigours of a life of migration, they became soft and subsequently degenerated over the generations. In the end, the ruling dynasty fell prey to a new tribal group with a stronger sense of *ʿaṣabiyya*. He thus uncovered a cyclical pattern and conceptual model for history: civilisation could not survive without military prowess, yet military prowess in itself was unstable. Only through close scrutiny and patient observation could one detect the pattern of social and political change as an explanation of what brought one dynasty to an end and its successor to power.

As an Islamicate cosmopolitan, Ibn Khaldūn stands out for his rigorous commitment to judge and advance arguments only after surveying all available evidence. He privileged geography among the sciences. The geographical lens of pre-modern civilisation focused on the spectrum of civilised life in what Hodgson called the Afro-Eurasian *oikumene*. As civilisation presupposed cities, commerce, travel and trade, as well as alliances and warfare, civilisation – and Islamicate civilisation in particular – encompasses the necessary components of cosmopolitanism. Yet it is not automatically and never securely cosmopolitan: every generation, like every dynasty, is in need of careful, critical self-reflection with a moral compass in mind to maintain its vitality and its integrity. And it is this combination of close scrutiny with moral high purpose that Ibn Khaldūn urges on his co-religionists.

Ibn Khaldūn's privileging of geography and critical self-reflection is suggestive of the wider ambit of Islamicate cosmopolitanism, of both its horizontal and vertical trajectories. It goes not only outward horizontally, encompassing multiple regions within the Afro-Eurasian *oikumene*, but also seeks a vertical path, across a transcendent realm that can be shared across cultures and centuries. It is this 'cosmos' in cosmopolitan (echoing Harvey)[10] that makes it necessary to define Islamicate by what came before Islam and the period of Ibn Khaldūn. Islamicate was a potential frame of thought and action before Islam. Though Hodgson argued about the importance of seeing Islam over a span of 1,500 years (500 CE–2000 CE), he also proffered an emplotment that was even longer (500 BCE–2000 CE). [11]

Here the interaction of the known world (ecumene, or *oikumene*) is crucial. It provides the potential for networks that criss-cross multiple zones or cultural core areas. By the middle of the first millennium BCE, the old world had crystallised into four cultural core areas: Mediterranean, Nile-to-Oxus, Indic and East Asian ('Sinic'). The Nile-to-Oxus, the future core of Islamdom, was the least cohesive and the most internally complex of the four. Whereas each of the other regions developed a single language of high culture – Greek, Sanskrit and Chinese, respectively – the Nile-to-Oxus region became a linguistic palimpsest of several Irano-Semitic languages: Aramaic, Syriac and Middle Persian. When the Nile-to-Oxus region became conjoined with the Arabian Peninsula through the expansion of early Muslim rule to neighbouring regions, the nature of the society, culture and religion that evolved was bi-directional. Even as the Arabs conquered, they were challenged and changed by the people, the institutions and the societies over which they ruled.

And so the formative period long precedes the rise of Islam. It is 800–200 BCE, known as the Axial Age. Why? Because the world's first religions of salvation developed in each of the four core areas, and from these traditions – for example, Judaism, Mazdeism, Buddhism and Confucianism – also sprang later forms of major religious traditions, including Christianity and Islam.[12]

Beyond that seminal period, however, in all the subsequent periods of history the pre-Islamic and the Islamic continued to interact. The Islamicate palimpsest – at once linguistic and cultural, social and religious – resulted from this cross-cultural, inter-regional translation. It was a fungible, flexible translation. Indeed, no contestant for political power ever succeeded in entrenching or imposing a winner-take-all outcome on the region. Time and space alike were subject to new interpretations, visions colluding and colliding with one another. What resulted was a sea of ambiguity, and it is in that sea that we must chart the course of Islamicate cosmopolitans.[13]

Ibn Khaldūn was himself alert to the diverse forms of cultural interpenetration and commingling that developed out of the myriad interactions of the Islamicate palimpsest, with all its ambiguities of interpretation and meaning. Reliance on metaphor allows Ibn Khaldūn, who was an *adīb* or litterateur as well as a *faqīh* or jurist, to demonstrate how the same word, like the same event or person, can be viewed differently over time and also from different places in the same time frame. Crucially, Ibn Khaldūn argues that historians alone can explain how Islam arose out of a context of orality and nomadism–primitivism (*badāwa*) in order to become a proponent of both writing and civilisation (*ḥaḍāra*). What had been speech and a habit became writing and a craft. Yet the very lifeline of Islam depended on maintaining the connection between literacy and orality, between writing and speech, as also between civilised and nomad.

Many have described Ibn Khaldūn's new science as critical history, comparative sociology or even 'supply-side economics'. But Ibn Khaldūn was also an Islamicate cosmopolitan, not least for his subtle, consistent use of the Arabic language to further empirical observation as the cornerstone for networked knowledge.[14]

Islamicate Cosmopolitanism, Coercion and Authority

And so Islamicate cosmopolitan is neither a badge of honour nor a lifetime achievement award. It is instead an unceasing, self-critical quest for truth. In the pre-modern period, it was marked by major elite male exemplars who were often scientists or historians, like Bīrūnī and Ibn Khaldūn. In the modern period they have numerous successors, women as well as men, artists as well as scientists, and in each instance one must contextualise their experiences and embodiments of cosmopolitanism within the structures, often state-directed and coercive, that sometimes elide but in other instances even support them. Geography intersects with temporality, and both dimensions – space as well as time – must be considered in accounting for the limits, as well as the benefits, of Islamicate cosmopolitanism.

The difficulties of this unceasing search for truth come into particularly sharp focus when juxtaposed with the messy realities of political rule exercised by Muslim rulers and empires in the *oikumene*. Consider the medieval Muslim concept of the 'Circle of Justice', which could, and did, frame rulers' patronage of figures like Bīrūnī and Ibn Khaldūn. This circle of justice was epitomised by the thirteenth-century political philosopher Naṣīr al-Dīn al-Ṭūsi (d. 1273), who projected a harmonious structure to permeate, and also sustain, state military and civilian bureaucracies. The circle of justice became the basis for Ottoman consciousness, but it also reflected the ideal for other pre-modern Islamic dynasties as well. Iranian by background and Persianate in outlook, Ṭūsi relied on a Sasanian social ethic that emphasised order, stability, legality and harmony among the theoretical four estates of priests, soldiers, officials and workers. Ṭūsi reinterpreted Sasanian principles within an Islamic programme. He projected a dual function: hierarchical duties mirroring a consensual reciprocity between different groups, each aware of their specific role in the hierarchy. While the loyalty structure is a pyramid, its function is projected as a 'circle of justice':

> There can be no royal authority without the military
> There can be no military without wealth
> The agriculturalists produce the wealth
> The sultan keeps the loyalty of agriculturalists by ensuring justice
> Justice requires harmony in the world
> The world is a garden, its walls are the state
> The state's axis is the religious law
> There is no support for religious law without royal authority.[15]

The elegance of this formulation belies its inner tension. The accent is on justice rather than right religion as the basis for effective rule, not eliminating conflict or violence but redirecting its force to the benefit of the state. While the ruler and the ruled depend on each other, theirs remains an asymmetric relationship, for the circle begins and ends with the state, and its supreme subject, the ruler. Only the middle line suggests that harmony and justice are coterminous one with the other, yet justice is not justice between equals but rather justice as 'just' rewards or allotted payments for participation in this hierarchical system. It never approaches parity, much less equality. The religious custodians of religious law required state support, just as the state, in turn, required the loyalty of the military classes who were its foundation. One could label this system as controlled coercion or the harmonious balance of competing self-interests. At the same time, it presupposed parity among rival dynasties, Muslim or non-Muslim, without which neither harmony nor cosmopolitan options would be possible.

Yet the options for self-determination and patterns of regional rivalry shifted dramatically with the onset of what Hodgson has labelled the 'Great Western Transmutation'. World historical processes from the eighteenth century on involved what William McNeill has etched as 'the rise of the West'.[16] While this process was not rapid, it was decisive. As Hodgson observed, 'the Western Transmutation, once it got well underway, could neither be paralleled independently nor be borrowed wholesale. Yet it could not, in most cases, be escaped. The millennial parity of social power broke down, with results that were disastrous almost everywhere.'[17]

It is necessary to recognise that the secondary impact of these changes involved not only colonial expansion through political, commercial and military power, but also the adoption of Euro-American ideologies, of which ethno-nationalism proved to be the most resilient and pervasive. It is to counter the force of ethno-nationalism that we must review, with contextual nuance, the relationship of different segments of the Islamicate world to cosmopolitan options.

Sample Genealogy of Indian Ocean Trajectories

There are many possible routes along which to theorise and expand the biographies of Islamicate cosmopolitans in the modern period.[18] Perhaps one of the best places for examining the intermingling of European and Islamicate worldviews, for understanding how cosmopolitans survived and even thrived in engagements with coercive power, can be seen beyond the limits of the Nile-to-Oxus regions of Hodgson's description, in the vast maritime arena just beyond it in the Indian Ocean world. One of the most thorough attempts to chart this legacy in terms of Southeast Asia and the modern trajectory of global Islam comes from Carool Kersten. His *Cosmopolitans and Heretics* demonstrates the need to look at the peripheries and not just at the core of Islamicate civilisation. [19] His approach complements another equally compelling temporal–spatial lens: the mid-twentieth-century prism of the Indian Ocean, sometimes referred to as the Bandung moment. Isabel Hofmeyr has drawn attention to the usefulness of the Bandung moment when she depicts:

> the hitherto unrecognised diversity of forms of transnational political community that emerge within the purview of the Bandung nations (largely the

> Indian Ocean arena). These involve the constellations of political community (and non-community) that have cut across the Asian–African divide for the twentieth and early twenty-first century and that transcend the political geographies and the imagination of the nation-state . . . Invoking the Bandung moment helps us examine the variety, complexity and wide-ranging geographies of Afro-Asian relations during the last century and their multiple histories of connection and contradiction.[20]

Yet underlying the Bandung moment is a fundamental cleavage: its opposition to prevalent ideologies outside Bandung, namely, the capitalist West and the communist East. How does one 'transcend the political geographies and the imagination of the nation-state' during the Cold War and its aftermath? In themselves the variety and complexity of Afro-Asian geographies and histories do not confirm an Islamicate cosmopolitan ethos. Ethno-nationalism, a by-product of colonialism but enhanced by independence movements, stressed the primacy of race and language as marks of national solidarity. In this sense, while the Bandung moment opens up the temporal spatial domain of the modern Indian Ocean, it engages neither the Islamicate nor the cosmopolitan.[21]

To make that connection one needs to locate the Indian Ocean *within* longer Islamicate world histories. But where does one find Islamicate world histories? Hardly anywhere. Looking at the range of contemporary specialists on Afro-Eurasian history, one might deduce that *The Venture of Islam* is an event still waiting to happen rather than one that has just marked its fortieth year of publication.[22] Among the very few who have tried to expand Hodgson's vision is the Ottoman economic historian Huri Islamoglu. In her essay 'Islamicate World Histories?', Islamoglu revisits Hodgson's pivotal insight, namely, that Islamicate is the surplus of value in the Afro-Eurasian *oikumene*, at once identified with a Muslim presence yet not limited to its religious expression:

> What is required is the rethinking of world history beyond bifurcation into domains of domination and subordination, East and the West, centre and periphery. If there is a common world historical context of continuous interactions across regions through trade, war, and exchange of ideas, then *one can imagine positioning non-European regions in a new kind of world*

> *history, according them a space comparable to that of Europe, judging them not simply by outcomes, but evaluating them in relation to the world historical processes they were part of and to which they responded – or failed to respond* (added emphasis).[23]

I italicised the last part of this quotation because it provides the link to reimagining Islamicate world history. What would 'a new kind of world history' be if it were both Islamicate and cosmopolitan? It would have to begin by underscoring the 'cosmos' in 'cosmopolitan'. As the cultural critic David Harvey noted in his critique of Martha Nussbaum, 'cosmopolitanism is empty without its cosmos'.[24] Finding the cosmos in 'cosmopolitan', however, can be, and often is, an elusive quest.

In a probing set of essays collected as *Iranian Identity and Cosmopolitanism: Spheres of Belonging*,[25] Lucien Stone stitches together essays from several contributors, many of them Iranian academics in exile, all of which both examine and contest the concept 'cosmopolitan'. They include an ironic meditation by Farhang Erfani, an Iranian-American philosopher focusing on the work of Paul Ricoeur. Erfani laments the fact that 'true' cosmopolitans are the Iranian community abroad, yet they participated in neither the Green Movement (June 2009) nor the Arab Spring, which began 18 months later (December 2010/January 2011). There is no integration, in Erfani's view, between the freedom to resist and to express resistance *abroad* with the repression and inability to change governance *at home*, in Iran itself. Hence, he concludes: 'The Capital (with a capital 'c') of cosmopolis often serves metropolitan and not cosmopolitan interests, and integration [of longing with belonging] remains an unattainable fantasy.'[26] In other words, for Erfani, as for most of the contributors to Stone's volume, there are no 'true' Islamicate cosmopolitans, at least with Iranian names, histories, belongings and longings.

One way out of the impasse between metropolis–cosmopolis is to move beyond the folds of Iranian diasporic history and to imagine instead how the dyad of metropolis–cosmopolis has played out in another cosmopolis, one etched in Arabic. Could the Indian Ocean be such a cosmopolis? Kersten has indicated possible new eastward directions in *Cosmopolitans and Heretics*, citing James Clifford's clarion cry for 'non-Western, or not-only-Western models for cosmopolitan life'.[27] Ronit Ricci has broached a similar argument.

In her celebrated monograph, *Islam Translated*, Ricci explores what she terms 'the Arabic Cosmopolis of South and Southeast Asia' as marked by 'shifting cosmopolitanisms'. This Arabic cosmopolis, we are told, 'was never a singular entity in the region: overlapping, waxing and waning cosmopolitan worlds existed and were not mutually exclusive'.[28] Yet she inscribes a persistent reifying trace in the qualifier 'Arabic'. Her cosmopolis remains an *Arabic* cosmopolis, and its core is lined to the lodestone of Islamic belief and practice: the Qur'ān. Anouar Majid, a Moroccan cultural critic teaching in the United States, tries to identify this Arabic core as a Qur'ānic idiom that goes beyond the actual history of Qur'ānic commentary or *tafsīr* and folds back into the surplus of meaning that derives from the original revelation. 'The cosmopolitan thought expressed in the Qur'ān,' argues Majid, was later reduced to 'a fictional ethnicity invented as a political ploy to contain dangerous foreigners attracted by the egalitarian and liberating promise of Islam,' thus serving to underscore much later conceptions of Arab ethno-nationalism. By contrast, the project of our era, according to Majid, should be a recuperation of that initial, defining moment of cosmopolitan Arabic liberation.[29]

But is it possible to recuperate in an 'Arabic' cosmopolis 'the egalitarian and liberating promise of Islam'? The centuries of verbal and historical conflation of Arabic language with Arab culture and ethnicity makes it difficult to imagine 'Arabic' separate from 'Arab' except for the cognoscenti. A more productive approach, in my view, would be to shift from 'Arabic' to 'Islamicate', and that requires some further elaboration of what Hodgson meant by the term. The set of comments, arguments and evidence above critiques an absence of deep commitment to Islamicate belongings and longings – in short, to the cosmopolitan option. Islamicate cosmopolitanism in a Hodgsonian idiom goes in the other direction: it sets forth the criteria that make the Islamicate cosmopolitan at once possible and desirable.

The eastern reaches of the Indian Ocean are remote from the Mediterranean Sea, or the Nile-to-Oxus region that preoccupied major pre-modern Islamic empires (apart from the Mughals). Yet while the content of Islamicate cosmopolitan is different for the Indian Ocean, its methodologies are shared with other regions, including the Middle East and North Africa (MENA). And it would seem that these same reverberations – our own past in mid-concert with all other pasts – also shape and reshape the Indian Ocean. We can, and should, examine Islamicate cosmopolitan beyond MENA without, however, privileging the Indian Ocean as itself a unique site of cosmopolitan experience.[30]

One of the first steps is to conceptualise the region not solely by national flags or the histories they convey, but also by large-scale continuities over the past two millennia. While no name is innocent of interest, some names couch what Braudel has labelled *la longue durée* in more expansive terms. Shinzo Hayase, for example, has written of the cosmopolitan formations of a region he refers to as 'East Maritime Southeast Asia'.[31] Hayase's study outlines the contours of a maritime world that is also an open society, one where networks criss-cross almost all prescribed boundaries, where the norm was amiable behaviour despite periodic warfare – though even warfare can produce unanticipated cultural synergies as well as long-term benefits.

Sundry Conclusions, with Three Accents

Belonging and Longing

Islamicate cosmopolitan becomes a useful analytical tool rather than an empty descriptor when it moves beyond dichotomous blinders. It is not the abandonment of the West and embrace of the East, it is neither a rejection of all things colonial nor an assertion of all norms and values, activities and dreams that are post-colonial. Instead, it is a pragmatic engagement with the end of empires, the rise of the modern West and the emergence of nation-states. All these world historical processes have to be problematised, but without either wholesale embrace or categorical rejection of the past. The Islamicate cosmopolitan, at once partisan and above party, pursues local idioms that refract pre-Islam and post-Islam through an Islamicate lens.

Never free of tension or contradiction, Islamicate cosmopolitan remains rooted in hope; it grows out of, even as it sustains, a deep, layered history – at once diachronic and trans-regional, not ad hoc and piecemeal but systematic and incremental. Instead of a pyramid, Islamicate cosmopolitan is a rhizome. It requires, and facilitates, constant engagement with difference. Travel is not the only vehicle to broader horizons, nor do tolerance and reciprocity as social reflexes suffice. To be or become cosmopolitan requires agonistic engagement – striving to be better through the other. It is a constant moral vision, never intent on one goal, never self-satisfied. There must be multiple, non-hierarchical entry and re-entry into spaces, communities and activities that are shared rather than isolated, mutual rather than exclusive in the challenges they offer and the benefits they confer.

Indian Ocean as Islamicate Cosmopolitan Regions

Because many regions participate, one would expect a hierarchy of regional value within those deemed to be Islamicate cosmopolitan. The Indian Ocean region, from South and Southeast Asia extending into the South China Sea, has given Islam a particular civilisational shape, making the Islamicate cosmopolitan a vital category for contemporary as well as historical analysis. What distinguishes the Islamicate cosmopolitan imaginary is in this sense aqua-centric thinking and living, belonging to an island yet criss-crossing and connecting many islands. Despite the hesitancy or demurral of some academics,[32] the central question about Asia remains vital: how do colonial, then nationalist, and now lingering, persistent patrimonial efforts to control Muslims in all the sub-regions of Asia also produce an unintended consequence? If conquest, warfare and systemic violence are inevitable, what are the implications accompanying their seeming failure to produce any new order, but merely perpetuate disunity, disorder and calamity? Might these not also be seen to include multiple mobilities, connections and ethical frameworks of mutual obligation and perpetual longing that can sometimes nevertheless emerge out of efforts to control, narrow and reduce the pluralist option? And what is the residue of such ebb and flow of proto-pluralism if not Islamicate cosmopolitan as a pervasive idiom of Indian Ocean history?

Islamicate Cosmopolitan as Process

Finally, Islamicate cosmopolitan is a process rather than a product: the constant commingling of the local with the national, the regional with the trans-regional, the aesthetic and the social with political and economic interests marked by a Muslim presence. East Maritime Southeast Asia, to quote Hayase again, will remain one of the crucial arenas in attempts to conceptualise Islamicate cosmopolitan longing. More than a topic to be explored, it is also an agent to be welcomed, an optic to be expanded. Through its presence in the Indian Ocean, Islam has become a pan-Asian cultural agent with potential yet untapped and unrealised. A detailed, critical set of empirical case studies, such as the current volume provides, demonstrates the ways in which particular formations of the Islamicate cosmopolitan take shape in specific times and places – shaped by both transcendent ethical imaginaries and this-worldly hierarchies and contestations of power.

Notes

1. See Appiah, Kwame Anthony, *Cosmopolitanism: Ethics in the World of Strangers* (New York: Norton/Penguin, 2006). Artfully framed, Appiah's thesis conceals what amounts to an Hellenic, European claim to cosmopolitanism as the high side of moral relativism. Central to his argument is the nineteenth-century explorer, Richard Burton, himself a successor to the Moroccan traveller, Ibn Baṭṭūṭa. Burton becomes for Appiah the epitome of moral relativists. Burton's views are projected through the figure Haji Abdu, who is alleged to have said: 'There is no Good, there is no Bad; these be the whims of mortal will' (p. 11). Later, the notion of firm belief and daily ritual observance are questioned through Appiah's own uncle, Uncle Aviv, a Muslim. Though Uncle Aviv dotes on him, Appiah writes about his uncle: 'I knew only that Uncle Aviv was a devout Muslim and that he was also tolerant and gentle' (pp. 148–51). Nothing more is said of this clustering of traits – 'devout', 'tolerant', 'gentle' – but the implication is clear: the devout is in tandem with tolerant and gentle but as stronger to weaker, more to less. The more you believe, the less you are tolerant, gentle or cosmopolitan in Appiah's unstated yet persistent hierarchy of values.
2. Aravamudan, Srinivas, 'East–West Fiction as World Literature: the Hayy Problem Reconfigured', *Eighteenth-Century Studies* 47(2) (2014): 198. I am indebted to Aravamudan for many stimulating discussions on Islamicate as a cosmopolitan qualifier across time and space, in Europe and Asia, in the eleventh, eighteenth and now twenty-first centuries.
3. Ahmed, Shahab, *What is Islam? The Importance of Being Islamic* (Princeton, NJ: Princeton University Press, 2016). According to Ahmed, the most fundamental, recurrent error in scholarship on Islam is to register law at the pinnacle in a hierarchy of truth. One must instead '*conceptualize the law in terms beyond the law itself* . . . within a larger perspective of social and discursive truth, meaning and value' (p. 455). And to accomplish that task Ahmed suggests a Persianate idiom: *madhhab-i ʿishq* (i.e., the frame of Love). Ahmed argues that precisely because the law – the notion of *sharīʿa* or *sharīʿa*-mindedness – has been overvalued,

there needs to be a new, higher law, a more lyrical and inclusive notion of Islam, one he labels *madhhab-i ʿishq*, literally, a way of moving, going, travelling that is prompted and informed by deep passion or radical love, at once transcendent and immanent. And the most ample, necessary resource for *madhhab-i ʿishq* is the centuries-old fount of lyrical creativity: Islamicate/Persianate poetry (p.38, fn. 99).

4. Hodgson, Marshall G. S., *The Venture of Islam: Conscience and History in a World Civilization*, vol. 1 (Chicago, IL: University of Chicago Press, 1974), p. 95, as quoted in Ahmed, *What is Islam?*, p. 170, fn. 131.
5. 'Rooted cosmopolitanism' is a central topic in Appiah's earlier book, *The Ethics of Identity* (Princeton, NJ: Princeton University Press, 2005), where he argues that one can be both a local citizen, i.e., a patriot, and also a global citizen, identifying with universal values and espousing a cosmopolitan outlook. The anecdotes, however, dodge the difficult choice that the deep, intertwined roots of both identities must, and do, often entail. Also, Appiah centres on the privileged individual and her or his choices to the exclusion of marginal, less privileged societies and their lack of choices.
6. Scham, Sandra Arnold, '"Time's Wheel Runs Back": Conversations with the Middle Eastern Past', in Lynn Meskell (ed.), *Cosmopolitan Archaeologies* (Durham, NC: Duke University Press, 2009), pp. 182–3.
7. Several examples of these nodes – their locations, their trajectories, their successes and failures – can be found in miriam cooke and Bruce Lawrence (eds), *Muslim Networks from Hajj to Hip-Hop* (Chapel Hill, NC: University of North Carolina Press, 2005).
8. In the initial iteration of this chapter, I had included two modern Muslim women as exemplar cosmopolitans. Both are artists, the Indonesian Arahmaiani and the Iranian-American Shirin Neshat. I have written about them elsewhere, Arahmaiani, *Who is Allah?* (Chapel Hill, NC: University of North Carolina Press, 2015), pp. 164–6; and Neshat, 'Islamicate Cosmopolitan: a Past Without a Future, or a Future Still Unfolding', available at: https://humanitiesfutures.org/papers/islamicate-cosmopolitan-past-without-future-future-still-unfolding, last accessed 7 February 2018.
9. Many are the secondary sources for pursuing the strands of knowledge that emanate from, and trace back, to Bīrūnī. The best is still in process: Malagaris, George E., *Biruni* (Oxford: Oxford University Press, forthcoming). I have done a popular essay, 'Al-Biruni: Against the Grain', in *Critical Muslims* 12 (2014): 61–71.

10. Harvey, David, 'Cosmopolitanism and the Banality of Evil', *Public Culture* 12(2) (2000): 554.
11. Hodgson had numerous successors in his accent on Jasper's notion of the Axial Age as itself axial for the comparative study of civilisations. Among the most notable is S. N. Eisenstadt in multiple articles and books, but especially *The Origins and Diversity of Axial Age Civilizations* (Binghamton, NY: State University of New York Press, 1986). Like Hodgson, Eisenstadt emphasised the double role of world religions, as both product and catalyst for the major civilisations with which they became identified.
12. I am relying here on an epitome by Hodgson's former student, Marilyn Waldman, in an essay for *Encyclopaedia Britannica*, titled 'The Islamic World'. Alas, due to Waldman's untimely, early death, in 1996, paralleling the experience of her mentor, Hodgson, the final section, including 'Islam and Globalization: The Age of Mobility', was written by Malika Zeghal.
13. Numerous are the blind alleys or false leads in the burgeoning but unmonitored field of cosmopolitan studies. For some of the most salient, and often grotesque, see my unpublished paper 'Muslim Cosmopolitanism in the Age of Globalization', delivered as a keynote address at the Michigan State University Conference on 'Beyond Islamic Studies: De-essentializing the Study of Muslim Societies', 7 April 2011. Similar critiques are also presented in my 'Afterwords: Competing Genealogies of Muslim Cosmopolitanism', the final chapter of Carl W. Ernst and Richard C. Martin (eds), *Rethinking Islamic Studies: From Orientalism to Cosmopolitanism* (Columbia, SC: University of South Carolina Press, 2010), pp. 302–23.
14. There are even more secondary sources on Ibn Khaldūn than on al-Bīrūnī. Two are especially notable: Alatas, Syed Farid, *Ibn Khaldun* (Oxford: Oxford University Press, 2013), and Dale, Stephen F., *The Orange Trees of Marrakesh: Ibn Khaldun and the Science of Man* (Cambridge, MA: Harvard University Press, 2015). I had compiled an earlier collection of essays highlighting his interdisciplinary appeal: *Ibn Khaldun and Islamic Ideology* (Leiden: Brill, 1984).
15. For the elaboration of this concept among Ottoman ruling elites, see Fleischer, Cornell, 'Royal Authority, Dynastic Cyclism, and "Ibn Khaldunism"', in Bruce B. Lawrence (ed.), *Ibn Khaldun and Islamic Ideology* (Leiden: Brill, 1984), pp. 48–51.
16. McNeill, William H., *The Rise of the West: a History of the Human Community* (Chicago, IL: University of Chicago Press, 1992).
17. Hodgson, Marshall and Edmund Burke III (eds), *Rethinking World History:*

Essays on Europe, Islam and World History (Cambridge: Cambridge University Press, 1993), p. 71.

18. The list could easily be expanded, and among recent works one should note, Aljunied, Khairudin, *Muslim Cosmopolitanism: Southeast Asian Islam in Comparative Perspective* (Edinburgh: Edinburgh University Press, 2016). The author applies the category cosmopolitan solely to Muslim actors, in and beyond Southeast Asia, with a welcome attention to juridical categories that have a strong ethical import, including *maqāṣid al-shariʿa.*
19. Kersten, Carool, *Cosmopolitans and Heretics: New Muslim Intellectuals and the Study of Islam* (New York: Columbia University Press, 2011).
20. Hofmeyr, Isabel, 'The Complicating Sea: the Indian Ocean as Method', *Comparative Studies of South Asia, Africa and the Middle East* 32(3) (2012): 589, here she is quoting Lee, Christopher, *Making a World After Empire: the Bandung Moment and Its Political Alternatives* (Athens, OH: Ohio University Press, 2010).
21. See Kersten, *Cosmopolitans and Heretics*, p. 199, for Arkoun's critique of the Bandung moment as itself a point of manipulating knowledge and power, glorifying revolution in the so-called Third World without seeing its ideological limits and anti-cosmopolitan potential.
22. On the absence of Hodgson's influence within cultural studies, including literary and artistic domains, see my online essay: 'Islamicate Cosmopolitan: A Past Without a Future, or a Future still Unfolding', at https://humanitiesfutures.org/papers/islamicate-cosmopolitan-past-without-future-future-still-unfolding, last accessed 8 February 2018.
23. Islamoglu, Huri, 'Islamicate World Histories?' in Douglas Northrop (ed.), *A Companion to World History* (Chichester: Wiley-Blackwell, 2012), pp. 457–9, here adapted to the sense of my argument.
24. Harvey, 'Cosmopolitanism', p. 554.
25. Stone, Lucian (ed.), *Iranian Identity and Cosmopolitanism: Spheres of Belonging* (London: Bloomsbury, 2014).
26. Erfani, Farhang, 'Cosmopolitanism: Neither For, nor Against, to the Contrary', in Lucien Stone (ed.), *Iranian Identity and Cosmopolitanism: Spheres of Belonging* (London: Bloomsbury, 2014), p. 157.
27. Kersten, *Cosmopolitans and Heretics*, p. 38, citing Clifford, James, *Routes: Travel and Translation in the Late Twentieth Century* (Cambridge, MA: Harvard University Press, 1997), p. 276. There are many efforts to pursue what Kersten identifies as 'the mapping of Indian Ocean networks linking maritime Southeast

Asia with centres of Islamic learning in the Middle East' (p. 7), and he has highlighted the importance of networks for new Muslim intellectuals, especially, but not solely, Madjid, Hanafi and Arkoun, as well as their connection to antecedent scholars both Muslim and non-Muslim. I am indebted to Kersten for many of the insights in this chapter on Muslim cosmopolitanism, or what I prefer to call, Islamicate cosmopolitan.

28. Ricci, Ronit, *Islam Translated: Literature, Conversion, and the Arabic Cosmopolis of South and Southeast Asia* (Chicago, IL: University of Chicago Press, 2011), p. 267.
29. Majid, Anouar, *Unveiling Traditions: Postcolonial Islam in a Polycentric World* (Durham, NC: Duke University Press, 2000), p. 53. I have modified the actual quote to fit the sense of my argument.
30. Among several efforts to debunk Indian Ocean cosmopolitanism is André Wink's review 'Cosmopolitanism and Xenophobia' (H-Asia, October 2010), a critique of Simpson, Edward and Kai Kresse (eds), *Struggling with History: Islam and Cosmopolitanism in the Western Indian Ocean* (New York: Columbia University Press, 2008), also available at: http://www.hnet.org/reviews/showrev.php?id=30792. Islamic(ate) cosmopolitanism, argues Wink, is 'the product, largely, of a combination of ignorance, willful distortion, and wishful thinking; it naively celebrates the Indian Ocean as the multicultural "cradle of globalization" – the maritime counterpart of the so-called silk road – and its cosmopolitan Islam as interfaith dialogue'. Yet Indian Ocean cosmopolitanism has both a commercial and cultural trajectory that is more than naive nominalism or empty religious rhetoric.
31. Hayase, Shinzo, *Mindanao Ethnohistory beyond Nations: Maguindanao, Sangir, and Bagobo Societies in East Maritime Southeast Asia* (Manila: Ateno de Manila University Press, 2007). On Hayase as a catalyst for projecting a new social meaning of Southeast Asia in the twenty-first century, see my earlier manifesto, *Islam in the Public Square: Minority Perspectives from Africa and Asia*, Youngstown Papers in Islamic Religion, History, and Culture 2 (Youngstown, OH: Youngstown State University, 2009), pp. 37–41.
32. See also Hanley, Will, 'Grieving Cosmopolitanism in Middle East Studies', *History Compass* 6(5) (2008): 1346–67; and Mills, Amy, *Streets of Memory: Landscape, Tolerance, and National Identity in Istanbul* (Athens, GA: University of Georgia, 2010). Wink focuses on the Indian Ocean, while Hanley surveys the entire Middle East, and Mills Istanbul, particularly the neighbourhood of Kuzguncuk. In my British Association for Islamic Studies (BRAIS) plenary

address of 10 April 2014 at the University of Edinburgh, I appreciated the critiques of both Hanley and Mills, as also the development of everyday cosmopolitanism by Bayat, Asaf, *Life as Politics: How Ordinary People Change the Middle East* (Stanford, CA: Stanford University Press, 2010). My chief difference from all of their approaches is to stress the broad-based, diachronic and multi-civilisational basis of an Islamicate cosmopolitan ethos, with special reference to the peripheries rather than the so-called core of the Afro-Eurasian *oikumene.*

3

Sufi Cosmopolitanism in the Seventeenth-century Indian Ocean: *Sharīʿa*, Lineage and Royal Power in Southeast Asia and the Maldives

A. C. S. Peacock

Sufi networks have been seen as constituting one of the prime means through which cosmopolitanism in a variety of senses was articulated in the pre-modern Islamic world. In emulation of the Prophetic *ḥadīth*, 'seek knowledge though it be in China', travel was one of the key duties of the Sufi, both in theory and in practice, and Sufi literature was permeated with the vocabulary of voyaging.[1] Through shared texts, holy men and genealogies both spiritual and blood, *ṭarīqa*s bound together the Islamic world in a way that political and commercial links never rivalled. Itinerant holy men criss-crossed the *dār al-Islām*, and from an early date some specifically sought out contested zones on the border with non-Muslims, far from the urban centres of Islamic civilisation, to devote themselves to contemplation and holy war.

As a type of religiosity that thrived on these contested peripheries, Sufism has often been characterised as especially receptive to non-Muslim influences,[2] which for some modern scholars constitutes a form of cosmopolitanism.[3] This presumed aspect of Sufism is often seen as underlying its alleged role in converting non-Muslim populations, by providing a sort of common ground whereby pre-Islamic practices could be incorporated into a Muslim society.[4] One scholar has written that analysis of Sufism in the Indian Ocean is 'more apt to speak of an acceptance of Islamic practices into pre-Islamic cosmology and customs rather than conversion to a new orthodoxy'.[5] However, as Nile Green has put it, 'to a very large extent, Sufism *was* Islam in its medieval form' and it cannot easily be detached from other forms of Islamic piety.[6] Sufi Islam encompassed a wide variety of practices, the distinctive unifying component being a belief in the efficacy of the blessing power (*baraka*) of holy men. Thus, whatever the reasons for the widespread appeal of Sufism to Muslims and converts throughout post-classical Islamic history, it would be wrong to assume that it was in any uniform sense especially (or at all) accommodating to pre-Islamic practices.

If claims that Sufism is cosmopolitan by virtue of openness to other religions are questionable, so is the idea that travel necessarily engenders cosmopolitanism, except perhaps in a very limited sense where it becomes little more than a synonym for itinerancy.[7] The early modern Indian Ocean, for instance, is characterised by an intensification of links between its various parts, with ever greater numbers of itinerant scholars and Sufis.[8] Yet these links, far from promoting openness to diversity, in fact brought an unsettling realisation of the variety of Muslim practices – often merely local variants rather than true survivals of pre-Islamic tradition – which in turn have been linked to a prevailing trend over the sixteenth to eighteenth centuries that sought to criticise and eradicate *bid'a* (innovation), or diversity in religious practice.[9] Some recent scholarship has sought to identify these competing interpretations of Islam as rival forms of cosmopolitanism, in the sense of cosmopolitanism as the challenge of 'how to create or envisage wider unity when faced with social diversity'.[10] In this sense, cosmopolitanism could thus constitute a religious or even a political project, and one far removed from the utopian ideas of open-mindedness and mobility that characterise many discussions of the phenomenon. Indeed, like many universalist religious and political projects, such a cosmopolitanism might overlap with, and indeed require, coercion. Although Sufis are characterised in some scholarship as other-worldly 'Muslim mystics', recent work has drawn attention to the intense political connections of Sufis in diverse areas of the Muslim world, such as, for instance, on the peripheries of the *dār al-Islām* where Sufis played an important role in turning frontier regions such as Bengal, the Deccan and the Balkans into Muslim space, receiving in return support and patronage from political elites, and thus participating in and facilitating imperial expansion.[11]

In at least some times and places Sufism supported imperial political power by offering through its philosophical theology a legitimation of sultanic authority. This is associated, in particular, with various developments of the thought of Ibn ʿArabī (d. 1240). In the sixteenth century, the Ottoman Empire claimed its very foundation had been predicted by this great Sufi thinker,[12] while in newly Islamising territories like Southeast Asia the doctrine of the perfect man (*al-insān al-kāmil*) associated with Ibn ʿArabī has been interpreted as offering a means of perpetuating the pre-Islamic, divine status of the ruler and justifying it in Islamic terms.[13] Studies of Southeast Asia have often seen this political function of Sufism as linked to an elite court culture. Martin Van Bruinessen argues that in Southeast Asia until the eighteenth or even the nineteenth century, Sufism had no wider appeal. For him, Sufism is intimately bound up with efforts to support the ruler's legitimacy, or as he puts it, 'The *tarékat* [i.e., *ṭarīqa*] was perceived as a source of spiritual power, at once legitimating and supporting the ruler's position. It was obviously not in the rulers' interest to make the same supernatural power available to all their subjects.'[14]

However, during the seventeenth century, a critical phase in the spread of Islam in the Indian Ocean region, a certain *sharīʿa*-minded Sufi piety was disseminated that had little connection with the speculations of the school of Ibn ʿArabī. This phenomenon, sometimes called 'neo-Sufism', has been attributed to the efforts of scholars from the Ḥaramayn, the two great Muslim holy cities of Mecca and Medina which in the seventeenth century were major intellectual centres,[15] and is often seen as associated with a more popular rather than courtly religiosity. As Michael Laffan puts it, 'Sufism was formally restricted to the regal elite, while adherence to the *sharīʿa* was commended to their subjects.'[16] Yet beyond constituting a reaction to the perception of *bidʿa* mentioned above, this *sharīʿa*-minded piety had profound political consequences, seeking to shape societies in accordance with the norms of an idealised Islamic Middle East and sweep away existing dynasties. Here cosmopolitanism, in the sense of an attempt to impose unity over diversity, appears as both a disruptive and a coercive force. Yet the political consequences of the rise of this *sharīʿa*-minded piety in the Indian

Ocean have received little attention. In this chapter, I focus on the sultanates of Banten in Java, Aceh in Sumatra and the Maldive Islands in the Indian Ocean. All fell outside the compass of the great imperial projects of the Asian mainland – the Mughal, Ottoman and Safavid empires; all were societies still undergoing a process of Islamisation (culturally, if not demographically); and all were, from the perspective of the Middle East, remote frontiers of Islam, even if their self-image was otherwise.[17] Furthermore, although geographically disparate, cultural and commercial ties – especially but not exclusively the spice trade – bound Banten closely to Aceh, and Aceh to the Maldives.[18] These lands thus shared a relationship with one another, as well as with the Middle East.

I will draw on some neglected Arabic texts to argue that promoting the universalist project of *sharīʿa*-minded Sufism was a prime concern not just of Ḥaramayn *ʿulamāʾ* but more importantly local actors, including royal courts. Promotion of *sharīʿa* was a component of efforts to promote themselves as Islamic, and sometimes more specifically as Middle Eastern-style, monarchies,[19] and in this sense can itself be seen as a cosmopolitan venture in the sense outlined in the previous paragraph. First, I will look at the evidence of the Arabic texts composed in the Hijaz for the royal library of the Banten sultanate, which can help us to understand better the Sufi interests of at least some Southeast Asian rulers, which are suggestive of the intimate relationship between the *sharīʿa*, Sufism and the court. I will then in the second part of this chapter develop the argument by turning to a practical example of a Sufi in action in late seventeenth-century Aceh and the Maldives, the Syrian Qādirī shaykh Muḥammad Shams al-Dīn, a descendant of the famed Baghdadi saint ʿAbd al-Qādir al-Jīlānī (d. 1166). While in both locations our Syrian Qādirī received the support of the political elite for a programme that aimed at enforcing a more rigorous interpretation of the *sharīʿa*, and rejection of local customs, he also played a part in destabilising royal power. Here another component of Sufism, genealogical links as embodied in a holy man, play a crucial role, as will be discussed in further detail below.

God's Law at the Royal Court of Banten: the Evidence of Texts

One of the early Islamic monarchies of Southeast Asia was Banten, a rich trading city on the island of Java whose commercial links stretched as far west as Mecca and as far east as Manila. From the sixteenth century onwards, the sultans of Banten sponsored the development of Islamic institutions in northeast Java. For instance, as van Bruinessen notes, the position of *qāḍī* was especially politically important in Banten compared with other Javanese sultanates where it had a more limited role. [20] Moreover, as the Javanese chronicle the *Sejarah Banten* relates, two sultans visited Mecca in person, receiving recognition from the Sharīf of Mecca; one, indeed, was subsequently known as Sultan Hajji. The *Sejarah Banten* also recounts how in 1638 a Bantenese embassy, after passing through the Maldives, the Coromandel Coast, Surat, Mocha and Jeddah, reached Mecca to ask the Sharīf to explain for them certain tracts. This report has attracted attention from scholarship because these tracts have been identified with the debates over the doctrine of *waḥdat al-wujūd* attributed to Ibn ʿArabī that rocked Southeast Asian learned circles. This has often been taken as further evidence for the association of courts, and that of Banten in particular, with a high-flown philosophical mysticism, evidence of Sufism's 'elite' nature and its appeal to royal legitimation strategies.[21]

An examination of the texts themselves, however, suggests rather different conclusions. The royal library of Banten, preserved in the National Library in Jakarta, contains copies of the works commissioned by the Sharīf from the leading Meccan scholar Ibn ʿAlān (d. 1647 or 1648) for the Bantenese embassy. The Bantenese had tried to persuade Ibn ʿAlān to make the long journey to Java with them but he declined.[22] Although Ibn ʿAlān was a well-known Hijazi scholar, some of whose works remain in print today, his compositions written at the behest of the sultan of Banten, Abū l-Mafākhir, apparently only circulated in Southeast Asia, for their titles never feature in biographical notices of Ibn ʿAlān from the Middle East, such as the detailed one given by the seventeenth-century biographer al-Muḥibbī in his *Khulāṣat al-Athār*.[23] Perhaps most importantly for the Bantenese purposes, Ibn ʿAlān was not just a well-known scholar, known as the *muḥyī al-sunna*, or 'reviver of the Prophet's custom', but possessed a distinguished lineage as a direct descendant of Caliph Abū Bakr.[24]

In an unpublished commentary on a work on eschatology attributed to al-Ghazālī, *al-Durra al-Fākhira*, Ibn ʿAlān provides a detailed account of how the work's composition came about, confirming the reality of the sultans' contacts with the Sharīfs. He starts by describing how Ghazālī's reputation reached Southeast Asia (Jakarta, MS A32, p. 3):

> And the *ʿulamāʾ* of distant regions (*ʿulamāʾ al-aṭrāf*) became aware of the precious fine pearls [of his writings] and wanted to copy these lights [of knowledge], and these delightful gems. The righteous, noble *ʿulamāʾ* of Java, highly respected, raised a petition to their king, the noble sultan who defends Islam and Muslims, whose task it is to spread noble justice over the succession of the years; the glorious, fortunate Abu l-Mafākhir ʿAbd al-Qādir [sultan of Banten]. The king contemplated and examined then cogitated and considered; he knew that light had not been granted to [al-Ghazālī] nor had he reached this knowledge except by the guidance of the Prophet Muḥammad, born in the Holy Land; and he realised that this [knowledge] could not be acquired except from the family of the Prophet . . .

The king therefore sought to acquire his desire, and 'the finest man of his age urged him to realise his desire' – this was, Ibn ʿAlān tells us, the Sharīf of Mecca, Zayd b. Muḥsin. The sultan wrote Zayd 'a letter which asked him, of his good grace, requesting what he wanted. His request was well-received, that the book entitled *al-Durra al-Fākhira fī ʿUlūm al-Ākhira* should be explained to him, along with the book *Naṣīḥat al-Mulūk* ("Advice for Kings").'

Ibn ʿAlān then relates how the Sharif Zayd b. Muḥsin chose him to undertake this task, being qualified by virtue both of caliphal descent and his learning. The commentary on *al-Durra al-Fākhira* survives only in this one manuscript, with occasional annotations in Arabic-script Javanese (*pegon*). The *Naṣīḥat al-Mulūk*, also by al-Ghazalī, was copied in Banten, and two manuscripts of the Arabic text survive in Jakarta.[25] In addition, Ibn ʿAlān supplied another work of his own composition, titled *al-Mawāhib al-Rabbāniyya ʿalā l-Asʾila al-Jāwiyya* ('The divine gifts in response to Javanese questions').[26] These questions, posed by Sultan Abū l-Mafākhir, all arise from the *Naṣīḥat al-Mulūk*, and *al-Mawāhib al-Rabbāniyya* in many ways reads like a commentary on the *Naṣīḥat al-Mulūk*.

The *Naṣīḥat al-Mulūk* is designed as a practical primer on how to govern in accordance with Islamic precepts. Many examples of this type of 'mirror for princes' are known, although some place much more emphasis on Persian courtly traditions. The central idea of the text is that 'the tree of faith has ten roots and ten branches, its roots being the beliefs of the heart and its branches actions of the body'. Al-Ghazālī outlines these ten roots of faith but devotes most attention to the ten 'branches' – that is, actions, which he illustrates with anecdotes usually drawn from early Islamic history. The *Naṣīḥat al-Mulūk* thus aims to show the sultan how to behave, above all how to act with justice. Through its anecdotes, it offers something of a manual for relatively recent converts to Islam, and its popularity in Mamluk times suggests that its appeal for new Muslims was enduring. It is easy to see then why it might have appealed to the rulers of Banten, at a time when it was still a peripheral area of the Muslim world.

The questions that Ibn ʿAlān addresses in his *al-Mawāhib al-Rabbāniyya* also revolve around justice and, in particular, the implementation of the *ḥudūd*, divinely prescribed punishments.[27] Just like al-Ghazālī, Ibn ʿAlān draws on *ḥadīth* and anecdotes of early Islamic history to illustrate his points, although he occasionally also relates anecdotes concerning the behaviour of recent Sharīfs of the Hijaz. Both the *Naṣīḥat al-Mulūk* and *al-Mawāhib al-Rabbāniyya* are thus designed as practical guides on how to behave, and in particular how to rule as a Muslim. The very lack of mystical content in *al-Durra al-Fākhira* has been noted and the texts described by its English translator as 'presenting a series of ethical teachings that are intended less as descriptions of the future life than as injunctions for the living of this life in order to be ready for the Day and the Hour'.[28] In a Southeast Asian context, it has also been noted that the works of al-Ghazālī are sometimes invoked precisely in opposition to Ibn ʿArabī and the doctrine of *waḥdat al-wujūd*.[29]

In other words, the evidence of these texts is that, for the court of Banten, Sufism was not a source of legitimacy through esoteric doctrines. On the contrary, the texts show a preoccupation with the *sharīʿa*, with the *ḥudūd* and with obedience to the external forms of Islam, not with metaphysical speculation. Moreover, Ibn ʿAlān's testimony suggests that the mission to Mecca was prompted ultimately by the *ʿulamāʾ* of Banten rather than by their court. Nonetheless, the preservation of these texts in the palace library, sometimes in fine presentation copies, with careful Arabic vocalisation alongside *pegon* translations, indicates their enduring importance for the royal court of Banten and suggests that they had ritual as well as purely functional uses, perhaps for public declamation.

The key point, though, as Ibn ʿAlān underlines in his introduction to his commentary on *al-Durra al-Fākhira*, is that these texts, and their transmission from Mecca via the agency of the Sharīf and Ibn ʿAlān, served to link them, and the dynasty of Banten, to the Prophet himself. In this context, it is worth recalling that, as one scholar has put it, 'Sufi Islam was a religiosity of embodied holy men who re-presented the blessing power that via genealogical memory believers traced through space and time back to the Prophet Muhammad in Mecca.'[30] When a physical holy man was lacking – or could not be persuaded to move, as in the case of Ibn ʿAlān – texts stood in for him and served to 're-present the blessing power', hence the emphasis Ibn ʿAlān gives to both his and the Sharīfs' lineage. In this sense, the example of Banten suggests that a simple disjunction between *sharīʿa* for masses and Sufism for the court is untenable, nor can we see these missions as simply an attempt to raise the standards of Southeast Asian Islam by Hijazi scholars and their sympathisers, as has been suggested.[31] Rather, embracing and supporting the *sharīʿa* and the *ḥudūd* as promoted by texts such as *al-Mawāhib al-Rabbāniyya* was a source of legitimacy, reinforcing the link to the sacred land of the Hijaz and to the family of the Prophet that was provided by the association with the Sharīf and Ibn ʿAlān. This is a point that we will see more clearly in our second case, that of the itinerant Qādirī preacher Muḥammad Shams al-Dīn.

Commanding Right and Forbidding Wrong in Late Seventeenth-century Aceh and the Maldives

The Qādirī Sufi *ṭarīqa*, taking its name from the Prophet's descendant ʿAbd al-Qādir al-Jīlānī (d. 1166), is often credited with a major role in the spread of Islam in Southeast Asia. As early as the fourteenth century, the Arabic author al-Yāfiʿī recalls being initiated into the Qādiriyya in Aden by a certain Masʿūd al-Jāwī, a Southeast Asian, and al-Yāfiʿī's Qādirī hagiographic texts such as the *Khulāṣat al-Mafākhir* obtained a widespread currency in the archipelago.[32] The poems of the sixteenth-century Acehnese mystic Ḥamzah Fanṣūrī in several places mention ʿAbd al-Qādir, suggesting Ḥamzah's affiliation to the Qādirī order. By the mid-eighteenth century *saraka* (investiture documents issued by the sultan) from Aceh were invoking ʿAbd al-Qādir al-Jīlānī directly after God, the Prophet and his four companions,[33] while allusions to ʿAbd al-Qādir may also be found in documents from the Minangkabau sultanate of south Sumatra.[34] The Qādiriyya may also have had an important place in the sultanate of Banten – van Bruinessen has suggested that the name of Sultan ʿAbd al-Qādir indicates an affiliation with the order. Similarly affiliated to the Qādiriyya (in addition to other *ṭarīqa*s such as the Rifāʿiyya) were two of the leading figures in seventeenth-century Southeast Asian Islam, Nūr al-Dīn al-Rānīrī (d. 1658) and Shaykh Yūsuf al-Maqassārī (1629–99).[35]

The careers of both al-Rānīrī and al-Maqassārī are emblematic of the interconnected nature of the Indian Ocean world in this period, the close association of leading *ʿulamāʾ* with royal power and the growing influence of *sharīʿa*-minded piety. Al-Rānīrī, born in Gujarat to a Hadrami family, made his career at the sultanate of Aceh, for whose ruler, Iskandar Thānī (r. 1636–1641), he composed a vast compilation of Arabic texts in Malay translation, the *Bustān al-Salāṭīn*, which aimed at promoting acculturation to a Middle Eastern Islamic cultural ideal.[36] Al-Rānīrī is notorious for launching a campaign against the teachings of two earlier Acehnese Sufis, Ḥamzah Fanṣūrī and Shams al-Dīn al-Sumatrāni, condemning them as unbelievers (*kāfir*) and burning their books.[37] Al-Maqassārī, meanwhile, was born into the royal family of the kingdom of Goa in Sulawesi, and was educated in the palace. He travelled to Banten and then Aceh, before continuing to Arabia to complete his education and to undertake the pilgrimage. One of his teachers was al-Rānīrī, who inducted him into the Qādirī order.[38] On al-Maqassārī's return to Southeast Asia, he was employed at the court of Banten and married into the royal family. After the revolution in 1682 in which Sultan Ageng was overthrown by the Dutch, al-Maqassārī himself was also captured. Regarding him as a grave security risk, the Dutch exiled him, first to Ceylon then to the Cape of Good Hope. Although al-Maqassārī's travels in his later life were thus coerced, he nonetheless remained part of Muslim networks. Indeed, the development of the Qādiriyya and Rifāʿiyya Sufi orders in the Cape has been attributed to his exile there.[39]

Both al-Rānīrī and al-Maqassārī emphasised a *sharīʿa*-minded piety,[40] yet the Qādiriyya *ṭarīqa* to which they adhered is often considered by modern scholarship to be in some sense opposed to *sharīʿa*-minded Islam. Anthony Reid remarks that 'An orthodox Muslim code of ethics from sixteenth-century Java warns its readers against the most popular of all the [Sufi] orders, the Kadiriyya',[41] while van Bruinessen, for instance, has noted the association between the reading of ʿAbd al-Qādir's *manāqib* and the *debus* cult of invulnerability involving the adept striking himself with metal spikes.[42] The *Encyclopaedia of Islam* entry on the Qādiriyya is also devoted almost exclusively to discussing such exotic practices.[43] In this sense, the Qādiriyya may be said to embody the tendency to view Sufism as in some sense opposed to *sharīʿa*. Such a view though, hardly does justice to the historical practice of the Qādirī *ṭarīqa*, which, following ʿAbd al-Qādir al-Jīlānī's own custom, emphasised adherence to the Qur'ān and *sharīʿa*, as is suggested by the activities of the seventeenth-century Qādirī Sufi Muḥammad Shams al-Dīn, who forms the focus of the remainder of this chapter.

Muḥammad Shams al-Dīn's career underlines the intricate relationship between Sufis and royal power. To my knowledge, the sole source to discuss him is the eighteenth-century Arabic chronicle of the Maldive Islands by Ḥasan Tāj al-Dīn, himself a disciple of Muḥammad Shams al-Dīn. Although an edition of the Arabic text was published in Tokyo in 1982, the chronicle seems to have attracted very little attention subsequently.[44]

Ḥasan Tāj al-Dīn relates that Muḥammad Shams al-Dīn was originally from Hama in Syria, where a famous branch of the descendants of ʿAbd al-Qādir al-Jīlānī had settled.[45] We are told that he had studied at the al-Azhar in Cairo, the premier institution of learning in the Arabic-speaking world, and then travelled with his brother Ṭāhā to Mocha in Yemen. From there they went to the Coromandel coast of India and on to Sumatra. Ḥasan Tāj al-Dīn recounts the circumstances of his arrival in Aceh:

> He sailed from Muḥammad Bandar [Parangipettai on the Coromandel coast] to Banda Aceh. When he arrived there the people of Aceh received him with the highest honours. As long as he was in Aceh, he used to command what is right and forbid what is wrong [*ya'muru bi l-maʿrūf wa-yunhī ʿan al-munkar*]. Many of its notables [*akābiruhu*] were his disciples [*murīdīn lahu*], and they gave him slaves and much money. He was brave and feared no one in abolishing things that are forbidden and

> destroying innovation [*bidʿa*] and in reviving the sublime practice [*sunna*] of the Prophet. He used to progress in the land, he and his brother carried on two thrones, accompanied by a great green flag on the middle of which was written the name of their ancestor Shaykh Muḥyī al-Dīn ʿAbd al-Qādir al-Jīlānī. Sayyid Muḥammad Shams al-Dīn would only go out under a great green parasol like a king of great rank. He continued to order what is right and forbid what is wrong, to abolish shameful innovation and detestable wrongdoing until he heard that the Maldives were worse than Aceh in terms of wrongdoing, innovation, corruption and promiscuous behaviour. So he sailed from Banda Aceh making haste with his army of slaves and disciples, and reached the Maldives . . . [Rabīʿi 1097/1686 CE].

Ḥasan Tāj al-Dīn's account of Muḥammad Shams al-Dīn's activities in Aceh draws our attention to several elements that will resurface in his more detailed account of the Maldives. First, his account explicitly compares this Sufi's conduct to that of a 'king of great rank', accompanied by his parasol and banner with the name of his illustrious ancestor; it underlines how Shams al-Dīn derived prestige from his lineage and suggests his potential to destabilise existing structures of rulership. In addition, the account suggests that Shams al-Dīn's *sharīʿa*-minded agenda of rooting out 'innovation' had an appeal both to the elite and the wider population. We are not told anything more of the direct consequences of Muḥammad Shams al-Dīn's visit, but it does serve to provide a context to the events that would follow shortly in Aceh, when sixty years of female rule was brought to an end and a Hadrami *sayyid* dynasty was brought to power.[46] Although in the early seventeenth century, Sultan Iskandar Muda (r. 1606–36) had attempted to create an autocratic monarchy in Aceh, albeit one in which the *ʿulamāʾ* had significant influence,[47] royal power there was rather weak in the second half of the century.[48] Doubts about the legitimacy of female rule under the four queens who reigned between 1641 and 1699 may have contributed both to this weakness and to the subsequent Hadrami coup, and the immigration to Aceh of Arabs with different ideas of political legitimacy may also have undermined the queens' position.[49]

The Hadrami coup was orchestrated by the Acehnese noble elites; doubtless, practical considerations may have played a part, but Tāj al-Dīn's account

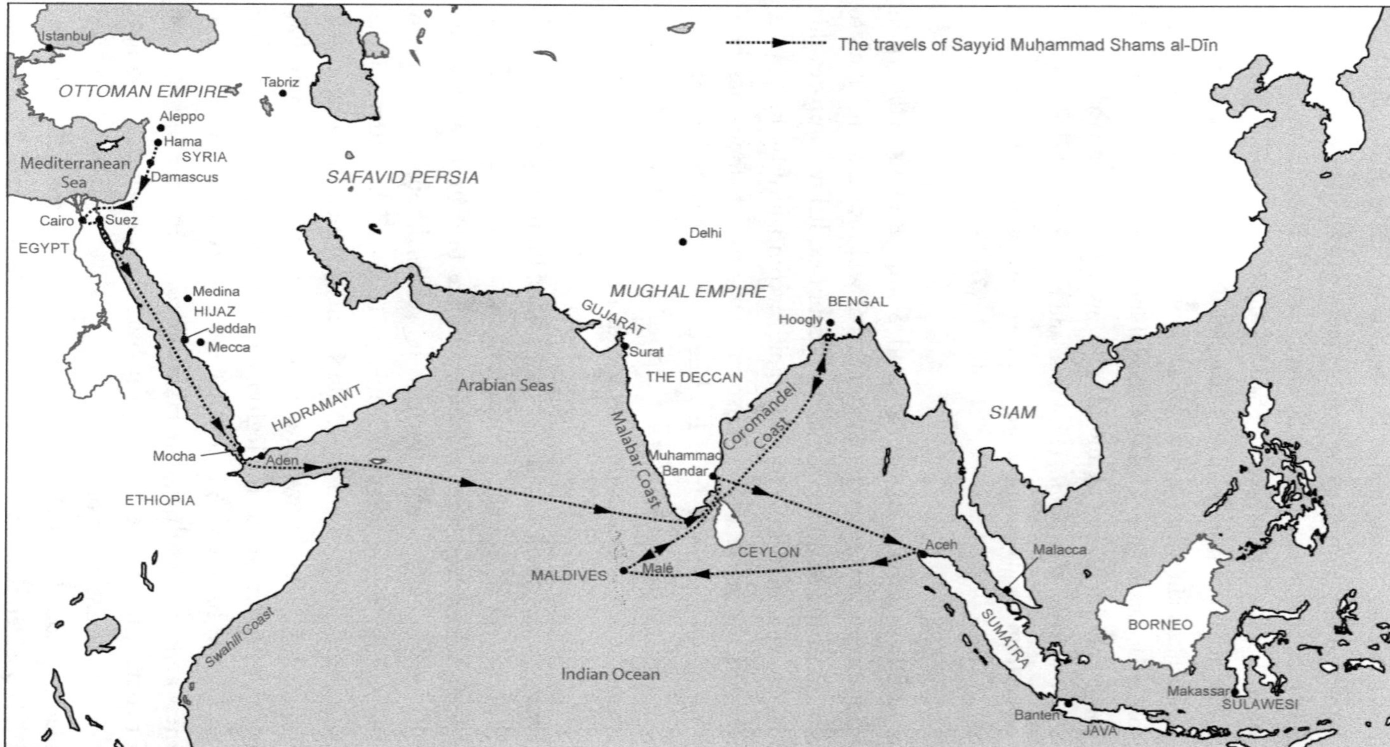

Map 3.1 The travels of Sayyid Muḥammad Shams al-Dīn, 1686–92.

also points to a thirst for *sharīʿa*-minded piety and leadership by a foreigner of noble, Prophetic lineage among this same constituency – the *akābir* (i.e., notables or *orangkaya*) who became Shams al-Dīn's *murīds*. Yet Muḥammad Shams al-Dīn's greatest effect was in the Maldives, where, in contrast, a strong monarchy under Sultan Ibrāhīm Iskandar portrayed itself as a vigorous defender of Islam. However, royal power was decisively undermined by Muḥammad Shams al-Dīn and the appeal of his *sharīʿa*-minded agenda and his prestigious lineage, as we shall see. Before examining Ḥasan Tāj al-Dīn's account in more detail, however, it is worth briefly reviewing the historical situation in the archipelago.

The Maldives have long served as an intermediary stop on routes linking Southeast Asia and the Middle East, although their importance seems to have developed especially from the sixteenth century as a consequence of the Portuguese disruption of established routes via India. The Maldivans themselves claim Islam was brought by a twelfth-century Sufi saint from Iran, Shams al-Dīn of Tabriz; the name points to connections both east and west, for Shams al-Dīn is also claimed by Javanese legend as one of the forerunners of Islam in Java.[50] The French traveller Pyrard de Laval visited in the early seventeenth century, leaving an account that attests the importance of Sufis in court and society.[51] Ḥasan Tāj al-Dīn's chronicle points to the late sixteenth century as a turning point in the Islamisation of the Maldives, with Jamal al-Din, a scholar from the main Maldivan town of Malé, returning after studies in Hadramawt in 1573, and founding a *khānqāh* (Sufi lodge) of his own at Vadu, which played a crucial role in the promotion of Islam in the archipelago.[52] Another factor in the increasing Islamisation of the Maldives was doubtless the bitter struggle with the Portuguese in the sixteenth and early seventeenth centuries, led by the prayer leader (*khaṭīb*) Muḥammad Takurufānu who founded a new ruling dynasty. The struggle also intensified the Maldives' links across the Indian Ocean, for Aceh was an important point from which the fort of Malé was supplied with munitions to defend itself against the Portuguese, and there were important commercial connections too between the two regions.[53]

These developments laid the ground for the reign of Sultan Iskandar Ibrāhīm I (1648–1687), who styled himself *ghāzī* (holy warrior) and sponsored the building of mosques and the endowment of *waqfs*. A *waqf* deed for the mosque of Gan Fat-Kolu island dated 1652/3 describes the sultan in traditional Indian terms as a *kshatriya*, the name given to members of the warrior elite, but its content is thoroughly Islamic, praising the destruction of pagan/Buddhist temples and relating the glorious conversion of the Maldives under Shams al-Dīn Tabrīzī.[54] Indeed, in the view of the local Maldives chronicle, Islam and military values seem to have been intertwined. Ibrāhīm studied in his youth with a shaykh who 'taught him the Qur'ān, the conditions of the obligatory rituals and pillars of Islam, and then the wisdom of cannon guns, arrows, the sword, shield and spear'.[55] During his reign, Ibrāhīm continued the marriage of Islamic and military values, as according to the chronicle: 'he was a teacher to the people of his time; from him people learned the wisdom of the sword, shield, arrows, cannon, guns and fighting, and he used to make the *'ulamā'* happy to teach the people knowledge [*al-'ilm*], so that the land should not be empty of *'ulamā'* out of fear of God's revenge'. As well as piety, practical politics may have encouraged Ibrāhīm's attempts to deepen the Islamic character of the Maldives, for his relatives, the descendants of the apostate Sultan Ḥasan IX who converted to Christianity and fled to Goa, had sought to topple him with Portuguese support.[56]

The Maldives also became ever more closely linked to the Middle East over the course of the seventeenth century. It was also a time of growing cosmopolitanism: 'the port of Malé in his times was a blessed port, a harbour to which ships from India, Aceh and other ports brought money, foodstuffs and other products'.[57] Sultan Ibrāhīm himself undertook the *ḥajj* in 1666, and his visit to the Hijaz may have inspired the import of Arabian architectural styles, for the chronicler notes that on his return he built a madrasa and a minaret 'in the style of Meccan minarets'.[58] He undertook a further visit to the Hijaz a few years later, in 1093/1683, the thirty-fifth year of his reign, visiting the tomb of the Prophet at Medina as well as Mecca for a second time.[59] Perhaps copying Middle Eastern rulers' practice, on the death of his wife Ibrāhīm resolved not to re-marry but instead adopted a series of concubines for his harem.[60]

With his cosmopolitan Islamic horizons, it is thus natural that Sultan Ibrāhīm should welcome the Syrian Muḥammad Shams al-Dīn, with his prestigious descent from 'Abd al-Qādir Al-Jīlānī, when he arrived in Malé from Aceh in Rabī' I 1097/1686, as Ḥasan Tāj al-Dīn describes:

> The sultan Ibrāhīm Iskandar lodged him in a blessed lodging, and honoured him as much as possible . . . When the sultan sat on his throne in the court of the palace [*dār al-salṭana*] he sent his ministers and soldiers with weapons and drums of honour to the *sayyid*, asking him to embrace him and kiss his hand. And *sayyid* Muḥammad came to him carried on his throne/litter [*sarīr*] with his green Qādirī flag before him and the parasol above his head, with his *murīd*s praising his ancestors the Prophet and ʿAbd al-Qādir al-Jīlānī before him, until they put the *sayyid*'s throne opposite that of the sultan.[61]

It was thus with the encouragement and support of the sultan that Muḥammad Shams al-Dīn started his campaign of 'commanding what is right and forbidding what is wrong, reviving the *sunna*, and destroying innovation, and abolishing customs contrary to Muhammadan *sharīʿa* in deed and word by force and strength'.[62] These included forbidding the shaving of beards and the wearing of silver belts, both of which were local customs. The latter prohibition was enforced by the *sayyid*'s brother Ṭāhā, who with his assistants 'would break the belt from the middle of any man they saw wearing it, whether he liked it or not. They did this as the *sayyid* ordered, not distinguishing between great and little people.'[63] Women were also ordered to cover their heads and stay at home. Despite this enforcement of a fairly rigorous interpretation of the *sharīʿa*, we are told Sayyid Muḥammad's popularity increased, and numerous Maldivans joined the Qādirī *ṭarīqa*. Next, Sayyid Muḥammad directly challenged Sultan Ibrāhīm, writing to him that:

> God created you, raised you, gave you kingship and entrusted you with the affairs of the Muslims. You were preoccupied, however, with other affairs, and were concerned with seizing their money by plunder and expropriation, and you have appointed corrupt viziers and adopted oppressive assistants, and have strengthened them in oppressing God's servants. You did not listen to the complaint of the oppressed but you prevented them from entering into your presence, and you veiled those in need from yourself. You rendered the mosques inactive with your seizure of their endowments of land and date palms, and prevented free women from marriage, and did not marry them but demanded they become your prostitutes . . .[64]

The sultan, unsurprisingly, reacted with fury (*ishtaddat ḥamiyyatuhu al-jāhiliyya*), attempting to ban the populace from frequenting the *sayyid*. This was, however, to no effect for, we are told, 'they listened to [Muḥammad Shams al-Dīn's] advice and entered his *ṭarīqa* and loved him very much, and they continued to attend the *sayyid* every Friday and Monday for Qādirī rituals'.[65] One of his adepts was the sultan's nephew, with whom he was staying, and whom the *sayyid* proclaimed to be the true sultan. Evidently, however, the Maldives became sufficiently uncomfortable that Muḥammad decided to leave for Hoogly (Calcutta) – other branches of the al-Jīlānīs were already established in India,[66] which may have made it an attractive location for him to continue his work.

Upon the holy man's departure, the sultan instituted the persecution of the Qādiriyya. However, shortly afterwards the sultan died of poisoning at the hands of his senior concubine (*umm walad*), Mariyam.[67] A period of turbulence followed, as his son, Sultan Muḥammad, was only six years old, and power ended up in the hands of the *umm walad* Mariyam – who was vehemently denounced by Ḥasan Tāj al-Dīn as a pleasure-loving fornicator who sought to corrupt the morals of the people and royal family. Sultan Ibrāhīm's nephew (also called Muḥammad) nevertheless remained faithful to the teachings of his *murshid*, Muḥammad Shams al-Dīn, and was imprisoned for resisting her. A number of *ʿulamāʾ* fled to India or Arabia, including the historian Ḥasan Tāj al-Dīn himself, while his shaykh, al-Khaṭīb Muḥammad Sirāj al-Dīn, was grievously persecuted by the *umm walad*'s regime.[68] Eventually, the *umm walad* and her son Sultan Muḥammad died in a fire in 1102/1691. The nobility then bestowed the throne on Muḥammad Shams al-Dīn's disciple, Sultan Ibrāhīm's nephew Muḥammad, with the regnal title Muḥyī al-Dīn. On gaining power, the latter immediately summoned his *murshid* from Hoogly, writing to him that 'The kingdom of the Maldives is mine, just as you predicted when you sat in my house; now I desire to see your blessed face, come in the next sailing season.'[69]

In his brief reign, Muḥyī al-Dīn sought to follow the example of his mentor by imposing Islamic law and trying to abolish local habits that were contrary to it. However, he died after only a year. Ḥasan Tāj al-Dīn recounts what happened next:

> When Sultan Muḥammad Muḥyī al-Dīn was buried next to his uncle Sultan Muḥammad son of Sultan Iskandar [Ibrāhīm] by the congregational mosque, Sayyid Muḥammad [Shams al-Dīn] proclaimed to them that, 'I am entitled to the succession/caliphate [*mustaḥiqq al-khilāfa*], you should not give oaths of obedience to anyone but me. For I am at your head in accordance with the Prophetic *ḥadīth*, "Let the Quraysh lead [do not lead them] (*qaddimū qurayshan al-ḥadīth*).''' Then they sought out the *sayyid* and gave oaths of obedience to him and seated him on the throne of kingship, and he took the title Sultan Muḥammad al-Sayyid Shams al-Dīn, and the oaths were given to him at the beginning of Jumada II 1103 [February 1692]. And he undertook the duties of the *khilāfa* perfectly, and was a generous, prudent king, and a noble, great, knowledgeable, virtuous, just, pious, and ascetic sultan. He ordered what is right and forbade what is wrong, and abolished customs contrary to *sharīʿa* . . . He preached to the people every night between *ʿishā* and *maghrib* prayers, and after *ʿishā* he taught Qāḍī Muḥammad, the Khaṭīb Muḥammad Sirāj al-Dīn and Ḥasan Tāj al-Dīn *fiqh*, grammar and other sciences.[70]

Even in the sympathetic account of Muḥammad Shams al-Dīn's pupil Ḥasan Tāj al-Dīn, it is clear that adherence to Islamic law had to be imposed by force. Ḥasan describes how his teacher:

> sent him out every Friday with the *qadi*'s assistants and a troop of soldiers to go around the streets of the town to command what is right and forbid what is wrong and to command the people to gather together to undertake the prescribed prayers at the first opportunity, and to reprimand anyone who opposed him. [He ordered him] to bring him anyone who failed to perform the prescribed prayers so that he could kill him with the shining sword of *sharīʿa*.[71]

As under Sultan Ibrāhīm, Muḥammad Shams al-Dīn's efforts to enforce the *sharīʿa* had to be accompanied by force. Coercion was a vital element in propagating *sharīʿa*-minded piety in the Maldives, as elsewhere in the expanding Muslim world of the seventeenth century.

Muḥammad Shams al-Dīn did not rule for long, dying after only six months. On his death he was afforded the signal honour of burial next to the tomb of the apostle to the Maldives, Shams al-Dīn of Tabriz. As he did not leave any descendants, only marrying Muḥyī al-Dīn's widow on his deathbed, he did not found a dynasty. Nonetheless, his prestige is reflected in the fact that his regnal title was adopted by two subsequent sultans,[72] and that on his death the nobles of Malé again sought to appoint a religious leader, the Khaṭīb Muḥammad, as sultan. Although the Khaṭīb refused, eventually a *qāḍī*, Muḥammad, was appointed as ruler, the first of the new Isdu dynasty. Muḥammad did have some distant royal ancestry as a descendant of Muḥammad Takurufanu (r. 1573–85), the leader of the sixteenth-century struggle against the Portuguese,[73] who had also been a *khaṭīb* – another indication of the extent to which the religious and royal establishments were intertwined.

Ḥasan Tāj al-Dīn's account of Muḥammad Shams al-Dīn's activities clearly must be treated with a certain degree of circumspection: the author was a student of, and clearly sympathetic to, the *sayyid*. Nonetheless, it does suggest several features to which we have alluded in the first part of the chapter. First, the sort of Sufism being espoused by this Qādirī was clearly *sharī'a*-orientated, and appealed both to and beyond the royal court. Although the universal adoption of this rigorous piety was evidently secured only by force, the chronicle repeatedly emphasises the popular appeal of Muḥammad Shams al-Dīn, while his conversion of the youthful future Sultan Muḥyī al-Dīn and the fact of his own apparently unchallenged rise to power suggests that he also won over the elite. Secondly, the chronicler underlines the importance of genealogy, in particular Prophetic descent, in providing a new form of legitimacy that could trump existing political structures: note how Muḥammad Shams al-Dīn even included his title of *sayyid* in his regnal *laqab*, underlining this point, as well as drawing on the authority of *ḥadīth* in his speech claiming the right to rule.

Sultan Ibrāhīm Iskandar's reign featured an attempt to turn the Maldives into an Islamic monarchy based on Middle Eastern patterns, suggested by a variety of reforms and innovations: the endowment of *waqfs*; the building of Meccan-style minarets; the abolition of sultanic marriage and the introduction of concubinage (polygyny being almost unknown in the Maldives);[74] and the consequent institution of *umm walad*. Yet far from securing the ruler's position as an autocrat (if that was the intention), bringing the Maldives closer in line with the Middle East had precisely the opposite effect, undermining the legitimacy of royal power and reminding the inhabitants that the thing they really lacked was a ruler of Qurayshi descent. Muḥammad Shams al-Dīn's challenge to Ibrāhīm seems to have been rooted not in any fundamental difference of approach, but rather in the fact that the holy man, with his distinguished lineage, more precisely embodied the Islamic values that the sultan had spent his reign promoting than the sultan himself did.

Conclusion

The story of Muḥammad Shams al-Dīn and his coup reminds us of the figure of the 'stranger-king', well known to the historiography of Southeast Asia. However, studies have tended to emphasise the ability of such strangers to seize power as resting in their ability to form marriage alliances with local elites and to impress the populace by performing impressive feats of magic.[75] In common with many of these stranger-kings Muḥammad Shams al-Dīn boasts his own prestigious *sayyid* lineage. However, his ancestor ʿAbd al-Qādir al-Jīlānī seems to have played an almost equally important role as his *sayyid* status. In both Aceh and the Maldives, Muḥammad Shams al-Dīn is paraded around under the great green banner with ʿAbd al-Qādir's name inscribed on it. His reception indicates that the name was already known and prestigious in both locations, suggesting perhaps a rather broader diffusion of the Qādirī *ṭarīqa* in the Indian Ocean in the seventeenth century than is sometimes admitted, and indeed the popular appeal of the cosmopolitan networks of Sufis that linked the Indian Ocean world to the Middle East.

This Sufi and *sharīʿa*-minded religiosity appealed to the elite, but also more widely, and rather than Sufism offering a way of combining pre-Islamic and Islamic practices and legitimising traditional royal power in Islamic terms, this chapter has suggested that on occasion we can see it achieving almost the opposite. Through *sharīʿa*-orientated Sufi texts and holy men, Indian Ocean courts sought to link themselves to the Hijaz and to the Prophetic *sunna*. In Banten, the texts stood in for the absent holy man, Ibn ʿAlān, but by virtue of being composed by a scholar of Caliphal descent, served to bestow some measure of their *baraka* on the royal court, as is indicated by the careful copies made of them in the eighteenth century. Yet, as Ibn ʿAlān states, this was ultimately a project of local, Bantenese origin, not the initiative of Ḥaramayn scholars. It was by emulating the practices of kings as laid down by al-Ghazālī, as implemented by the Sharīfs of Mecca and as interpreted and explained by Ibn ʿAlān that the sultans of Banten aspired to assert their legitimacy. In our second case, the holy man in person is embraced and honoured by Sultan Ibrāhīm Iskandar, doubtless seeking to harness him for his own purposes of building a Middle Eastern-style monarchy in the Maldives. Yet this project rebounded against the sultan, suggesting that this emergent *sharīʿa*-orientated piety had a popular purchase that in fact allowed it to undermine traditional power structures, as is also suggested by the *sayyid* coups in both the Maldives and Aceh at the close of the seventeenth century. (The case of Banten is rather different as royal power was sapped by effectively being made into a Dutch protectorate in the same period).[76]

Finally, it is worth noting that this phenomenon of a rising *sharīʿa*-orientated piety is of broader currency in the seventeenth-century Muslim world, often with similar consequences. The Ottoman Empire was convulsed for much of the seventeenth century by the partisans of the *sharīʿa*-minded Kadızadeli movement, whose leaders achieved great influence in the palace – and the period is noted for the dissipation of sultanic power.[77] In Safavid Iran, the late seventeenth century sees the growth of an increasingly powerful clerical movement led by Muḥammad Bāqir Majlisī (d. 1699), which dominated the court and politics; this clerical dominance has often been attributed with a decisive role in the fall of the dynasty.[78] In India, too, the last great ruler of the Mughal dynasty, Aurangzeb, is generally thought to have espoused a much more *sharīʿa*-orientated piety than his predecessors.[79] Whether the occurrence of these comparable phenomena in these disparate places is not coincidental or needs further research, Sufi networks certainly seem to have ensured that Islam's frontier in the Indian Ocean world was increasingly integrated into the broader Muslim world and its political and religious trends.

Acknowledgement

I am very grateful to the editors of this volume, Michael Feener and Joshua Gedacht, as well as to Annabel Teh Gallop and Alan Strathern for comments on earlier drafts of this chapter.

Notes

1. Green, Nile, 'Saints, Rebels, Booksellers: Sufis in the Cosmopolitan Western Indian Ocean, ca. 1780–1920', in Edward Simpson and Kai Kresse (eds), *Struggling with History: Islam and Cosmopolitanism in the Western Indian Ocean* (London: Hurst, 2007), p. 159; for an example of the connection between Sufism, scholarship and travel in one *ṭarīqa*, see Le Gall, Dina, *A Culture of Sufism: Naqshbandis in the Ottoman World, 1450–1700* (Albany, NY: State University of New York Press, 2007), pp. 17–23, 169–75; and in general on travel and piety in Islam, see the essays in Eickelman, Dale F. and James Piscatori (eds), *Muslim Travelers: Pilgrimage, Migration, and the Religious Imagination* (Berkeley, CA: University of California Press, 1990).
2. See, for instance, Ricklefs, M. C., *Mystic Synthesis in Java: a History of Islamization from the Fourteenth to the Early Nineteenth Centuries* (Norwalk, CT: Eastbridge, 2006), esp. pp. 21–2.
3. For a discussion and critique of various conceptions of cosmopolitanism in the field, see Hanley, Will, 'Grieving Cosmopolitanism in Middle East Studies', *History Compass* 6(5) (2008): 1346–67.
4. See, for instance, Letvzion, Nehemia, 'Toward a Comparative Study of Islamization', in Nehemia Levtzion (ed.), *Conversion to Islam* (New York: Holmes & Meier, 1979), pp. 16–18. For ideas of syncretism in more recent scholarship, see, for example, Green, Nile, *Sufism: A Global History* (Oxford: Oxford University Press, 2012), pp. 102–3, and see also the discussion by Simon Kemper, Chapter 4, this volume.
5. Prange, Sebastian R., 'Like banners on the Sea: Muslim Trade Networks and Islamization in Malabar and Maritime Southeast Asia', in R. Michael Feener and Terenjit Sevea (eds), *Islamic Connections: Muslim Societies in South and Southeast Asia* (Singapore: Institute of Southeast Asian Studies, 2009), pp. 36–7, citing Parkin, David, 'Inside and Outside the Mosque: A Master Trope', in D. Parkin and S. C. Headley (eds), *Islamic Prayer across the Indian Ocean: Inside and Outside the Mosque* (Richmond: Curzon, 2000), p. 3.
6. Green, *Sufism*, p. 126. For this reason, in this chapter I deliberately do not make the distinction between *ʿulamāʾ* and Sufis that we find in some scholarship; if certainly not all Sufis were *ʿulamāʾ*, yet in one sense or another almost all *ʿulamāʾ* were Sufis. See also note 77 below.
7. See, for instance, the comments in Simpson, Edward and Kai Kresse, 'Cosmopolitanism Contested: Anthropology and History in the Western Indian

Ocean', in Edward Simpson and Kai Kresse (eds), *Struggling with History: Islam and Cosmopolitanism in the Western Indian Ocean* (London: Hurst, 2007), p. 13, and for a more detailed critique of reductive ideas of cosmopolitanism, see Hanley, 'Grieving Cosmopolitanism'.

8. For a discussion of some of these links, see Azra, Azyumardi, *The Origins of Islamic Reformism in Southeast Asia: Networks of Malay–Indonesian and Middle-Eastern 'ulamā' in the Seventeenth and Eighteenth Centuries* (Honolulu, HI: University of Hawaii Press, 2004); Tschacher, Torsten, 'Circulating Islam: Understanding Convergence and Divergence in the Islamic Tradition of Ma'bar and Nusantara', in R. Michael Feener and Terenjit Sevea (eds), *Islamic Connections: Muslim Societies in South and Southeast Asia* (Singapore: Institute of Southeast Asian Studies, 2009), pp. 48–67; Laffan, Michael, *The Makings of Indonesian Islam: Orientalism and the Narration of a Sufi Past* (Princeton, NJ: Princeton University Press, 2011), esp. ch. 1.
9. Green, *Sufism*, pp. 155–6.
10. Simpson and Kresse, 'Cosmopolitanism Contested', p. 3, for quotation and see further discussion on pp. 24–6; cf. Hanley, 'Grieving Cosmopolitanism', pp.1346–7.
11. Green, Nile, *Making Space: Sufis and Settlers in Early Modern India* (New Delhi: Oxford University Press, 2012); Eaton, Richard, *The Rise of Islam and the Bengal Frontier, 1204–1760* (Berkeley, CA: University of California Press, 1993); Barkan, Ömer Lüfti, 'İstila devirlerinin Kolonizatör Türk Dervişleri ve Zaviyeleri', *Vakıf Dergisi* 2 (1942): 279–353.
12. See Masters, Bruce, *The Arabs of the Ottoman Empire 1516–1918: a Social and Cultural History* (Cambridge: Cambridge University Press, 2013), pp. 114–20.
13. See Gibson, Thomas, *Islamic Narrative and Authority in Southeast Asia: From the 16th to the 21st Century* (London: Palgrave Macmillan, 2007), ch. 2; Milner, A. C., 'Islam and the Muslim State', in M. B. Hooker (ed.), *Islam in Southeast Asia* (Leiden: Brill, 1983), pp. 23–49.
14. Van Bruinessen, Martin, 'The Origins and Development of Sufi Orders (*tarekat*) in Southeast Asia', *Studia Islamika: Indonesian Journal for Islamic Studies* 1(1) (1994): 1–23.
15. Azra, Azyumardi, 'Opposition to Sufism in the East Indies in the Seventeenth and Eighteenth Centuries', in Frederick de Jong and Bernd Radtke (eds), *Islamic Mysticism Contested: Thirteen Centuries of Controversies and Polemics* (Leiden: Brill, 1999), pp. 665–86.
16. Laffan, *The Makings of Indonesian Islam*, p. 24.

17. The description of Aceh by the secretary to the seventeenth-century Iranian embassy to Siam starts off by praising the wealth of the place but soon moves on to describe it as an alien and remarkable land, remarking how 'the king and people have a very strange sense of morals and proper behaviour . . . On the island of Aceh stealing is most common and this basic flaw of character has infected all the inhabitants, young and old.' Moreover Aceh is described as equipped with wonders such as a booming mountain. Likewise, while the Maldives is reported to have a Muslim king who seats his Qur'ān on an amber throne, the author remarks that 'they do their trading with various bits of broken sherds' (*The Ship of Sulaiman*, trans. J. O'Kane (London: Routledge, 1972), pp. 177, 178, 225).
18. On Aceh–Banten links, see Lieberman, Victor, *Strange Parallels: Southeast Asia in Global Context, vol. 2: Mainland Mirrors. Europe, Japan, China, South Asia, and the Islands* (Cambridge: Cambridge University Press, 2009), pp. 849–50; Kathirithamby-Wells, J., 'Banten: A West Indonesian Port and Polity', in J. Kathirithamby-Wells and John Villiers (eds), *The Southeast Asian Port and Polity* (Singapore: National University of Singapore, 1990), pp. 107–25, esp. p. 117. On the Maldivian connection to Aceh, which at times also seems to have been political, see Maloney, Clarence, *People of the Maldive Islands* (Hyderabad: Orient Blacksong, 2013), pp. 111–14, also n. 53 below.
19. This is not, of course, to suggest that contemporaries thought specifically of a Middle East; yet disparate influences such as the prestige of Ottoman royal power, of the holy cities of Arabia, of descent from the Prophet, and of Persian culture and even literature, which were to make themselves felt in Southeast Asia and other parts of the Indian Ocean world in this period are most conveniently summed up under this neologism.
20. For an overview, see van Bruinessen, Martin, 'Shariʿa Court, Tarekat and Pesantren: Religious Institutions in the Sultanate of Banten', *Archipel* 50 (1995): 165–99; and also Yakin, Ayang Utriza, 'Undhang-Undhang Bantĕn: a 17th- to 18th-century Legal Compilation of the Qadi Court of the Sultanate of Bantĕn', *Indonesia and the Malay World* 44(130) (2016): 365–88.
21. Van Bruinessen, 'Shariʿa Court', p. 193, n. 10, for the proposed identity of these three treatises. Laffan, *The Makings of Indonesian Islam*, p. 17, with further references; Djajadiningrat, Hosein, *Critische Beschouwing van de Sedjarah Banten* (Haarlem: Joh. Enschiedé en zonen, 1913), pp. 50–1.
22. Djajadiningrat, *Critische Beschouwing*, p. 50.
23. Al-Muḥibbī, *Khulāṣat al-Āthār fi Aʿyān al-Qarn al-Ḥādī ʿAshar*, ed. Muḥammad

Ḥasan Ismāʿīl (Beirut: Dār al-Kutub al-ʿIlmiyya, 2006), vol. 4, pp. 183–8; for further references, consult al-Hayla, Muḥammad al-Ḥabīb, *al-Ta'rīkh wa'l-Mu'arrikhūn bi-Makka* (London: Mu'assasat al-Furqān, 1994), pp. 314–30.

24. Al-Muḥibbī, *Khulāsat al-Āthār*, vol. 1, pp. 185–6; vol. 4, p. 183. His uncle was also a well-known Naqshbandi, known as the 'imām al-taṣawwuf fī zamānihi' (ibid., vol. 1, p. 186), and this may have provided a further link to the Banten court, where the Naqshbandi *ṭarīqa* was much in vogue (on this point, see van Bruinessen, 'Shariʿa Court', pp. 178–80).
25. National Library, Jakarta, MSS A102 and A103.
26. National Library, Jakarta, MS A105. For a more detailed discussion of this text, see Tim Peneliti, 'Sultan Maulana Hasanuddin' Banten, 'Al-Mawahib ar-Rabbaniyah 'An Al-As'ilah al-Jawiyah dan Etika Kekuasaan', in Fadhal A. R. Bafadal and Asap Saefullah (eds), *Naskah Klasik Kegamaan Nusantara: Cerminan Budaya Bangsa II* (Jakarta: Pulitbang Lektur Keagamaan Badan Litbang dan Diklat, 2006), pp. 55–96.
27. Also on the *ḥudūd* in Banten, see Yakin, '*Undhang-Undhang Bantĕn*', pp. 382–83.
28. Smith, Jane Idleman, *The Precious Pearl: a Translation from the Arabic* (Cambridge: Scholars Press, 1979), pp. 8–9.
29. Laffan, *The Makings of Indonesian Islam*, pp. 9–10; cf. Azra, 'Opposition to Sufism', pp. 671, 682.
30. Green, *Making Space*, p. 1.
31. Azra writes that Sultan Abū l-Mafākhir 'Abd al-Qādir 'had a special interest in religious matters; he sent inquiries about religious matters not only to al-Raniri but also to scholars in the Ḥaramayn, which resulted in special works being written by those scholars, answering his questions. As a result, Banten became known as one of the most important Islamic centres on Java', *The Origins of Islamic Reformism*, p. 89. Of his son Sultan Ageng, Azra writes that 'he had a special interest in religion' (ibid., p. 98).
32. Feener, R. Michael and Michael F. Laffan, 'Sufi Scents across the Indian Ocean: Yemeni Hagiography and the Earliest History of Southeast Asian Islam', *Archipel* 70 (2005):185–208.
33. Gallop, Annabel Teh, 'Sultanah Tajul 'Alam's *tarakata* of 1666: the Earliest Known Original Royal Decree from Aceh', in M. Hasbi Amiruddin, Kamaruzzaman Bustaman-Ahmad and Baiquni (eds), *Yusny Saby Sang Motivator: menelusuri karakter pemimpin jujur dan ikhlas dalam membangun umat* (Banda Aceh: Lembaga Studi Agama dan Masyarakat Aceh, 2009), p. 319.

34. Gallop, Annabel Teh, 'Royal Minangkabau Seals: Disseminating Authority in Malay Borderlands', *Indonesia and the Malay World* 43(126) (2015): 284.
35. Van Bruinessen, Martin, 'Shaykh ʿAbd al-Qadir al-Jilani and the Qadiriyya in Indonesia', *Journal of the History of Sufism* 1/2 (2000): 362–5, 367; also Gibson, *Islamic Narrative and Authority*, pp. 55, 60–3. The Leiden collection of manuscripts from Banten, many of which also have a royal connection, contains the following manuscripts that deal with the Qādiriyya in some form: Or 5601, Or 5658, Or 5660, Or 5669, Or 5701.
36. On al-Rānīrī and the contents of the *Bustan al-Salāṭīn*, see Wormser, Paul, *Le Bustan al-Salāṭīn de Nuruddin ar-Raniri: réflexions sur le rôle culturel d'un étranger dans le monde malais au XVIIe siècle* (Paris: Cahiers d'Archipel, 2012), p. 41.
37. al-Attas, Syed Muhammad Naguib, *Rānīrī and the Wujūdiyyah of 17th Century Acheh* (Singapore: Monographs of the Malaysian Branch of the Royal Asiatic Society, 1966), pp. 14–17; Azra, *The Origins of Islamic Reformism*, pp. 66–9; Laffan, *The Makings of Indonesian Islam*, pp. 12–17.
38. On this point, see Azra, *The Origins of Islamic Reformism*, pp. 66, 89; also see Laffan, *The Makings of Indonesian Islam*, p. 248, n. 61.
39. On Maqassāri's travels and career, see Azra, *The Origins of Islamic Reformism*, pp. 87–108; Ward, Kerry, *Networks of Empire: Forced Migration in the Dutch East India Company* (Cambridge: Cambridge University Press, 2009), pp. 199–208, 231–6; Laffan, *The Makings of Indonesian Islam*, pp. 19–22.
40. Azra, *The Origins of Islamic Reformism*, pp. 66–7, 107–8.
41. Reid, Anthony, 'The Islamization of Southeast Asia', in Anthony Reid, *Charting the Shape of Early Modern Southeast Asia* (Chiang-Mai: Silkworm Books, 2000), p. 20.
42. Van Bruinessen, 'Shaykh ʿAbd al-Qadir', pp. 374–5.
43. D. S. Margoliouth, 'Ḳādiriyya', *Encyclopaedia of Islam*, 2nd edn (Brill online), available at: http://referenceworks.brillonline.com/browse/encyclopaedia-of-islam-2.
44. Yajima, Hikoichi (ed.), *Ḥasan Tāj al-Dīn's The Islamic History of the Maldive Islands* (Tokyo: Institute for the Study of the Languages and Cultures of Asia and Africa, 1982), (hereafter Ḥasan Tāj al-Dīn, *History*). The *History* was summarised in English by Bell in his classic study: Bell, H. C. P., *The Maldive Islands: Monograph on the History, Archaeology and Epigraphy* (Malé: Novelty Printers and Publishers, 2002; originally Colombo: Ceylon Government Press, 1940), pp. 18–43. However, the activities of Muḥammad Shams al-Dīn are

treated only very scantly in this summary. Unfortunately, the chronicle is the sole narrative source for many aspects of Maldivian history, including the activities of Muḥammad Shams al-Dīn, so it is not possible to compare its information against other sources.

45. Although both the earlier and later history of the Hama Jīlānīs is well known, the seventeenth and eighteenth centuries represent something of a black hole. See Khenchelaoui, Zaïm and Thierry Zarcone, 'La famille Jîlânî de Hamâ (Syrie): Bayt al-Jîlânî', *Journal of the History of Sufism* 1/2 (2000): 53–77.
46. Khan, Sher Banu A. L., *Sovereign Women in a Muslim Kingdom: the Sultanahs of Aceh, 1641–1699* (Singapore: NUS Press, 2017), pp. 248–53.
47. Takeshi, Ito, 'The World of the *Adat Aceh*: a Historical Study of the Sultanate of Aceh', PhD thesis, Australian National University, 1984, pp. 248–62.
48. Takeshi, 'The World of the *Adat Aceh*', pp. 31–2, 66–8. For a different interpretation see Khan, *Sovereign Women*, p. 226, who argues that the consensual style of rulership practised by Aceh's queens accorded with Malay tradition and was a sign of exemplary behaviour. Nonetheless, Khan does agree that the exercise of power by the queens was qualitatively different that that practised by rulers such as Iskandar Muda; cf. Khan, *Sovereign Women*, pp. 247, 255–6.
49. Khan, *Sovereign Women*, pp. 251–3.
50. Djajadiningrat, *Critische Beschouwing*, pp. 188–97; see also Kalus, Luvik and Claude Gilliot, 'Inscriptions islamiques en arabe de l'archipel des Maldives', *Archipel* 70 (2005): 15–52, at pp. 39–40. A conflation with Shams al-Dīn al-Tabrīzī, the great companion of Rūmī, has prompted suggestions that Sufism in the Maldives was Mevlevi in orientation (see also n. 51 below). It seems unlikely, however, that this aristocratic Ottoman order, which had a limited presence outside Anatolia, would have spread to the Maldives.
51. de Castro, Xavier (ed.), *Voyage de Pyrard de Laval aux Indes orientales (1601–1611)*, vol. 1 (Paris: Chandeigne, 1998), pp. 163–5; Nasheed, Mohamed, *Maldives: a Historical Overview of the Traditional Dhivehi Polity, 1800–1900* (Malé: Orient Academic Centre, 2003), pp. 51–6.
52. Nasheed, *Maldives*, pp. 47–69; Ḥasan Tāj al-Dīn, *History*, vol. 1, p. 24.
53. Ḥasan Tāj al-Dīn, *History*, vol. 1, p. 28; further on trade links between Aceh and the Maldives, see Takeshi, 'The World of the *Adat Aceh*', pp. 332–3 nn. 141, 144, p. 429, n. 29.
54. Bell, *The Maldive Islands*, pp. 190–3. Formulas praising the ruler as a *kshatriya* (an Indic term denoting a warrior) continued to be used in Maldivan *waqf* documents into the twentieth century. See Ahmed Nazim Sattar, *King Kalaafaan*

Manuscripts (Malé: National Centre for Linguistic and Historical Research, 2009), pp. 67, 68, 70. I am very grateful to Michael Feener for providing me with a copy of this publication. Cf. the discussion of the term *ghāzī* by Simon Kemper in Chapter 4, this volume.

55. Ḥasan Tāj al-Dīn, *History*, vol. 1, p. 29.
56. Ibid., vol. 1, p. 30.
57. Ibid., vol. 1, pp. 30–1.
58. Ibid., vol. 1, p. 32: *thumma ibtada'a binā' al-mināra wa banā hādhihi al-mināra fi uslūb al-manābir al-makiyya.*
59. Ibid..
60. Ibid.
61. Ibid., vol. 1, p. 35.
62. Ibid.
63. Ibid.
64. Ibid., vol. 1, p. 36.
65. Ibid.
66. Khenchelaoui and Zarcone, 'La famille', p. 71; Buehler, Arthur, 'The Indo-Pakistani Qadiriyya: An Overview', *Journal of the History of Sufism* 1/2 (2000): 339–60, at pp. 345–53.
67. Ḥasan Tāj al-Dīn, *History*, vol. 1, p. 37.
68. Ibid., vol. 1, pp. 39–40.
69. Ibid., vol. 1, p. 44.
70. Ibid., vol. 1, p. 45.
71. Ibid.
72. Shams al-Dīn Muḥammad II (r. 1773–4); Shams al-Dīn Muḥammad III (1893, 1903–1934). See Bell, *The Maldive Islands.*
73. Bell, *The Maldive Islands*, pp. 27, 33.
74. Maloney, *People of the Maldive Islands*, pp. 336, 342.
75. See, for example, Kathirathamby-Wells, Jeyamalar, '"Strangers" and "Stranger-kings": the Stranger-king in Eighteenth-century Southeast Asia', *Journal of Southeast Asian Studies* 40 (2009): 567–91.
76. Cf. Kemper's discussion of the power of *karamat* at the court of Mataram, Chapter 4, this volume.
77. On the Kadızadelis and their Sufi links, see Le Gall, Diana, 'Kadızadelis, Naksbendis and Intra-Sufi Diatribe in Seventeenth-century Istanbul', *Turkish Studies Association Journal* 27 (2004): 1–28. For the circulation of texts by the proto-Kadızadeli Ottoman author Birgevi in Southeast Asia (Sumatra), see

Fathurahman, Oman, 'New Textual Evidence for Intellectual and Religious Connections between the Ottomans and Aceh', in A. C. S. Peacock and Annabel Teh Gallop (eds), *From Anatolia to Aceh: Ottomans, Turks and Southeast Asia* (Oxford: Oxford University Press, 2015), pp. 306–7.

78. Matthee, Rudi, *Persia in Crisis: Safavid Decline and the Fall of Isfahan* (London: I. B. Tauris, 2011), pp. 201–2, 248.
79. Pirbhai, M. Reza, *Reconsidering Islam in a South Asian Context* (Leiden: Brill, 2009), pp. 91–116.

4

The White Heron Called by the Muezzin: Shrines, Sufis and Warlords in Early Modern Java

Simon C. Kemper

Seven *sayyida* sisters await Shaykh Yūsuf al-Maqassārī (henceforth al-Maqassārī) in front of the East Javanese Giri shrine court around 1680. All have similar features and one cannot be told from the other. They pose a challenge to Shaykh Yūsuf, who had long neglected the folklore of Javanese shrine polities on his journey to acquire knowledge of and initiation into the brotherhoods of overseas Islam. This journey took him from his birthplace in Makassar to cosmopolitan ports like Banten and Aceh, and finally to the Islamic heartland of Damascus and Ḥaramayn (i.e., Mecca and Medina). To followers of the Giri shrine, however, the teachings from these seminal religious hubs are relevant only to the extent that they fit into their established framework of Javanese mystic cosmology. Only this cosmology, they maintain, can determine the true friends of God (*wali*). To test Shaykh Yūsuf's worthiness, the saintly lord of Giri – also known as Puspa Ita – challenges him to point out his wife among the seven sisters in sight. The shaykh only blinks. As he immediately identifies the wife of the Giri lord. Puspa Ita cannot but stutter: 'Indeed this [shaykh] is a *wali*'. According to texts from South Sulawesi, it took hovering eggs and parting the Java Sea for al-Maqassārī to reach the Giri court in the first place, but with this final feat his mystical powers (*karāmāt*) finally proved strong enough to compete with those of the Javanese shrine lords.[1]

This tale derives from South Sulawesian textual traditions which extoll the saintly powers and miracles of Shaykh Yūsuf al-Maqassārī. For nearly two centuries such texts were passed on in Makasar and Bugis households as potent heirlooms.[2] These tales depicted the shaykh as an enchanted figure in ways rather different from how he comes across in the body of Arabic texts in the Islamic religious sciences that he authored during his lifetime. Over the past half century some modern Indonesian writers have directed their attention towards more 'sober' aspects of his biography, rather than on his purported performance of miracles.[3] While still hagiographic in nature, these works dismiss perspectives which – as in the anecdote above – reveal parallels between traditional Southeast Asian conceptions of sources of power and authority that were often attributed to both Sufi scholars like al-Maqassārī and saints of magical prowess like Puspa Ita. Today, al-Maqassārī is often cited as representing trans-regional Islamic cosmopolitanism through his Sufi networks stretching from ports in the Indonesian Archipelago to Sri Lanka, the Arabic Middle East and South Africa. Moving across this seascape, al-Maqassārī appears not as a man of magic, but one advocating the Muslim cause through the trans-regional transmission of texts in Arabic acknowledged by authoritative religious leaders and inspiring armed resistance to European colonial expansion. More so than Puspa Ita, his formal knowledge of the Islamic religious sciences supported his authority in campaigns of Islamic resistance to the spread of European imperialism. Such readings of the life of al-Maqassārī situate his life and work in modern, rationalised frameworks that are more relevant to the lives of many contemporary Indonesian Muslims and that support the identification of common ground with other Muslim communities, especially in South Africa.[4] In contrast to al-Maqassārī, the legacy of Puspa Ita was never revised in such ways, nor are his custodians interested in elevating him to a figure of more than local appeal. At first sight, it thus appears that a lack of research has turned the lord of Giri into a flat character standing beside a shaykh who is now renowned for bringing cosmopolitan Sufi brotherhoods to the Malay Archipelago and South Africa.

The limited interest in Puspa Ita in modern Islamic literature is not coincidental. He represents a vernacular, shrine-centred form of Islam often seen as being at odds with the ideals of scriptualist piety that have become increasingly prevalent in the modern period. As this chapter shows, both al-Maqassārī and Puspa Ita stood at different ends of early modern Sufism, the first being empowered by his trans-oceanic networks, the other by emplaced traditions. This is reflected in the extant source material. Shaykh Yūsuf al-Maqassārī left a corpus of Arabic writing in established disciplines of the Islamic religious sciences, while we only know of the myths of the lords of Giri. A bias crops up because of this, since it is impossible to conduct the same theological and biographic studies on Puspa Ita as have been done on al-Maqassārī's life and works. A solution lies in searching beyond formal treatises to alternative source bases to develop better understandings of other dimensions of religious power and authority in early Muslim Southeast Asia. As this chapter demonstrates, the complexities of Sufism in history involved not only ascetic practice and metaphysical cosmology, but also demonstrations of spiritual prowess, military accomplishment and political allegiance. War reveals that the trans-regional Islamic cosmopolitanism of al-Maqassārī and the more locally 'emplaced' Islam of Puspa Ita's mystic and military power comprise two contrasting, albeit overlapping, hierarchies in the early modern Malay Archipelago. To gather troops, al-Maqassārī appealed to the Islamic community (*umma*) at large. His call, however, was apparently perceived differently by at least some Muslims who were more rooted in the local geographies of shrine clientelism and power. By examining the career of one of these shrine patrons – namely, Puspa Ita – this chapter demonstrates that shrine spaces and networks played a decisive role in mobilising troops during the Mataram and Banten wars which tore Java apart in the late seventeenth century. As can be seen on Map 4.1 below, the influence of shrine polities like that of the Giri shrine in East Java ranged as far overseas as Ternate in North Maluku, while remaining embedded within particular regional geographies.

By underlining the durability and wide appeal of a vernacular shrine-based Islam, this chapter offers a contrast that complements the view presented by A. C. S. Peacock in Chapter 3, this volume. Whereas Peacock highlights the ways in which universalist conceptions of normative *sharīʿa* resonated strongly in Banten, Aceh and the Maldives, these concerns were

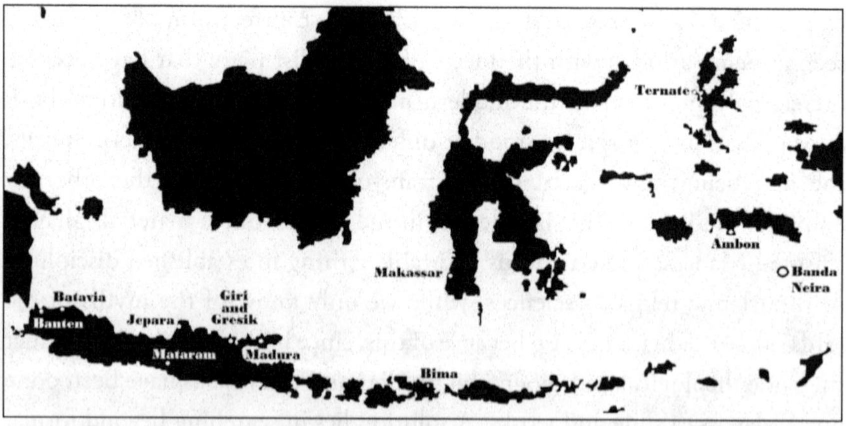

Map 4.1 The network of Giri ranged from East Java to North Maluku. The ports of Jepara, Banten and Batavia and the court of Mataram would become competitors of Giri in the late seventeenth century. (*Source:* Simon C. Kemper.)

apparently not as compelling for Muslims inhabiting the shrine landscapes of Central and East Java at the same time. The first section of this chapter, on the Mataram and the Banten wars, demonstrates the extensive imprint of shrine clientelism on these conflicts. The second section, on 'Holy War', examines the limits of appeals to trans-regional Muslim solidarity and normative textual authority in mobilising resistance to European expansion. The third section ('Spice War') discusses how the roots of Giri's shrine clientelism can be traced to its political-economic power, which derived from the spice trade. The fourth section ('Mystical War') illustrates how different discourses redefined Giri as a primarily religious polity after its conquest by Mataram; while the fifth section (the Giri War) reveals how Puspa Ita used the appeal of his shrine to marshal troops of different backgrounds and how this led to his downfall. Finally, the last section ('Sufi Warfare') demonstrates the ways in which the campaigns of al-Maqassārī and Puspa Ita reveal two different modes of Sufi authority and mobilisation, respectively: one trans-regional and cosmopolitan the other locally emplaced and vernacular.

The Mataram and Banten War

These conflicts occurring between 1675 and 1683 led to the downfall of both the Central Javanese sultanate of Mataram and that of Banten in West Java.

Both al-Maqassārī and Puspa Ita played important roles in these conflicts. After returning from Mecca in the early 1670s, Shaykh Yūsuf al-Maqassārī had become both *qāḍī* and *muftī* at the court of Banten and married the daughter of the sultan. Unlike the previous royal religious adviser (nearly always Javanese who often bore the title *Pakik Najmuddin*), al-Maqassārī dealt with matters ranging from law to the conduct of war and enjoyed considerable autonomy in his decision-making.[5] Judging from his treatises, two concerns stood central in his policies: first, the encroaching Dutch East India Company (VOC) based in the neighbouring port of Batavia and, secondly, the spread of vernacular Sufism, which grounded its power in rituals ranging from shrine visits to cockfights. Unlike claims found in the myths of the seven *sayyida* sisters of Giri, al-Maqassārī strove to empower Banten by connecting it to overseas Sufi networks rather than to Javanese shrine communities. His affiliations with trans-regional Sufi brotherhoods served as a foundation for fostering connections across the Indonesian Archipelago and beyond to the wider *umma*, while also elevating the authority of religious scholars within the sultanate.[6] Due to the support of his patron, Sultan Tirtayasa (1631–92), al-Maqassārī went a long way towards achieving his goals only to face a royal succession crisis and subsequent invasion by the VOC in 1682. He personally commanded troops during this conflict and continued a guerrilla war for nearly a year after his patron was captured. But the struggle was eventually lost. In the aftermath, the VOC exiled him first to Sri Lanka and eventually to South Africa, where he both authored many of his Arabic texts and played an important role in the establishment of new local Muslim communities.[7]

The reputed military accomplishments of the Giri lords were even greater. Puspa Ita, for instance, was not known as a writer or an orator, but chiefly as a late heir of the Giri saint empowered by the shrine he protected.[8] His claim to authority derived from his lineage, as well as from his custodianship of the shrine of his ancestors. From the mid-seventeenth century until 1680, he guarded the Giri shrine polity in East Java.[9] In the two centuries since its founding in the late fifteenth century, the Giri shrine had gained wide esteem. By 1581, the Giri lord Sunan Prapen reached a summit of power by giving his blessing to the recently established Central Javanese Islamic realm Pajang, resulting in a complicated alliance with the Pajang successor-state Mataram over the decades that followed.[10] As Mataram gained strength, however, Giri suffered. In 1635–6, the belligerent Sultan Agung of Mataram ordered his son-in-law to move against the powerful shrines that were seen as potential rivals. Giri was well prepared and enjoyed the support of the Chinese – likely Fujian – Muslim Endraséna and his 250 trained musketeers. Only after much bloodshed did the Mataram force defeat the Giri lord and behead Endraséna. In the wake of this conquest, Giri was turned into a vassal and the shrine lord a mere nobleman.

The successors of the fifth Giri lord gained the courtly titles of Panembahan and, eventually, the submissive *pangeran* (prince). The tables were now turned: earlier Mataram rulers received their titles from the shrine polities, whereas now they assigned them to the latter as a token of royal sovereignty.[11] For instance, the religious title of *Sunan* initially referred to the followers of the Prophet's path or the *Sunna* and the proselytisers of Islam on Java, who are now known as the *wali sanga* ('nine saints'). In the wake of Sultan Agung's conquests, *Sunan* became a royal appellation and the lords of Giri but one of the 'younger brothers of the ruler' (*para yayi* or shortened *priyayi*).[12] These titles thus became a means to demonstrate the subordination of the Giri shrine to the Mataram court. In contrast, the sovereigns of Mataram now designed genealogies in which they comprised the axis of the universe (*qutb*) around which even *wali* orbit.[13] This situation persisted for decades, until Pangeran Giri Puspa Ita sought to revive the shrine's former glories.

Puspa Ita saw an opportunity to do so by supporting an insurgency from the rival states of Makassar and Madura which reduced the Mataram court to ashes in 1677. Unfortunately for these insurgents, the surviving Mataram crown prince obtained assistance from the Dutch VOC and its allies. This turn of events forced Puspa Ita to loosen his ties with the Makasar and Madurese warlords and continue his resistance covertly. The situation slowly unravelled and in 1680, Puspa Ita launched an open revolt against Mataram and their VOC benefactors. In a final campaign, he encouraged his followers to run amok with daggers and talismans while outnumbered by the thousands of pike men, musketeers and elite soldiers from Mataram and the VOC.[14] What characterised Puspa Ita's war efforts throughout these years was a concern for regaining sovereignty over his local shrine polity. He did not long for a position as religious official of the Mataram court, but rather tried to restore his position at the axis of the Javanese–Muslim Giri cosmology. In honour of his shrine, Puspa Ita rejected the authority of the sultanate and marshalled his own army of devotees. His Islam was locally embedded in Giri and could not be ruled by 'outsiders'. In this his struggle against the Dutch and their clients in seventeenth-century Java was elaborated in terms rather different from that of al-Maqassārī and his appeals to Islamic textual authority and trans-regional visions of Muslim solidarity.

Holy War

Both al-Maqassārī's and Puspa Ita's war efforts, nevertheless, ultimately resulted in failure and defeat at the hands of the VOC and their allies. This has led some scholars to identify them in broad-brush as defeated rebels of a 'pan-Islamic resistance' or holy war.[15] Their claims to authority and the legitimation of militant action in these two cases were, however, much more complicated than can be explained by recourse to abstracted conceptions of *jihād*.[16] Shaykh Yūsuf, for instance, described 'Holy War' mainly as a spiritual attempt to 'repent and resist your forbidden desires' assisted by the 'enormous army' of Allah.[17] At the same time, he declared fighting to be required as a form of dedication to Sufi masters in the name of the *umma*. To unite Muslims in this cause, al-Maqassārī looked not to the frameworks of shrine communities, but rather to the more cosmopolitan fraternity of Sufi brotherhoods.[18] These trans-regional networks were already established in some parts of the Islamic world, but still of limited influence in most areas of the Indonesian Archipelago during the seventeenth century.[19] 'Sufism' in many parts of the region largely took the form of shrine-based practices. The forms of Sufism characteristic of this milieu are, however, absent from al-Maqassārī's writings, where cosmopolitan Sufi brotherhoods (*ṭuruq*, sing. *ṭarīqa*) dominate. His treatise the *Safinat al-najā* expounds several brotherhoods he joined, ranging from his beloved Shaṭṭāriyya to his stint with Kubrāwiyya.[20] He personally made copies of treatises associated with these brotherhoods and urged his readers to pledge an oath of allegiance to a Sufi master or shaykh (*bayʿa*) and obediently follow his example if they desire to receive God's blessing (*baraka*).[21]

For instance, his *Ḥabl al-warīd li saʿādat al-murīd* recommends that his followers seek support from Sufi masters during times of war. As mentioned earlier, Shaykh Yūsuf al-Maqassārī spearheaded the guerrilla war himself after his patron, Sultan Tirtayasa of Banten, was arrested by the VOC. During a year of hardship, he led approximately 2,000 Bugis, Makasar and Bantenese troops as well as one of the sultan's sons through mud, forests and mountains with hostile forces on his trail.[22] The *Ḥabl al-warīd* is a reflection on this campaign written in exile in Sri Lanka at the request of his followers who were left on both Java and South Sulawesi. It refers to the military authority to which al-Maqassārī resorted when commanding his company of 2,000 warriors in Banten. This authority was, moreover, built to a considerable extent upon appeals to scriptural injunctions and buttressed by imaginations of Muslim solidarity joined through Islamic networks reaching all the way to Mecca and beyond.[23] Al-Maqassārī stressed that war requires guidance from cosmopolitan courts or preferably scholars to oppose the 'infidel Dutch'.[24] True believers are implored to respect their shaykh like a father and do anything he wishes, even if this entails drinking wine or sleeping with strange women. It takes this level of love and trust to follow one's shaykh, for he holds spiritual authority and serves as the Prophet's caliph (*khalīfa Rasulullah*). Sultans and lords of this world are not to be ignored, but in dire straits the authority of the shaykh takes precedence.[25] The treatise does not refer to mystical powers or *karāmāt* obtained from shrines which were traditionally resorted to for obtaining invulnerability on the battlefield.[26] Al-Maqassārī's peer from Giri, however, could not do without such powers and indeed saw them as the very basis for his legitimacy.

While alive, Puspa Ita and Shaykh Yūsuf were thus worlds apart, particularly in their views on shrine-based religiosity and devotional practice. In a rather ironic twist, however, al-Maqassārī's dead body was entombed in multiple sites across the Indian Ocean world from South Africa to Sulawesi in what became active sites of popular veneration visited for their reputed sacred potency.[27] To posterity, the shaykh's miracles (*karāmāt*) counted more than his writings.[28] Sultans and servants alike enshrined monuments to his memory in ways similar to established cults of earlier Islamic pioneers such as the fabled nine saints (*wali sanga*) in Java or the three Datuks (Dato' Tallua Makasar) in South Sulawesi.[29] Whereas the shaykh's *Ḥabl al-warīd* insisted on guidance from living teachers, his followers found it around his scattered shrines instead.

Al-Maqassārī became a founding figure for the Makasar Khalwatiyya-

Yūsuf *ṭarīqa* as well as South African Islam in general.[30] His influence persists in Banten, where he had a thousand followers, as well as Madura, where he had none. It is at these sites that the shaykh's descendants laud his 'good morals' based on diplomacy rather than on confrontation.[31] Mystical prophecies, courtly ties and travels to Mecca and 'Rome' (*Rūm*, i.e., Istanbul) are judged more important than his military campaigns in Banten.[32] According to the current custodian of his mausoleum in Makassar, al-Maqassārī intended to advocate for the *sharīʿa* among both the VOC and the Bantenese sultan. While the shaykh requested the former to respect Islamic territory, he urged the latter to cease impious activities such as the cockfights popular amongst gamblers and traders.[33] All of the shaykh's shrine custodians simultaneously portray him as cosmopolitan figure bringing knowledge from overseas as well as a saint embedded in the particular location of his tomb.

At times, however, the narrative traditions circulating through and around his shrine site provide a range of depictions of Shaykh Yūsuf al-Maqassārī which reveal the complexities of intersections and overlap between appeals to trans-regional models of textual normativity and local conceptions of mystical power in the establishment of Sufi authority. On the one hand, the report of his spiritual powers (*karāmāt*) resemble those of the earlier Islamic proselytisers such as the fifteenth-century founder of the Giri shrine: Sunan Giri. The Islamic-influenced martial arts of Java and Sulawesi, for instance, still seek to access powers of invulnerability through al-Maqassārī's spiritual legacy.[34] At the same time, he is commonly held to have been more concerned with *sharīʿa* than his predecessors. His crusade against cockfights, for example, implies that earlier legends in which the *wali sanga* had reportedly used such gambling matches as a tool to spread the faith had now come to be seen as an aspect of local Islamic practice in need of reform.[35] Likewise with al-Maqassārī's insistence on the need for a living teacher in *Ḥabl al-warīd,* devotion to the holy dead is demeaned. He appears to have acknowledged shrine pilgrimage as an honourable deviation from the Prophetic Example (*bidʿa ḥasana*) but did not advocate the practice.[36] His legacy of *karāmāt* thus does not derive from his own works or teaching in life, but rather from long-lasting and trans-regional pilgrimage traditions attempting to emplace the blessing of saints that came to be associated with him after his death.

By the late seventeenth century both the landscapes of Java and South

Sulawesi were prominently marked with shrines and sacred sites. The grave shrines in particular were more than meeting grounds; they were also sites that facilitated access to the mystical power (*karāmāt*) of the saints buried there. Commoners, kings and warriors alike prayed at these sites for healing, physical powers, spiritual enlightenment and other this-worldly benefits. Lords controlling these sites were esteemed as descendants and thus channels of their forefather's *karāmāt.* It was this, rather than the textual knowledge and cosmopolitan connections to a wider world of Islam that comprised their primary claim to religious as well as military authority. Before taking to the battlefield, warriors visited shrines and associated sacred spaces in preparation for an honourable death. These shrines ranged from venerated gravesides (Jv. *punden* /Sd. *kabuyutan*) to spiritually potent sites of nature (e.g., *punden berundak*). Shared lineages also connected shrines to religious tax-free villages (*pradikan*), mosques and religious endowments (*waqf*, pl. *awqāf*), all of which boosted prestige and manpower.[37]

By the time Shaykh Yūsuf al-Maqassārī was teaching his students in Banten, Puspa Ita already ruled over a large Javanese shrine polity on top of the Giri hill on the opposite end of Java.[38] At the central hill stands the grave of Sunan Giri, one of the so-called *wali sanga* who founded the sanctuary in 1487 and built one of the first Javanese mosques there.[39] The graves of his followers and family surround his tomb. At a distance along the same range of hills lies Sunan Prapen, the ruler who bought the shrine polity to the height of its power by supporting the Pajang realm in 1581 and its successor Mataram afterwards. What is more, he reconstructed the shrine of his forefathers and further elevated the prestige of Giri by establishing a shrine polity appealing to kings and merchants alike.[40] The heart of political power was established on another hill opposite the shrine of Sunan Giri, where the ruins of the former court remain visible to this day. There Sunan Giri and his descendants reputedly governed as both secular (*nata*) and religious (*pandita*) leaders. Encircled by backstreets, little houses and the remains of mansions of the former complex (*dalem*), the top of the hill served both as a place of religious instruction and as a court called the Giri Kedaton.

Figure 4.1 The side plateau of the Giri Kedaton.
(*Source:* Simon C. Kemper.)

Spice War

The durability of vernacular shrine polities like that of Giri should not, however, be taken for granted. As A. C. S. Peacock shows in Chapter 3 of this volume, other archipelagos like the Maldives did shed their embedded Islam for a cosmopolitan one of trans-regional Sufi or *sharīʿa* authority over the course of conflicts in the late seventeenth century.[41] The strength of the Giri shrine before its conquest in 1635–6 was drawn not only from religion, but also from its involvement with inter-island regional trade. Puspa Ita gained both his worldly and his religious authority from the Giri shrine and the traditions of mysticism surrounding the *wali sanga*. At the same time, his power was also not unlike that of early modern *ghāzī* in Anatolia and South Asia. While known as 'warriors of faith' offering their services for holy war, *ghāzī* were often charismatic chiefs of war-bands gathered around shrines while wandering in search of booty at least as much as of blessings.[42] The

Figure 4.2 The grave of the *kris* maker *Empu* Supo V at the Giri Kedaton. (*Source:* Simon C. Kemper.)

myths of the *wali sanga* likewise supported the consolidation of rites, cults, loot and miraculous entertainment to establish shrines as centres of worship as well as military recruitment. Giri's spiritual weapons were both physical and intangible: including supernatural daggers and other manifestations of spiritual powers (*karāmāt*). Similar to the legendary tales of South Asian *Sajjada Nashins* or *khalīfa*, the Javanese shrine custodians (*juru kunci*) attest to the supernatural powers of the Giri saint by pointing to lineages, miracles and potency.[43] During the mid-seventeenth century, Puspa Ita served as custodian as well as shrine lord. In that position he was expected to demonstrate both spiritual power and the ability to provide material resources for his followers. His predecessors had relied on the spice trade to support the latter, but those sources of wealth had begun to run dry during his day.

For a shrine like Giri, religious renown was often concomitant with commercial wealth. The hilly Giri cannot therefore be separated from littoral Gresik. The nearby harbour of Gresik was a major early modern trade hub and its shoreline, which is visible from the uphill Giri court, was crowded with merchants.[44] When the harbour of Gresik came under Giri's control halfway through the sixteenth century, the shrine lords came to enjoy greater wealth and prestige, allowing them access to ports across the Indonesian Archipelago as far as Ambon and Banda Neira.[45] The Sasak of Lombok attribute the Islamisation of their community to Sunan Prapen, and one of their chronicles even has it that the proselytisers of Makassar studied Islam in Giri.[46] Similarly, Ternatan oral history also asserts that knowledge of Islamic jurisprudence (*fiqh*) and Islamic mysticism (*taṣawwuf*) reached northern Maluku from Giri.[47] The religious and economic networks of the Giri shrine thus enfolded many of the major ports of the Spice Islands.

In 1565, the Ambonese Hitu kingdom had allied with Giri to attack the Portuguese, and Giri troops roamed Ambon for three years before returning to Java.[48] In 1622, a group of exiles in Batavia sent letters to Giri and Mataram urging them to join in a coordinated campaign against the VOC.[49] Giri's maritime network presented a significant challenge to the VOC in the early seventeenth century. Company officers were not pleased to discover that Javanese, Madurese and Chinese vessels from Gresik and adjacent ports plied the Spice Islands of Maluku on behalf of the Giri 'popes'.[50] Their attempts to restrict spices to the tiny island of Banda Neira and thereby build a trade monopoly were challenged by these Asian Muslim merchants. The Senior Buyer and council member Hans de Hase visited Gresik for nearly two months in late 1611 and came to the conclusion that if the VOC was to create a monopoly on spices this would lead to war with Gresik. He warned the lords of Gresik that 'we will attack them if they send any [vessels] to Banda Neira'.[51] The conquest of Gresik and Giri by Sultan Agung two decades later postponed a war between the VOC and Gresik for half a century. Yet de Hase's reports already highlight the ways in which struggles between Muslims and Christian powers in the Indonesian Archipelago were animated as least as much by economic concerns as they were by religious difference.

The spice trade was enmeshed within networks of religious genealogies and a topogeny of related shrines all over the archipelago in which Giri served as the core and thus enjoyed authority as a teacher over the ports where its students could be found.[52] Today, Giri remains acclaimed across the region from the grave of Kyai Gede in Kotawaringin in Kalimantan to that of Sultan Zainal Abidin in Ternate. Over time, however, this network came to be thought of primarily in terms of its religious significance, with reference to Giri teachers of *taṣawwuf* and *fiqh*. Followers equally elaborate on how the Giri school combined Islam with Hindu–Buddhist elements.[53] The custodians of the Giri court point, for example, at the 'Srivijayan design' of its architecture and basins and how the Giri graves emulate those of Majapahit in contrast to the marble Cambay (Rajasthan) tombstones found at the Gresik graveside of Sunan Giri's predecessor, Malik Ibrahim.[54] This relative amnesia of Giri's earlier economic and political power reflects the

Mataram court's conquest of Giri in 1635/6, which curtailed the shrine polity's economic and political autonomy and reduced the lord of Giri to a ceremonial religious figure. However, the Giri shrine was not forgotten as a source of spiritual power that remains venerated to this day, which gave it a durability unmatched by sites of vernacular Sufism such as those in the Maldives discussed in Chapter 3 by A. C. S. Peacock, this volume.

The Mystical War

The Mataram sultanate in the interior of Central Java derived much of its cultural style and symbolic power from the *Pasisir* Muslim port polities of Java's north coast. Prior to Sultan Agung's campaign, Gresik as well as nearby Surabaya and Tuban had become cultural hubs connecting the art, folklore and etiquette from Mataram's antecedent, the former Hindu–Buddhist realm of Majapahit (*c.* 1290–*c.* 1527), with that of the Muslim merchants from China, India and the Middle East.[55] By inviting master craftsmen from the hinterlands, these polities supported the development of Javanese cultural forms, including *wayang* shadow puppetry, *gamelan* orchestras and the making of *kris* daggers in new cosmopolitan port settings where they came to take on distinctly Islamicate forms. When these coastal East Javanese polities were defeated by Sultan Agung in the early seventeenth century, the Mataram sultanate imported this coastal hybrid culture of Javanese Islam and added new martial elements to it.[56] This gave rise to new forms of mystical and ascetic warfare that sprang from, but also further transformed, those of polities like Giri.

Giri traditions reformulated vernacular mysticism and warfare in ways that drew on aspects of pre-Islamic cosmology and ritual practice, as well as perhaps on models of shrine grave lineage prominent in ʿAlawi *sayyid* traditions.[57] *Karāmāt* were important sites and sources of power in struggles against *gawat* (evil), grounding practices including *kanuragan* rituals performed to attain invulnerability.[58] War and magic complemented each other. As in South Asia during this same period, world renunciation went hand in hand with armed prowess.[59] Both 'nobles' and 'devotees' participated in this broad cultural matrix in which mystic warfare connected warlords to sacred lineages and divine aims.[60] In Giri, such sacred lineages and magic powers became part of the physical landscape as well as literary traditions – and in the process became associated with ascetic warfare.

Military threats were present from the onset. By the early sixteenth century, the Hindu–Buddhist Majapahit started attacking Giri and other coastal Islamic communities. Stories of commanders converting to Islam or warriors being chased away by swarms of bees were meant to warn opponents of Giri's *karāmāt*.[61] Visitors to the Giri Kedaton are immediately reminded of these powers when approaching the court via the main staircase. There the grave of a famed *kris* dagger-maker stands. He was but one in a long line of royal blacksmiths crafting daggers, or *krisses*, with *karāmāt* potency for Majapahit and later for Mataram. As these blacksmiths brought their skills and wares to Madura and the coastal areas of Java (*pasisir*), they frequented the Giri court and distributed powerful daggers, including the Kalamunyeng *kris* used by Sunan Giri to fight entire armies single-handedly. Named after a pre-Islamic *gawat*, the original dagger was believed to have been transformed from Sunan Giri's pen (*qalam*). In other words, Islamic piety turned *gawat* into *karāmāt*, after which it could be replicated by mystically potent blacksmiths (*empu*).[62] The *kris* maker buried at the court, *Empu* Supo V, happened to pass away there during his journey in the early seventeenth century.[63] This coincidence turned his grave into a testimony of the mixed spiritual and martial interests of the lords of Giri, both of which were emplaced into localised Sufi genealogies enmeshed within Hindu–Buddhist traditions. Yet it is only by the second half of the seventeenth century that Giri's claims to military power became exclusively associated with mysticism. Puspa Ita was a crucial actor in establishing this association.

To understand Puspa Ita's adaptation of his shrine's military powers in the late seventeenth century, it needs to be elaborated how the legend of these powers took shape over time. For the century following Sunan Giri's death, the strength of the polity was chiefly attested on Java through the graves of his successors and disciples on the two central hills with the tomb and the court. Unlike the military conquests of Central Javanese Demak, Giri mainly extended its realm through the 'soft power' of *karāmāt*.[64] To avoid friction with powerful neighbouring polities like Surabaya and Tuban, no offensive campaigns like those in Ambon were launched on Java itself. Instead, several natural sites were marked as sacred through narrative myths and the building of tombs. Sunan Giri was believed to have shaped a rock resembling the head of an elephant, to have dug a well by knocking his cane against the soil, to have summoned a lake for ablution and to have moved the Anyar hill with his mother's grave from the eastern tip of Java to the surroundings of Giri.[65] All these sites are still visible today, and the centuries-old graves of students and soldiers in their vicinity indicate their importance through the early modern period. The grandchild of Sunan Prapen, for instance, was buried on the Anyar hill in reverence to Sunan Giri's miracle. Most important, these graves not only signified miracles, but also extended the area of Giri's influence in the direction of its competing local polity in Surabaya. The Giri polity did not draw rigid borders, but instead moved further into the hinterlands through new tales of wild spaces touched by the *karāmāt* of the Giri lords and the assignation of their own graves as tokens of his blessing. Territory was defined by burial grounds, which indicated an ongoing Islamic proselytisation.[66]

Strikingly, the tales end with the onset of the Mataram and Banten wars, and artefacts cease to be constructed as these conflicts started raging. The custodians blame the gap in oral history to a lack of knowledge or – as some informants claim – fear of offending Dutch or Sulawesian inquirers.[67] The last reason for silence alludes to the collapse of Giri and the destruction of Gresik between 1675 and 1680.[68] The late seventeenth century saw Giri under pressure, especially from Mataram and Batavia. Yet it was because of this pressure that the ideal of the ascetic warrior became more prominent. The assaults on Gresik between 1675 and 1680 were first undertaken by exiled Makasar warriors and only afterwards by the VOC together with Mataram. Yet claims to resilience were not made based on how these various groups were fended off, but rather on how the *karāmāt* of Giri remained venerated by all of them.[69]

The esteem of the Giri community was preserved through literature and oral myths. This included tales of a local hero capable of assisting, as well as resisting, Mataram: Kyai Sindujoyo. While Kyai Sindujoyo was a disciple of Sunan Prapen distinguished by his piety, he became romanticised as an ascetic warrior roaming around Java half a century after Sunan Prapen's death. Facing armies, winning cockfights and riding crocodiles, he defeats the reputedly invulnerable lord of the Central Javanese Banyumas region in the name of the Mataram sovereign.[70] In the tale, royal rewards are bestowed upon him, but the *kyai* only wishes an albino buffalo in whose stomach he meditates for forty days. This act of asceticism impresses the Mataram sovereign so much that he grants a royal title to the *kyai* as a token of his superior *karāmāt*. The two graves of Kyai Sindujoyo still testify to the exceptional military strength believed to have been derived from his piety, and both were probably already pilgrimage sites in the seventeenth century.[71]

Central Javanese court literature also boasts of the ascetic military prowess of Giri. The retelling of Sultan Agung's conquest of Giri describes the army of 500 Giri disciples as a 'sovereign white heron' ready to take off and run amok at the call of the muezzin and in complete obedience to God as well as to the mighty lord of Giri.[72] Earlier references to military ascetics and devoted troops from Giri are scarce and the shrine polity only seems to have become associated with armed expertise at the moment its autonomy was challenged in 1636. The ascetic and saintly Giri warrior thus appears to be a product of the second half of the seventeenth century onward. More specifically, it relates to the turn of the century, which, according to the Javanese calendar, took place in 1677 CE.

The Giri War

In 1677, the turn of the Javanese century portended disaster as it entailed an overhaul of hierarchies. Volcanic eruptions, famine and a lunar eclipse increased anxieties about looming destruction and inspired prophets of doom. A warlord from Madura Island off the northwest coast of Java, now known as the Young Conqueror Trunajaya, took his chance to subordinate the dominant Central Javanese kingdom of Mataram. He succeeded in sacking the court in 1677 but only with the assistance of three crucial auxiliaries: (1) a band of noble refugees from the overseas region of Makassar in South Sulawesi; (2) the saintly lord Raden Kajoran from the Central Javanese shrine of Tembayat; and, finally, (3) Pangeran Puspa Ita of Giri.[73] Whereas they initially launched a unified and devastating assault, their campaign floundered after the court was conquered. They lost the war as quickly as they had initiated it, and indeed Giri itself would soon fall in the ensuing chaos. This last section returns to the downfall of Giri which occurred between the Mataram and Banten wars. It considers how the Giri army was defeated and contrasts this to al-Maqassārī's campaigns – imagined as the latter were along the lines of a more global vision of an Islamic frontier.

The Mataram War started with internal court intrigue and treachery. The

Mataram crown prince had made a pact with the Madurese lord Trunajaya to overthrow his father; however, in 1676 he was betrayed and the plot failed, allowing Trunajaya to ready his own army of Madurese, Makasar and Javanese troops to attack the court, which subsequently fell in 1677.[74] The Mataram sovereign Amangkurat I died while fleeing from the devastation, and the crown prince succeeded as Amangkurat II without a court, land or followers and only the VOC to turn to. Trunajaya took the loot and regalia to East Java to establish his own realm. But he would not have been able to do so without the assistance of the shrine lords of Kajoran and Giri, as both their shrines mobilised troops. Raden Kajoran recruited the Central Javanese warriors besieging the court, while Puspa Ita provided forces to raid the coastal periphery of Mataram.[75]

Similar to Raden Kajoran, Puspa Ita used his spiritual and political power to meddle with the allegiance between Trunajaya of Madura and his Makasar warlords.[76] To this day, shrine custodians of Giri extol how Puspa Ita fought alongside both parties until the bitter end.[77] Matters were not this simple, however, and Puspa Ita both established and spoiled this allegiance. He quickly alienated the Makasar forces. The Madurese were closely affiliated with the Giri shrine and shared genealogies with it, but the Makasar stood at a distance from it and would at most claim that the three Datuks who proselytised Islam in South Sulawesi once studied in Giri. The leaders of the Makasar troops, Admiral Karaeng Bontomarannu (d. 1677) and Karaeng Galesong (likely the son of Sultan Hasanuddin, 1655–80), soon found themselves caught up in a scheme of Puspa Ita to reassert autonomy over the shrine lands.[78] Despite being Muslims, the Makasar remained outsiders in these plans and less reverential towards Giri's *karāmāt*. Within a few months this led to a break-up between the forces.

Initially, the Mataram sovereign tried to keep Puspa Ita apart from the Madurese and Makasar insurgents. To do so, he assigned the crown prince to keep the shrine under surveillance; something he was quickly to regret. In January 1675, he discovered that the crown prince was not loyal to his cause, but rather 'allowed and approved . . . the Makasar robberies' in East Java by asking the Giri and Gresik regents to support them. The Mataram sovereign therefore executed several regents in Giri and sought to hand power over Gresik back to Puspa Ita. But the latter did not intend to serve Mataram and instead preferred to 'continue his priestly and honourable life'.[79] Facing a coup inside his court, the Mataram sovereign likely tried to win over Puspa Ita to retain his grasp over the East Javanese coast. However, Puspa Ita's genealogical ties with Madura were stronger than those with Mataram.[80] Direct opposition was too dangerous, so Puspa Ita attempted to regain autonomy by secretly inviting the Madurese and Makasar warriors to join his struggle. He pretended to be attacked by these forces to cover up the military alliance.

In the wake of the executions of the Giri regents in January, the Madurese lord Trunajaya chose to strengthen his ties with the Makasar exiles to undermine Central Javanese rule over the area surrounding Giri. As Raden Trunajaya explains himself, 'he offered to wed his daughter to Karaeng Galesong, on the condition that Galesong would conquer Surabaya and Gresik for him.' The descendants of Karaeng Galesong assume Trunajaya did actually wed his cousin, but the pact remains clear in both cases: wife for land.[81] Initially, rumours of raids struck great fear in the hearts of the coastal Javanese. Three European trading vessels harboured in Gresik witnessed how the Makassar 'landed there with 25 heavily armed vessels . . . carrying about 500 armed men, all equipped with machetes [*goloks*], pistols and round shields. At the sight of this landing, residents reportedly fled to the nearby mountains.' The European witnesses, however, halted the siege by simply warning the Makasar not to commit any hostilities. Surprisingly, the Makasar troops raised the white flag in response and accepted this command in return for fifteen jars of gunpowder and three hundred bullets.[82] The Makasar troops chose spoils of war over a profitless assault. The first attempt to liberate the shrine lands from Mataram's grasp thus failed utterly, providing the first sign of larger conflicts to come.

In rage and dismay over these developments, Karaeng Bontomarannu of Makassar called his troops 'spineless'.[83] The larger plans for obtaining Gresik and Giri were pursued once more a few months later, without Europeans present and under the command of Karaeng Galesong. Lacking their own eyewitnesses to this campaign, the VOC was easily alarmed by hearsay reports, as a VOC regent in Jepara wrote on 14 November 1675:

> The Makasar started to expose their murderous nature to the Javanese at the Bay of Gresik and the Madura Straits . . . those from Gresik have palisaded

> the beaches around the city with bamboo, and even retreated to the Giri mountain with their families, and left a small number of men in the city, from there the [lord] of Giri advised the Susuhunan [i.e., the Mataram sovereign] to ensure the unbearable rabble shall face the revenge of his majesty's force and, possibly, that all the Makasar will be evicted from the island of Java . . .[84]

Sources from Giri, however, reveal that Puspa Ita burned down his own palace to falsely claim that he had been attacked. No blood was shed.[85] Puspa Ita's advice to the Mataram sovereign was a deliberate act of manipulation: a diplomatic trick to avoid suspicion and secretly unite the forces that planned to sack the Mataram court. Without the Mataram sovereign realising, the Makasar and Madurese lords united with Puspa Ita and were ready to march inland. After the siege, Puspa Ita prophesised that 'soon a big change would come to the Mataram realm' from East Java and convinced many to join the insurgency.[86] In 1676, Puspa Ita further appealed to his own lineage as a source of spiritual authority in an attempt to convince Mataram to sever its ties with the VOC.[87]

The coalition between Giri and Trunajaya, however, quickly ran to the detriment of Karaeng Galesong, Karaeng Bontomarannu and their Makasar troops. Whereas the Madurese enjoyed a central role in the prophecies of Puspa Ita, the Makasar remained alienated from it and sought loot rather than the blessing of the Giri shrine polity. Puspa Ita must have foreseen this. A few weeks after the November siege, he started spreading rumours aimed at spoiling the ties between Trunajaya and the Makasar. He appears to have faced difficulties in keeping the latter in check, likely because the Makasar nobles had no reason to respect a shrine polity largely unrelated to their own Gowan and Taloqan traditions. After all, while one of the three Datuks who spread Islam in Makassar reportedly studied in Giri, the shrine is not mentioned in Makasar pedigrees.[88] For the Makasar nobles, Giri was a polity outside their own Sulawesi-centred sacred topography.[89] Their participation in Trunajaya's campaigns thus appears to have been mostly driven by the promise of material reward, and the Makasar troops turned to plundering traders out of apparent dissatisfaction with the limited spoils received from the fake siege.

Whereas the two sieges in April and November 1675 were largely bloodless, the one in December 'put Gresik . . . to ashes'.[90] The Malay ship *Sutana* happened to have been anchored in port at the same time violence erupted. Although out of town during the day of pillage, on his return to the ship shortly after the captain found his vessel burned and counted an army of 800 Makasar, 300 Bugis and 1,000 Malay men sailing 150 vessels. Their lords 'carried the seal and credentials of the [crown prince], the display of which ensured no one dared to intervene'.[91] Still, Giri would not submit. After laying the land around Giri to waste, threatening shrine polities like Tuban into submission and seeking support among Surabayan nobles, the Makasar lords retreated eastwards to Dẹmung, Panarukan and their supply hub on the island of Sumbawa.[92] From their new bases, the largest part of the Makasasr forces challenged Trunajaya's command up till the point of demanding rule over Gresik and Giri.[93] The Makasar outsiders seem to have realised that they could undermine Puspa Ita's authority simply by taking his shrine. Puspa Ita did not appear to be bothered by this and continued attracting new followers, while the brotherhood between the Madurese and Makasar turned sour.

By early 1677, the close ties between the Madurese and Makasar warriors were in ruins, while the marital ties between them had been violently cut. Trunajaya abducted and poisoned Galesong's wife and child, who were his own kin. Karaeng Galesong buried both of them on a hill next to which his own corpse would be laid to rest three years later.[94] But Trunajaya also faced pressure. VOC delegates who visited his headquarters discovered that he felt trapped in his Surabaya stronghold: 'as I have no one to whom I can entrust my provinces'. It is reported that at that moment his servants brought in 'two severed Makasar heads which [Trunajaya] observes while speaking: these heads belong to a people who I sheltered and assisted, for they are the people of my brother [Karaeng Galesong], yet because they opposed [me] and bit the hand that feeds, I have been forced to treat them like this'.[95] Trunajaya's attempts to build a new court and crown himself Sultan Intraprista were likely frustrated by the increasing conflict with Puspa Ita, who gradually expanded his own power over the coast and even Madura.[96] Eventually, he made his own alliance with the VOC in an attempt to regain control over East Java. In the end, the united alliance of Muslim forces from Giri, Madura and Makassar, which is celebrated in Giri and Malang today, turned out to be largely illusory – a later ideological imposition upon the narrative that obscures both the friction between diverse Muslim militias and the shifting relationships of various parties with the emerging Dutch power in the region. Instead of building an Islamic frontier, Puspa Ita reluctantly switched sides to the VOC and its partner.

Giri's allegiance with the VOC and Mataram was strained. Overwhelmed by the VOC forces, Puspa Ita assigned his nephew Tuampel to chase Trunajaya down. His own sons even joined the VOC forces with '400 armed Javanese and 100 bearers'.[97] In return, he was to receive forty-one cannons, which were captured from Trunajaya's headquarters and functioned as both arms and royal regalia. The Mataram troops, however, prevented the arrival of this gift by secretly bringing the guns to Central Java. Angered by this, the Dutch VOC commander tried to return them to Giri but to no avail.[98] Conversely, Trunajaya's lords showed none of Mataram's contempt and instead sent Puspa Ita a valuable black Madurese horse. These diplomatic exchanges awoke fears among the VOC officers that Giri had once more 'allied to the Madurese, and at the moment [the VOC commander] leaves Surabaya [Puspa Ita intends] to attack the city and destroy everything in it'.[99] Months later the rumour that Puspa Ita claimed Madura and the areas surrounding Surabaya only sounded further alarm bells.[100] By the middle of 1680, war erupted as the eighty-year old Puspa Ita flatly refused to recognise Amangkurat II as the legitimate heir of the Mataram sultanate.[101]

On the penultimate day of May 1680, Amangkurat II and his courtiers moved on Gresik to demand an audience with Puspa Ita. As Puspa Ita denied this request, a Javanese-speaking Scottish VOC commander named Couper surrounded the Giri shrine and demanded his submission once more. On behalf of Amangkurat II, he apparently also demanded the transfer of Giri's sacred regalia *kris* Kalamunyeng.[102] Puspa Ita once again refused to recognise any sovereign, claiming that he served none but his predecessor Sunan Giri whose grave he guarded. Amangkurat II was furious and loath to return humiliated to Surabaya if he were unable to force Puspa Ita to submit. Together with Couper he marched 1,100 Javanese and 450 VOC troops to the gates of the Giri palace. There, Puspa Ita appeared holding a plate filled with benzoin incense. Standing inside the incense smoke he mumbled several sentences before speaking out loud:

> I have spoken to the lord of the free spirits residing in the smoke, who promised me that a thousand spirits will protect every single one of my sons so that no enemy can hurt them [thus] allowing [them] to attack the enemy bravely and without fear, for the sovereigns of Mataram shall stem from my bloodline.

On cue, hundreds of his followers stormed downhill:

> spurred to such feverous [assault] as never has been beheld during this Javanese war . . . as they fear shots nor strikes in this attack but act like maniacs on the ongoing calls to run amok from the old Pangeran [Puspa Ita], who commanded all his troops personally, hitting us from all sides with such fury [that they killed] six Europeans and ten Javanese men and [injured a] dozen others [while pushing] the Susuhunan's Madurese and Javanese [troops to flee while they] bump into each other in confusion, [thus bringing] two of our white companies into disorder and the third one into retreat.[103]

In the midst of this chaos, Couper gathered the reserve troops and broke through the enemy lines, killing several lords and troops. Invulnerability proved to be short-lasting and after a second failed strike on Couper's force, Giri's troops fled to the forests. As the smoke of the lord of the free spirits was driven away by that of gunpowder, the commoners marshalled by Puspa Ita all abandoned him, leaving only some dozen intimates behind. Puspa Ita was struck in his right leg twice, but despite the wounds and his age fled with his kin to the graves of his descendants one hill further away. There the Madurese forces of Amangkurat II surrounded and captured him and his twenty-five sons, grandsons and nephews – the religious lord was not celibate after all – and brought them to Amangkurat II who had them all executed. Only the oldest son of Puspa Ita was pardoned as several nobles claimed him to be innocent.[104] Amangkurat II thus preserved one descendant of Sunan Giri for his own prestige. He was, however, never able to obtain the legendary Kalamunyeng *kris* – a primary symbol of Giri's mystical and military power.[105]

Despite the death of Puspa Ita, religious resistance against Amangkurat II persisted. When Puspa Ita's Madurese supporters heard about his execution, they started a revolt on both the west and east side of the island.[106] Other revolts erupting in Bangil – a town south of Surabaya – resulted in sieges of Surabaya and required prolonged efforts by the VOC before they were finally quelled.[107] Amangkurat II himself was hardly capable of resisting these opponents, and reference to the legitimacy of Puspa Ita's bloodline through his co-opted nephew Mas Tuampel thus became an integral part of his strategy for controlling Gresik and Giri. Unlike Puspa Ita's followers, Mas Tuampel had fought fervently on Mataram's side. This loyalty eventually cost him his life. In the midst of the siege of Giri, Mas Tuampel was poisoned by his uncle Puspa Ita and passed away nearly two months later. Amangkurat II promptly decided to marry Mas Tuampel's widow to his preferred regent of Gresik and Giri in order to keep control over the shrine land.[108] Nonetheless, he was not confident in his capabilities to control hallowed places like Giri. Even prior to attacking the shrine, Amangkurat II lost trust and reportedly stated 'that he w[ould] never become Sunan of Mataram, and even if that happen[ed], he would put his son on the throne and end his life in Mecca close to Mohammed's grave'.[109] The ongoing religious resistance and a worsening fever once again evoked his ascetic yearning, and he told the VOC commander Couper that 'he was looking forward to finding a potent spot close to Cirebon so he could end his life there as a hermit, since it appeared to him the Mataram Sultanate would never be in peace again.'[110] While outgunning Giri, Amangkurat II's prowess still paled next to that of Puspa Ita. Not only did Amangkurat II lack religious charisma but also diplomatic and economic guile. Whereas the Mataram sovereign had difficulties accepting this personally, his scribes tried to depict both men as equals in their account of the conquest of Giri written for the epic court chronicle.

As shown above, Puspa Ita was a shrewd religious leader pulling the strings of East and Central Javanese politics. The Mataram scribes emphasised Puspa Ita's genealogies, regalia and reputed magical powers to symbolise his wide-ranging esteem. Throughout the tale, Amangkurat II lays claim on all these merits too. For instance, the court description of the final attack on Giri by Mataram is characterised by references to Giri's Kalamunyeng dagger, which Amangkurat II desired for himself. Moreover, both armies were reputedly backed by heirs of the *wali sanga* and laid claim to ascetic prowess similar to that of Kyai Sindujoyo.[111] In other words, religious claims to supernatural powers were not peculiar to the Giri troops, nor separate from conceptions of military charisma. The call of Giri's muezzins intertwines with the beat of war drums to boost morale and promise invincibility. Only in one instance is the term 'holy war' (*perang sabil*) used, but it describes the fierce intentions while preparing for battle rather than a planned struggle against unbelievers. Just like the assault of Sultan Agung in the early seventeenth century, the followers of Giri act like a white heron through the quick and furious attack flying towards the enemy. The term holy war becomes a near synonym of '*amok*' in the account of the Giri assault in the Javanese chronicle *Babad Keraton*.[112]

The Mataram clerks and scribes equally ensured that Amangkurat II adapted part of the genealogy (*silsila*) of Giri. At his coronation, Amangkurat II added the phrase 'Zainal Kubra' to his royal title. Zainal Kubra is a literal device used to stress a Kubrawiyya *silsila* with 'Jumadil Kubra' (i.e., Najmuddīn al-Kubrā) and the Prophet's family. The Gresik chronicle as well as legends from surrounding areas cherish the Kubrawiyya *silsila* and even claim Jumadil Kubra to be the grandfather, or sometimes the father, of Sunan Giri himself.[113] The Cirebon chronicle also connects related saints to Jumadil Kubra.[114] By adding Kubrawiyya elements to his royal title, Amangkurat II and his scribes proclaimed that God's blessing (*baraka*) had now fallen on him and his new court instead of Giri or any of the other shrine polities. After conquering Trunajaya's headquarters in Kediri, Amangkurat II is told to seek acknowledgement of his saintly title by visiting the grave of the senior *wali sanga* Sunan Ampel and sending a delegate to Puspa Ita. As mentioned earlier, however, Puspa Ita refused to recognise these infringements on his spiritual authority and *karāmāt*. Instead, he considered Amangkurat II to be a pretender and the son of the VOC admiral Cornelis Speelman in disguise.

Since the military strength of the VOC and particularly the conqueror Speelman were envied in Java, Amangkurat II's connections with the Dutch served to enhance the Javanese Muslim ruler's image as a leader with access to extraordinary sources of power, albeit foreign and bewitching ones. Indeed, they were dangerous too; as Amangkurat II attacked and burned Gresik and Giri to the ground, its autonomy was to be permanently lost.[115] From its ashes rose a new saintly protector of Mataram: the heirs of the 'tenth saint' Sunan Kalijaga.[116] Royal blessing moved from one holy figure to another in return for saintly supernatural powers.

Sufi Warfare

Connections to broader trans-regional worlds of Islam were present in Giri without fundamentally changing its vernacular and embedded Islam. This becomes clear when comparing Puspa Ita's recruitment of troops with that of Shaykh Yūsuf al-Maqassārī. Throughout the conflict, Puspa Ita shifted allegiances to regain power over his shrine, whereas al-Maqassārī shifted places to recruit his followers. If the former thrived by keeping his forces ethnically divided in order to obtain diplomatic gains, the latter invoked a vision of Islamic solidarity uniting an *umma* stretching across the Indonesian Archipelago and beyond to confront the encroachment of European colonial power over Muslim lands. As I explained elsewhere, al-Maqassārī and his patron Sultan Tirtayasa of Banten never succeeded in assembling an Islamic army.[117] The shrine polities defining early modern Java did not celebrate tolerance of culturally diverse populations, but rather produced denominations that could clash as easily as cooperate.[118] These diversities were not so much dichotomous as factional, albeit within contexts of a shared belief in saints and *karāmāt*. Courts and ports alike depended on shrines for authority; still today the sultanate of Yogyakarta distributes lists of recommended shrine visits. Such lists not only hold religious claims, but also attempt to establish control over peripheries of what has now become a province of the Republic of Indonesia.[119]

Shaykh Yūsuf al-Maqassārī tried to overcome the divisive Javanese landscape by using his scholarly and courtly authority to amass followers from among Islamic communities stretching widely across the Indian Ocean world. Despite his stressing of the importance of living Islamic teachers as legitimate sources of religious knowledge, in the end his own dead body was transformed into a source of *karāmāt*. Blessing remained magical and so did warfare. Warfare, in this sense, remained fractional, as can be seen from the divisions among the troops gathering around Giri in the advance against Mataram.[120] Notions of Islamic solidarity here obscure the clientelism characterising the fragmented nature of Muslim armies and allegiances fighting in the wars of seventeenth-century Java. Whereas *sayyids* overturned the hereditary monarchy of the Maldives (see Peacock, Chapter 3, above), shaykhs, *ḥajis* and travellers (*musāfir*) generally had less prominent political profiles than the emergent Muslim polities scattered across early modern Java.

Two different forms of Sufi warfare resulted: one in which court and religious networks were resorted to for the sake of opposing the extension of Batavia and resilience of minor polities; the other centred on sacred places and aimed to increase the autonomy of former shrine polities vis-à-vis sultanates. The latter form of warfare referred to a different Islam than the one of trans-regional Islamic solidarity advocated by al-Maqassārī. The local shrine lords remained thoroughly embedded in Java and retained power through a fundamentally vernacular orientation towards Islam. The economic networks of these shrine lords extending to the Spice Islands counted in some ways more than connections to centres of Islamic learning and devotional life in the Holy Land. Puspa Ita reputedly married a *sayyida*, but he showed little concern for ties to the Ḥaramayn. Inevitably, overseas Islamic elements reached the port near Giri, but they were consistently shaped and adapted to Javanese politics and cosmology aimed at attracting Sufis and warlords. In other words, the call of the muezzin echoed in Giri but did not direct the flight of the white heron when its nest was under threat. Attention to the specific dynamics of military mobilisation and alliances in this context thus opens up critical space for reflections on the contours of, and constraints on, particular historic formations of Islamic cosmopolitanism. Shrines, Sufis and warlords formed myriad frontiers.

Notes

1. Manyambeang, Abdul Kadir, *Syekh Yusuf dalam Perspektif Lontaraq Gowa* (Makassar: La Galigo Press, 2014), pp. 93–5, 313–17.
2. In accordance with a growing consensus among scholars, Makasar with one 's' serves as an adjective, whereas Makassar with two of them refers to the place.
3. Feener, R. Michael, 'Shaykh Yusuf and the Appreciation of Muslim "Saints" in Modern Indonesia', *Journal for Islamic Studies* 18/19 (1999/98): 112–31.
4. Joppie, Saarah, 'Many Makassars: Tracing an Africa–Southeast Asian Narrative of Shaykh Yusuf Taj al-Khalwati al-Maqassari', in Scarlett Cornelissen and Yoichi Mine (eds), *Migration and Agency in a Globalizing World: Afro-Asian Encounters* (London: Palgrave Macmillan, 2018).
5. Van Bruinessen, Martin, 'Shariʿa Court, Tarekat and Pesantren: Religious Institutions in the Banten Sultanate', *Archipel* 50 (1995): 165–6, 168.
6. Kemper, Simon C., 'The Umbilical Cord of Threats: The Catastrophic but Seminal Securitization of Infidel Attacks on the Early Modern Banten

Sultanate, Indonesia', in Eberhard Crailsheim and María Dolores Elizalde (eds), *Representations of External Threats in History* (Leiden: Brill, forthcoming).

7. Feener, 'Shaykh Yusuf', pp. 112–31.
8. Note that Puspa Ita does not have a shrine custodian, which shows his lower rank in the Giri lineage. Only when he was alive and watched over the graves of his pre-descendants was honour bestowed upon him.
9. Both al-Maqassārī and Puspa Ita were aged over fifty by the late 1670s. Notice that oral traditions disagree whether Puspa Ita or Pangeran Wira ruled during this time or whether they might have ruled together. It is clear, however, that the Panembahan or Pangeran Giri referred to in Javanese and VOC sources is a single person and most likely Puspa Ita. Moreover, Puspa Ita was directly related to Sunan Giri and not merely a Mataram courtier as is suggested by the sign in front of the Giri Kedaton court. Mochtar Djamil (Kyai, pesantren head in Gresik and Giri expert consulted by the *juru kunci* of Giri Kedaton), in discussion with the author, 25 September 2015; and Wiselius, J. A. B. (trans.), 'Stamboom en geslachtsregister van de Regenten van Sidajoe en Grissee van Madureesche afstamming' (Gresik, 1872), D Or. 228, Special Collections, Leiden University Library.
10. The Sunan Gunungjati-inclined Cirebon chronicle claims recognition was gained via Demak, which underlines different narratives are shaped by varying saint cults, see de Graaf, Hermanus Johannes, 'Tjirebonse overlevering over Sjeich Ibn Maulana bij Valentijn', DH 1055–24, Special Collections, Leiden University Library, 1; de Graaf, Hermanus Johannes and Theodore Gauthier Pigeaud, *De Eerste Moslimse Vorstendommen op Java: Studiën over de Staatkundige Geschiedenis van de 15de en de 16de Eeuw* (The Hague: Martinus Nijhoff, 1974), pp. 150–1; and de Graaf, Hermanus Johannes, *De Regering van Panembahan Sénapati Ingalaga* (The Hague: Martinus Nijhoff, 1954), pp. 62–4.
11. de Graaf, Hermanus Johannes, 'Titels en namen van Javaanse vorsten en groten uit de 16de en 17de eeuw', *Bijdragen tot de Taal-, Land- en Volkenkunde* 1 (1953): 62–82; Pigeaud, Theodore Gauthier and Hermanus Johannes de Graaf, *Islamic States in Java 1500–1700: Eight Dutch Books and Articles by Dr H. J. de Graaf* (Leiden: KITLV Press, 1976), pp. 9, 15.
12. Bertrand, Romain, *État colonial, noblesse et nationalisme à Java: la Tradition parfaite (XVIIe–XXe siècles)* (Paris: Karthala, 2005), pp. 19–120, 189–260, 293–346, 375–449; Carey, Peter, *The Power of Prophecy; Prince Dipanagara and the End of an Old Order in Java, 1785–1855* (Leiden: KITLV Press,

2008), p. 843; Lombard, Denys, *Le Carrefour Javanais, essai d'histoire globale: L'héritage des royaumes concentriques*, vol. III (Paris: Éditions de l'École des hautes études en sciences sociales, 1990), pp. 66–71; Woodward, Mark, *Java, Indonesia and Islam* (New York: Springer, 2011), p. 175; Sutherland, Heather, *The Making of a Bureaucratic Elite: the Colonial Transformation of the Javanese Priyayi* (Singapore: Heinemann Educational Books, 1979).

13. Jaques, Robert Kevin, 'Sajarah Leluhur: Hindu Cosmology and the Construction of Javanese Muslim Genealogical Authority', *Journal of Islamic Studies* 17(2) (2006): 151; de Graaf and Pigeaud, *De Eerste Moslimse*, pp. 154–5, 168; de Graaf, Hermanus Johannes, *De Regering van Sultan Agung, Vorst van Mataram (1613–1645) En Die van Zijn Voorganger Panembahan Séda-Ing-Krapjak (1601–1613)* (The Hague: Martinus Nijhoff, 1958), pp. 205–22.
14. de Haan, Frederik, *Dagh-Register Gehouden Int Casteel Batavia Vant Passerende Daer Ter Plaetse Als over Geheel Nederlandts–India Anno 1679* (The Hague: Martinus Nijhoff, 1909), pp. 496, 520, 522.
15. This is not to claim these authors perceived a difference between Javanese and Islamic culture, for as Ricklefs rightly points out, they attempted to prove the opposite (see Ricklefs, Merle Calvin, 'Rediscovering Islam in Javanese History', *Studia Islamika* 21(39) (2015): 397–418). Nonetheless, even in the sophisticated research of Ricklefs, courtly opposition keeps being portrayed as a singular Islamic force. de Graaf, Hermanus Johannes, *De Regering van Sunan Mangku-Rat I: Tegal-Wangi, vorst van Mataram, 1646–1677: Opstand en Ondergang* (The Hague: Martinus Nijhoff, 1962), p. 64; Knaap, Gerrit, 'Islamic Resistance in the Dutch Colonial Empire', in David Motadel (ed.), *Islam and the European Empires* (Oxford: Oxford University Press, 2014), pp. 213–27; Knaap, Gerrit, Henk den Meijer and Michiel de Jong, *Militaire Geschiedenis van Nederland: Oorlogen Overzee, Militair optreden door compagnie en staat buiten Europa 1595–1814* (Amsterdam: Boom, 2015), pp. 116–21; Ricklefs, Merle Calvin, 'Balance and Military Innovation in 17th Century Java', *History Today* (1990): 40–7; Ricklefs, Merle Calvin, *Mystic Synthesis in Java: a History of Islamization from the Fourteenth to the Early Nineteenth Centuries* (Norwalk, CT: East Bridge Signature Books, 2006), pp. 36, 67; Ricklefs, Merle Calvin, *War, Culture, and Economy in Java, 1677–1726: Asian and European Imperialism in the Early Kartasura Period* (Sydney: Allen & Unwin, 1993), pp. 29, 40.
16. In fact, 'holy war' was rare throughout the region. Federspiel, Howard, *Sultans,*

Shamans & Saints: Islam and Muslims in Southeast Asia (Chiang Mai: Silkworm Books, 2008), pp. 35–6.

17. Quotes taken from Shaykh Yūsuf's *An-Nafhatu as-Sailaaniyah* in which the shaykh himself quotes from scripture. For an Indonesian translation, see Hamid, Abu, *Sheikh Yusuf Makassar: Seorang Ulama, Sufi dan Pejuang* (Jakarta: Yayasan Obor Indonesia, 1994), pp. 290–1. Only Darusman suggests a violent *jihād* is part of Shaykh Yūsuf's writing, but he does not back this up in any way. Darusman, Lukmanul Hakim, 'Jihad in Two Faces of Shariah: Sufism and Islamic Jurisprudence (*fiqh*) and the Revival of Islamic Movements in the Malay Word: Case Studies of Yusuf al Maqassaary and Dawud al Fatani', PhD dissertation, Australian National University, 2008.
18. This is not to claim that Shaykh Yūsuf was a neo-Sufi, but rather that he brought new scholarly discussions and brotherhoods to the Malay Archipelago, see Azra, Azyumardi, *The Origins of Islamic Reformism in Southeast Asia Networks of Malay–Indonesian and Middle Eastern Ulama in the Seventeenth and Eighteenth Centuries* (Sydney: Allen & Unwin, 2004), pp. 87–108.
19. This is in partial contrast to what Michael Laffan argues in *The Makings of Indonesian Islam: Orientalism and the Narration of a Sufi Past* (Princeton, NJ: Princeton University Press, 2011), pp. 16, 24.
20. These *ṭuruq* include Naqsyabandiyya, Qādiriyya, Shaṭṭāriyya, Ba'alawiyya and Khalwatiyya for which he could teach officially (a right granted through an *ijāza*), and Dasuqiyya, Shadziliyya, Chisytiyya, 'Aydarusiyya, Ahmadiyya, Madariyya and Kubrawiyya, as well as several less known ones into which he was once initiated. Van Bruinessen, Martin, *Kitab Kuning, Pesantren dan Tarekat* (Jakarta: Gading, 2015), p. 234.
21. Van Bruinessen, *Kitab Kuning*, pp. 27, 49–50, 114, 185, 265–7, 274, 334–6, 459–60.
22. Other numbers are often blindly quoted by scholars, but those mentioned here derive from several VOC reports. Azyumardi Azra suggests that Shaykh Yūsuf retreated to the village Karang in Tasikmalaya early on, but thereby ignores VOC reports of him and his troops still roaming around West Java. See Azra, *Origins of Islamic Reformism*, p. 96. See '25 January 1683 till 7 February 1683', Bundle 2495, pp. 129–83, Arsip Nasional Republik Indonesia (ANRI).
23. Feener, 'Shaykh Yusuf', p. 119. Azra's assumption that Shaykh Yūsuf did not use his *tarīqa* network for political purposes can hence be dismissed. Azra, *Origins of Islamic Reformism*, pp. 49, 91, 103–8.
24. Feener, 'Shaykh Yusuf', p. 121.

25. My gratitude goes to Professor Fuad Jabali (Syarif Hidayatullah State Islamic University in Jakarta) for pointing the *Ḥabl al-warīd* out to me and helping to interpret it.
26. Tudjimah, *Syekh Yusuf Makasar: Riwayat Hidup, Karya dan Ajarannya* (Jakarta: Departemen Pendidikan dan Kebudayaan, 1987), pp. 20–1.
27. For legends stressing his otherworldly abilities, see the example given in Chambert-Loir, Henri (ed.), *Naik Haji di Masa Silam Tahun 1482–1890* (Jakarta: Kepustakaan Populer Gramedia, 2013), pp. 157–207. Gibson suggests this but obscures the legacy by separating it from the shrine polities and abstracting it to: 'Islamic religious knowledge and the charismatic authority of cosmopolitan *shaikhs*'. Gibson, Thomas P., *Islamic Narrative and Authority in Southeast Asia from the 16th to the 21st Century* (New York: Palgrave Macmillan, 2007), pp. 1–2, 67–71, 85–109.
28. The term shrine is preferred over *keramat* to keep the distinction between saintly locations and the associated potency clear. As the Malay form of the Arabic *karāmāt*, *keramat* does not refer to places per se.
29. As is well known, Sultan Abdul Jalil requested that the corpse of Shaykh Yūsuf be buried in Lakiung. Cummings, William, *The Makassar Annals* (Leiden: KITLV, 2011), p. 20; Sunyoto, Agus, *Atlas Wali Songo* (Jakarta: Mizan, 2012).
30. Van Bruinessen, Martin, 'The Tariqa Khalwatiyya in South Celebes', in Harry A. Poeze and Pim Schoorl (eds), *Excursies in Celebes. Een bundel bijdragen bij het afscheid van J. Noorduijn als directeur-secretaris van het KITLV* (Leiden: KITLV Uitgeverij, 1991), pp. 251–69; Cummings, *Makassar Annals*, pp. 7–39, 63–4, 100, 149–212, 298; Ward, Kerry, *Networks of Empire: Forced Migration in the Dutch East India Company* (Cambridge: Cambridge University Press, 2009), pp. 1–12, 23–5, 42–5.
31. Mujib (Custodian at the Makassar graveside of al-Maqassārī), in discussion with the author, 28 August 2015.
32. On *Rūm* see Ricci, Ronit, *Islam Translated: Literature, Conversion, and the Arabic Cosmopolis of South and Southeast Asia* (Chicago, IL: University of Chicago Press, 2011), p. 226.
33. Mujib in Makassar (2015); Pudjiastuti, Titik, *Menyusuri Jejak Kesultanan Banten* (Jakarta: Penerbit Wedatama Widya Sastra, 2015), pp. 147–51.
34. Van Bruinessen, *Kitab Kuning*, p. 272.
35. Mujib in Makassar (2015) and Abdul Halik Daeng Mabe (middle-aged *juru kunci* at the royal graveside of Gowa in Makassar), in discussion with the author, 1 September 2015 and 9 December 2015.

36. Mujib in Makassar (2015) and Abdul Halik Daeng Mabe, *op. cit.* For the early modern notion of *bid'a*, see Green, Nile, *Sufism: A Global History* (Oxford: Blackwell, 2012), pp. 155, 174–6.
37. Guillot, Claude and Henri Chambert-Loir, 'Indonesia' and 'Makam Sunan Gunung Jati', in Henri Chambert-Loir and Claude Guillot (eds), *Ziarah dan Wali di Dunia Islam* (Jakarta: Jakarta: École Française d'Extrême-Orient, 2007), pp. 333–65; Guillot, Claude, 'La symbolique de la mosquee javanaise, a propos de la "Petite Mosquee" de Jatinom', *Archipel* 30 l'Islam en Indonésie II (1985): 4; Guillot, Claude, 'Le rôle historique des perdikan ou "villages francs": le cas de Tegalsari', *Archipel* 30 l'Islam en Indonésie II (1985): 153–7; Guillot, Claude, 'The Tembayat Hill: Clergy and Royal Power in Central Java from the 15th to the 17th Century', in H. Chamber-Loir and A. Reid (eds), *The Potent Dead: Ancestors, Saints and Heroes in Contemporary Indonesia* (Sydney: Allen & Unwin, 2002), pp. 141–59; Lombard, Denys and Claudine Salmon, 'Islam et sinité', *Archipel* 30 L'Islam en Indonésie II (1985): 81–3; Djatnika, Rachmat, 'Les wakaf ou "Biens de mainmorte" à Java-est: etude diachronique', *Archipel* 30 l'Islam en Indonésie II (1985): 121–8.
38. The importance of the elevation of the Giri shrine is visible from the name 'Giri' itself, which, in literary usage, means mountain in Javanese.
39. See *Precis de la Tradition Javanaise dur Giri et Son Criss* (1820), H227, Section KITLV Special Collections, Leiden University Library; Wiselius, J. A. B., 'Historisch Onderzoek naar de Geestelijke en Wereldlijke Suprematie van Grisse op Midden- en Oost-Java gedurende de 16de en 17de eeuw', *Tijdschrift voor Indische Taal-Land- en Volkenkunde* 23 (1876): 470–3.
40. de Graaf and Pigeaud, *De Eerste Moslimse*, pp. 149–51.
41. Parker, Geoffrey, *Global Crisis: War, Climate Change and Catastrophe in the Seventeenth Century* (New Haven, CT: Yale University Press, 2014).
42. For instance, Green, Nile, *Islam and the Army in Colonial India: Sepoy Religion in the Service of Empire* (Cambridge: Cambridge University Press, 2009), pp. 18–59; Green, Nile, *Indian Sufism since the Seventeenth Century: Saints, Books and Empires in the Muslim Deccan* (New York: Routledge, 2006), pp. xiii–xv, 10, 16–55; Kolff, Dirk A. H., *Naukar, Rajput and Sepoy: the Ethnohistory of the Military Labour Market in Hindustan, 1450–1850* (Cambridge: Cambridge University Press, 1990), pp. 42–56; Moin, A. Afzar, *The Millennial Sovereign: Sacred Kingship and Sainthood in Islam* (New York: Columbia University Press, 2012), pp. 8–24, 225.

43. Mochtar (Senior Juru Kunci Giri Kedaton), in discussion with the author, 25 September 2015.
44. The Portuguese writer Tomé Pires, for instance, did not even notice Giri's presence in 1515. See de Graaf and Pigeaud, *De Eerste Moslimse*, pp. 142–3.
45. Their main competitor over Gresik was Surabaya. See Valentijn, François, *Oud En Nieuw Oost-Indiën, Vervattende Een Naaukeurige En Uitvoerige Verhandelinge van Nederlands Mogentheyd in Die Gewesten: Beschryving van Groot Djava Ofte Java Major*, 5 vols (Dordrecht: Joannes van Braam, 1726), vol. 4, p. 65.
46. de Graaf, *Panembahan Sénapati*, pp. 60–1.
47. Early modern manuscripts from Giri are rare; I found two in the private collection of Oemar Zainuddin. Court tales from other islands give the strongest indication of Giri's legal network. Prince Hidayat of Ternate (Prince of Ternate from the first wife of Sultan Ḥajj Muzaffar Shah I, lecturer at the University Khairun Ternate and writer on Ternaten religion and culture), in discussion with the author, 6 December 2015; and Ḥajj Ridwan Daro (*qāḍī* of Ternate, writer on Ternaten religion and history, army official), as well as Prince Hidayat of Ternate, in discussion with the author, 7 December 2015; and Chambert-Loir, Henri, 'Dato' ri Bandang. Légendes de l'islamisation de la région de Celebes-Sud', *Archipel* 29 (1985) : 158–61.
48. de Graaf, *Panembahan Sénapati*, p. 61.
49. de Graaf, *Sultan Agung*, pp. 206–8, 218.
50. Tuban and Surabaya were looked at suspiciously, too, although its networks apparently depended on Giri. The Portuguese used Javanese skippers to trade in Banda Neira, but it is not known how they were affiliated to Gresik or Giri. My gratitude goes to Tristan Mostert for pointing out the reports of Hans de Hase and contemporary authors. See 'Versaemen discreeten de heer Jaques l'Hermits, oppercoopman in Bantam, 22 Augustus 1608 in Gresik'; Hans de Hase, 'Brief aan de Bewindhebbers vanuit Bantam, 12 augustus 1614'; van der Meer, '12 October 1608 in Gresik', '12 October 1608 in Gresik'; '8 December 1608 in Gresik'; Adam Claessen van Driel, '19 October 1610 in Gresik'; Adam Claessen van Driel, '25 December 1610 in Gresik'; Andries Soury, '8 August 1612 in Gresik', Section 1.04.02 (VOC), Bundle 1057 (62 pp.), Nationaal Archief in The Hague (NA).
51. J. W. Ijzerman (ed.), *Cornelis Buijsero te Bantam, 1616–1618: zijn brieven en journaal* (The Hague: Martinus Nijhoff, 1923), pp. 197–200; *Hans de*

Hase, Brief aan de Bewindhebbers vanuit Bantam, 12 augustus 1614, Section 1.04.02 (VOC) Bundle 1057, folio 66r, NA.

52. For the concept of topogeny, see Fox, James J. (ed.), *The Poetic Power of Place: Comparative Perspectives on Austronesian Ideas of Locality* (Canberra: ANU Press, 2006).
53. These handbooks were found in the private collection of Oemar Zainuddin. Juru kunci Kyai Gede (middle-aged *juru kunci* at Kyai Gede's grave in Kotawaringin), in discussion with the author, 9 September 2015; Ḥajj Ridwan Daro as well as Prince Hidayat in Ternate (2015).
54. Ironically, one tale contradicts these views. In it, Sunan Giri refuses to adapt to old Hindu–Buddhist customs, while his saintly peer and relative in Tuban believed that the Javanese were not ready for complete conversion and needed to be convinced via non-Islamic traditions. The origins of this perspective seem to lie in the report made by a Malang research team in 1975, which is still widely read in Giri today and was republished some years ago. Muhdlor, H. Ahmad and Mohammed Wiyono (eds), *Penelitian dan Pemugaran Sunan Giri* (Malang: Lembaga Research Islam Malang, 1974). For the Cambay graves of Gresik, see Lambourn, Elizabeth, 'From Cambay to Samudra-Pasai and Gresik: the Export of Gujarati Grave Memorials to Sumatra and Java in the Fifteenth Century C.E.,' *Indonesia and the Malay World* 31(90) (2003): 221–8, 244–51.
55. Further west on the island, the sultanates of Kudus, Pati, Jepara, Demak, Cirebon and Banten formed similar hubs.
56. Carey, Peter, 'Civilization on Loan: the Making of an Upstart Polity: Mataram and its Successors, 1600–1830', *Modern Asian Studies* 31(3), Special Issue: The Eurasian Context of the Early Modern History of Mainland South East Asia, 1400–1800 (1997): 711–22.
57. Mandal, Sumit K., 'Popular Sites of Prayer, Transoceanic Migration, and Cultural Diversity: Exploring the Significance of *keramat* in Southeast Asia', *Modern Asian Studies* 46(2) (2012): 355–72.
58. See Guillot, 'Le rôle historique', p. 156; Woodward, *Java, Indonesia and Islam*, pp. 7, 91–4, 102–3; de Grave, Jean-Marc, *Initiation rituelle et arts martiaux: trois écoles de kanuragan javanais* (Paris: l'Harmattan, 2001).
59. Green, *Islam and the Army*, pp. 12, 34; Moin, *The Millennial Sovereign*, pp. 26, 56–60, 90; Pinch, William R., *Warrior Ascetics and Indian Empires* (Cambridge: Cambridge University Press, 2006).
60. For similar historiographical elite-centred biases in Middle East studies, see

Hanley, Will, 'Grieving Cosmopolitanism in Middle East Studies', *History Compass* 6/5 (2008): 1358–61.

61. De Graaf and Pigeaud, *De Eerste Moslimse*, pp. 144–7.
62. See 'Dokumen Keramat' in possession of Dukut Imam Widodo in Malang (27 October 1772, copied on 21 October 1919). A replica was also made in honour of Sultan Hamengkubuwono VIII of Yogyakarta in the early twentieth century, and was obtained and sold by private traders in early 2013 (see Mas Rodin, 'Keris Kala Munyeng Mataram (16th–18th Century CE)' (5 January 2013) *IndoMagic*, available at: http://www.indomagic.com/store/#!/-/product/category=5216040&id=18713810, last accessed 10 August 2017). The latter *kris*, however, is unlikely to resemble the original one. The name of the Kalamunyeng dagger is also related to the spinning movement that Sunan Giri's pen-point was believed to make while *empu* Pangeran Sedayu tried to hit it with his hammer as it lay on his iron anvil. Most likely, this tale superseded the association between spinning and *gawat*. As for all folklore, origins and time order are nearly impossible to determine with certainty.
63. The sign at the Giri Kedaton suggests the *empu* Supo who made the Kalamunyeng *kris* is buried at Giri, but this is contested by the shrine custodian. The government likely put the sign there in 2005 without consulting the shrine custodian. Mochtar (Senior juru kunci Giri Kedaton), in discussion with the author, 25 September 2015; de Graaf and Pigeaud, *De Eerste Moslimse*, pp. 285–6.
64. Sunan Prapen did travel to Kadiri to proselytise, but he appears not to have used many troops doing so. de Graaf and Pigeaud, *De Eerste Moslimse*, pp. 43–85, 146, 149.
65. 'Anyar' means new in Javanese, and stresses how this hill came to Giri later than the others.
66. While it is often difficult to trace the origins of local legends, the popular myths captured in local literature like the *Sang Gresik* or *Grisee Tempo Doeloe* give a good indication of how wild spaces became part of a single Giri narrative. Mochtar Djamil in Gresik, in discussion with the author, 23 February 2016; and the grave custodians of the Anyar hill, in discussion with the author, 23 February 2016. Dukut Imam Widodo (ed.), *Grissee Tempo Doeloe* (Gresik: Pemerintah Kabupaten Gresik, 2004); Dukut Imam Widodo and Henri Nurcahyo (eds), *Sang Gresik: Kisah-Kisah Kearifan Lokal Gresik Tempo Dulu* (Gresik: PT Smelting & Mataseger, 2014).
67. Juru Kunci Sunan Giri (Senior *juru kunci* at the grave of Sunan Giri), in discus-

sion with the author, 23 September 2015; Juru Kunci Sunan Prapen (Young *juru kunci* at the grave of Sunan Prapen), in discussion with the author, 23/4 September 2015; Mochtar in Giri (2015); Mochtar Djamil in Gresik (2015); Muhdlor and Wiyono, *Penelitian dan Pemugaran*, p. 153; Umar Hasyim, *Sunan Giri* (Kudus: Menara Kudus, 1979).

68. Although it equally indicates obscurity as enquiries by others revealed little more.
69. Mochtar Djamil in Gresik (2015).
70. This narrative is based both on the original tale and the annual performance of it in Lumpur, Gresik. See Serat Sindujoyo or Babad Sindujoyo by Ki Tarub Agung in 1850 in Gresik, illustrations by Kyai Buder as obtained from the private collection of Oemar Zainuddin.
71. One is located in Karang Poh, Gresik, and the other next to the grave of Sunan Prapen in Giri.
72. Sunjata, Pantja, Ignatius Supriyanto and J. J. Ras, *Babad Kraton I: Sejarah Keraton Jawa Sejak Nabi Adam Sampai Runtuhnya Mataram*, vol. 1 (Leiden/Yogyakarta: Penerbit Djambatan, 1992), pp. 287–9. This section deals with the attack on the Surabayan army of Sultan Agung.
73. Notice that diplomatic letters send by the 'Makasar' warlords, as well as the hierarchical relations between them, show there was much less division between them than previously assumed. To classify these troops and warlords as Makasar is therefore appropriate. See fn. 66, above, also.
74. See M. C. Ricklefs, *Jogjakarta under Sultan Mangkubumi, 1749–1792: a History of the Division of Java* (Oxford: Oxford University Press, 1974), pp. 176, 420–1.
75. De Graaf, Hermanus Johannes, 'Het Kadjoran-vraagstuk', *Djawa* 20 (4/5) (1940): 279, 285–97; Guillot, 'The Tembayat Hill', pp. 141–59; Wiselius, 'Historisch Onderzoek'.
76. Andaya's article on the Makasar exiles ignores these struggles, see Andaya, Leonard Y., 'The Bugis-Makassar Diasporas', *Journal of the Malaysian Branch of the Royal Asiatic Society* 68(1) (1995): 119–38.
77. Notice that no further explanations are given on how this cooperation occurred. As stated earlier, this time period is obscured in Giri's oral history. Hasyim, *Sunan Giri*, pp. 98–100; Karaeng Ngabehi Mangoenadirdjo, *Serat Sedjarah Gresik* (Gresik, 1932); Muhdlor and Wiyono, *Penelitian*, pp. 153–7; juru kunci Sunan Giri from Giri (2015).
78. On the titles and names of these Makasar nobles, see I Mapparessa Daeng

Mangunedjuengi and I Mappakaya Daeng Madjarre, *Daftar Susunan Pemangku Hadat/Kerajaan Galesong* (Galesong: Jajasan Galesong, 1954); A. J. Bostan Karaeng Mama'dja, *Karaeng Galesong Yang Pantang Mundur* (Galesong: Jajasan Galesong, 1961).

79. The crown prince was later forgiven. Everardt van der Schuur to Batavia, 21 February 1675, Section 1.04.02, Bundle 1313, Java NO-kust, folio 620–621, NA; and Wijbrandt Dubbeldecop to Batavia, 16 March 1675, Section 1.04.02, Bundle 1313, Java NO-kust, folio 624, NA.
80. Wiselius, 'Historisch Onderzoek', p. 497; Mochtar in Giri (2015) and Mochtar Djamil in Gresik (2015).
81. Leonard Andaya arbitrarily assumes the wedding to have occurred in autumn 1675, taking de Graaf's assertions for granted. Given the circumstances, early 1675 appears more likely. Leonard Andaya, *The Heritage of Arung Palakka: a History of South Sulawesi (Celebes) in the Seventeenth Century* (Leiden: Springer, 1981), pp. 213–14. Arab Piru to Cornelis Speelman, 24/5 February 1677; Section 1.04.02, Bundle 1329, Java NO-kust, folio 1606–1614, NA; Aminuddin Salle (descendant of the Galesong lineage and professor of law at the University of Hasanuddin), 2 September 2015, in discussion with the author.
82. van der Schuur to Batavia, 31 April 1675, pp. 627–9.
83. Ibid.; Abdul Halik Daeng Mabe in Makassar (2015).
84. Jacobus Couper to Batavia, 14 November 1675, Section 1.04.02, Bundle 1314, folio 149–152, NA.
85. Wiselius, 'Historisch Onderzoek', p. 497; Mochtar in Giri (2015) and Mochtar Djamil in Gresik (2015). Some manuscripts of the Gresik chronicle do not contain this narrative, but move from Sunan Prapen to VOC hostilities, see Serat Babad Gresik (1936), D H 1055-16, Special Collections, Leiden University Library, p. 51.
86. de Graaf, *De Regering*, vol. 2, pp. 110–11.
87. Jacob Couper to Batavia, 1 May 1676, Section 1.04.02, Bundle 1321, Java NO-kust, folio 1090–1093, NA.
88. Suriadi Mappangara, A. Rasyid Asba, H. A. B. M. Yusman Batara Aji, A. Azis Tenrigau, Anwar (eds), *Silsilah Kekerabatan Raja-raja Sulawesi Selatan-Barat* (Jakarta: PT Buku Pintar Indonesia, 2015). Notice Suriadi conducted the lion's share to the research for this bundle and thus deserves a first mention; unfortunately, Indonesian publishers at times add names arbitrarily to their credit lists to distribute royalties.

89. Gowa did appear to have maintained ties with the Sunan Gunung-Jati cult in Cirebon, see Valentijn, *Groot Djava*, p. 15; Abdul Halik Daeng Mabe in Makassar (2015). For the proselytisation of South Sulawesi, see Chambert-Loir, 'Dato' ri Bandang', pp. 137–63.
90. de Graaf sees the attacks between November and December as one siege, but friction between the Makasar and Giri make this unlikely. Note that rumours might again have affected the report on the third siege. Yet, even if its scale was exaggerated, the breach between Bontọmarannu and Giri is indicated in other VOC sources also, as is shown below. de Graaf, *Sunan Mangku-Rat I: Opstand en Ondergang*, pp. 87–8; Mang Jacobus Couper to Batavia, 7 and 28 December 1675, Section 1.04.02, Bundle 1314, Java NO-kust, folio 151–152, NA.
91. de Graaf, *Sunan Mangku-Rat I: Opstand en Ondergang*, p. 88.
92. A third fortification at Ulubuan is mentioned too, but might refer to any harbour (*pelabuhan* in Malay). Jacobus Couper to Batavia, 24 March 1676, Section 1.04.02, Bundle 1321, Java NO-kust, folio 1077–1081, NA; Jan Fransen Holsteijn and council of Lasum to Batavia, 25 March 1676, Section 1.04.02, Bundle 1321, Java NO-kust, folio 1084–1087; Jacobus Couper to Batavia, 11 April 1676, Section 1.04.02, Bundle 1321, Java NO-kust, folio 1089; Jacobus Couper to Batavia, 10 July 1676, Section 1.04.02, Bundle 1321, Java NO-kust, folio 1098–1100, NA; de Graaf, Hermanus Johannes, *Het Geslacht der Djangrana's 1680–1704* (1742), D H 1055-25, Section KITLV Special Collections, Leiden Library, pp. 57–60a.
93. Andaya belittles the demand for power over Gresik and Surabaya. Andaya, *Heritage Arung Palakka*, pp. 214–16; de Graaf, *De Regering*, vol. 2, pp. 109, 134–7.
94. This hill is located near Ngantang in Malang, East Java. See H. J. de Graaf and J. J. Briel, *De expeditie van Anthonio Hurdt: Raad van Indië, als Admiral en Superintendent naar binnenlanden van Java sept.–dec. 1678*, (The Hague: Martinus Nijhoff, 1971), pp. 8–9; H. J. de Graaf, 'De Opkomst van raden Truna-Djaja', *Djawa* 20 (1940): 56–86; de Graaf, *De Regering*, vol. 1, pp. 146, 165–6; de Graaf, 'Het Kadjoran-vraagstuk', p. 323; Ricklefs, *War, Culture*, p. 55.
95. Arab Piru to Cornelis Speelman (1677), 1606r–1607l, 1612l.
96. Jacobus Couper and the council of Surabaya to Batavia, 12 and 19 January 1680, Section 1.04.02, Bundle 1360, Java NO-kust, folio 2043–2047, NA; Jacobus Couper and the council of Surabaya to Batavia, 13 March 1680, Section 1.04.02, Bundle 1360, Java NO-kust, folio 2054–2066;

Johan Jurgen Briel and Macquelijn to Jacobus Couper, 24–8 December 1679 and 13 March 1680, Section 1.04.02, Bundle 1360, Java NO-kust, folio 2066–2074, NA. For Trunajaya's entitlements, see de Graaf, 'De opkomst', pp. 28–9. For the neglect of these ties, see Ricklefs, *War, Culture*, p. 40.

97. de Graaf, *De Expeditie Hurdt*, pp. 232–3.
98. de Haan, *Dagh-Register 1679*, pp. 97 (17 March) and 109 (26 March).
99. de Haan, *Dagh-Register 1679*, p. 167 (6 May).
100. de Haan, *Dagh-Register 1679*, pp. 317 (16 July) and 330 (2 June).
101. de Haan, *Dagh-Register 1680*, pp. 306–7 (30 May).
102. de Haan, *Dagh-Register 1680*, p. 331 (2 June).
103. de Haan, *Dagh-Register 1680*, p. 324 (2 June).
104. de Haan, *Dagh-Register 1680*, p. 331 (2 June).
105. Ibid.
106. de Haan, *Dagh-Register 1680*, pp. 324–5, 328 (2 June); 522 (31 July).
107. de Haan, Frederik, *Dagh-Register Gehouden Int Casteel Batavia Vant Passerende Daer Ter Plaetse Als over Geheel Nederlandts-India Anno 1681* (The Hague: Martinus Nijhoff, 1919), p. 632 (23 October).
108. de Haan, *Dagh-Register 1680*, p. 522 (31 July).
109. de Haan, *Dagh-Register 1679*, p. 543 (29 November).
110. de Haan, *Dagh-Register 1680*, p. 523 (31 July).
111. The heir of Sunan Kalijaga (considered by some to be the tenth *wali sanga*) joined the Mataram army, his title is Panembahan Natapraja from Adilangu. Sunjata, Pantja, Ignatius Supriyanto and J. J. Ras, *Babad Kraton II: Sejarah Keraton Jawa sejak berdirinya Kartasura sampai perang Cina*, vol. 2 (Leiden/Yogyakarta: Penerbit Djambatan, 1992), pp. xviii–xix.
112. Sunjata et al., *Babad Kraton II*, pp. 44–7. My interpretation differs from that of Ricklefs in his *Mystic Synthesis*, p. 65, likely because Ricklefs attempts to fit these references into his mystic synthesis hypothesis.
113. Mochtar Djamil in Gresik (2015).
114. Notice Jumadil Kubra's legend is found throughout Java among court as well as shrines, yet his *silsila* is predominately associated with the *wali sanga*. Van Bruinessen, Martin, 'Najmuddin al-Kubra, Jumadil Kubra and Jamaluddin al-Akbar: Traces of Kubrawiyya influence in early Indonesian Islam', *Bijdragen tot de Taal-, Land- en Volkenkunde* 150 (1994): 319–26; Wiselius, 'Historisch Onderzoek': pp. 467–8; James J. Fox, 'Ziarah Visits to the Tombs of the Wali, the Founders of Islam on Jawa', in M. C. Ricklefs (ed.), *Islam in the Indonesian*

Social Context (Clayton, Victoria: Centre for Southeast Asian Studies, Monash University, 1991), pp. 25–8.

115. The Javanese royal charter of 1742 further inhibited all shrine polities through restraints on the military activities of religious freeholds (*pradikan*) and indirectly shrines. Ras, J. J., *Babad Tanah Jawi. Javaanse Rijkskroniek. W. L. Olthofs vertaling van de prozaversie van J. J. Meinsma, lopende tot het jaar 1721* (Dordecht: Floris, 1987), pp. 203–4; M. C. Ricklefs, 'De Verenigde Oost-Indische Compagnie en de geweldddadige wereld van het vroegmodene Azië', in Gerrit Knaap and Ger Teitler (eds), De Verenigde Oost-Indische Compagnie tussen oorlog en diplomatie (Leiden: KITLV Press, 2002),pp. 355–78; Ricklefs, *Jogjakarta,* pp. 27–30; Wiselius, 'Historisch Onderzoek', pp. 499–505.
116. Sunjata et al., *Babad Kraton II*, pp. xviii–xix.
117. Kemper, 'The Umbilical Cord of Threats'.
118. Mandal, 'Popular Sites of Prayer', pp. 355–72.
119. For one of these guides, see Suwarsono, L., *Petunjuk Singkat Tentang Makam dan Tempat Keramat di Daerah Istimewa Yogyakarta dan Sekitarnya* (Yogyakarta: Penerbit Lumintu, 2002).
120. This in contrast to the contemporary potential of shrines described by Mandal, 'Popular Sites of Prayer', p. 369.

5

Variations of 'Islamic Military Cosmopolitanism': The Survival Strategies of Hui Muslims during the Modern Period

Tatsuya Nakanishi

While classical doctrinal formulations of *jihād* declare it a duty incumbent upon the Islamic community, Muslims have not always hastened to the front line of the *umma* when they faced non-Muslims who exhibited aggression or threatened oppression.[1] Rather, following other provisions of the *sharīʿa*, they sometimes chose to coexist alongside the outsiders without regarding them as enemies. Likewise, the rallying of Muslims to the armed defence of Islam did not necessarily exclude their affiliation with a non-Islamic state. These cases comprise alternative forms of what might be regarded as 'Islamic military cosmopolitanism'; that is, interconnection of Muslims with non-Muslims as a result of lawful Islamic responses to aggression or external domination. Cosmopolitan situations created by Muslims who suffered hostility from non-Muslims varied depending on the historical context or the ways in which they coped with stress and violence emanating from beyond the *umma*.

This chapter explores variations of 'Islamic military cosmopolitanism' in the historical contexts of the Hui, Chinese-speaking Muslims of China, during the modern period. The first purpose of this exploration is to illuminate the coercive dimensions of majority power, warfare, and the nation-state in formations of cosmopolitanism in ways that problematise the unreflective use of the term as shorthand for tolerant interactions of people across ethnic and cultural boundaries.[2] The second objective is to illustrate that in conceptualising specifically military forms of Islamic cosmopolitanism, we need to recognise that this did not always assume a universalistic form that required exclusive allegiance to the Islamic moral community and the rejection of other sources of authority – including even non-Islamic forms of law and statecraft. This is done here through an examination of the way in which Hui Muslims formulated historically contingent ideas of 'Islamic military cosmopolitanism' in the context of Chinese history.[3]

This study begins with a discussion of arguments presented by Ma Anyi (1870–1943),[4] a Hui Muslim scholar who classified China as *dār al-ḥarb* – and thus outside the *dār al-Islām*, the territory of the *umma* where the *sharīʿa* is in force. Thus, he legally exempted Hui Muslims from the fight against non-Muslim Chinese people and enabled the Hui to mingle in non-Islamic Chinese society while retaining their 'Muslim-ness'. An important backdrop to Ma Anyi's work was the antagonism between Muslims and non-Muslims during and after the Yunnan Muslim rebellion (1856–1874), the repercussions of which threatened the very survival of the Huis in China. In grappling with the violent context and continuous tensions underlying relations between the minority Hui and the Chinese state, Ma Anyi's work presents a compelling example of a conciliatory form of 'Islamic military cosmopolitanism' within a broader, non-Islamic state context.

From there, this chapter turns to discuss how Hui intellectuals thought of the anti-Japanese campaigns of the Second Sino-Japanese War (1937–45). At the beginning of this conflict, the Hui regarded it as an anti-imperialist struggle that the Chinese nation, including its Muslim members, pursued along paths parallel to those of other Islamic communities. However, another voice soon arose. While some Hui scholars went so far as to refuse to acknowledge the existence of the single universal Muslim community, others argued that the patriotic fight of Chinese Muslims was a part of the holy war which 'the Islamic nation (*huijiao minzu*)', or the trans-national Muslim community (*umma*) waged to liberate itself from colonial occupation. In this reading of the politics of anti-colonialism it was not just the Hui, but by extension Muslims everywhere, who could be justified in *sharīʿa* terms for their support of China against the Japanese. Here, we see a reconciliation of 'Islamic military cosmopolitanism' with Chinese nationalism, presented against the harsh realities of national development and warfare as its historical background.

Withdrawal from 'Islamic Military Cosmopolitanism'

Ma Anyi and his Arabic Work, the Taḥqīq al-īmān

Ma Anyi was born in Yunnan province in 1870; he was the second son of Ma Lianyuan (1841–1903), who later became one of the leading Islamic intellectuals of Yunnan. Ma Lianyuan studied the Islamic sciences under Ma Dexin (1794–1874), one of the most esteemed Hui Muslim scholars, who is regarded as one of 'the four greatest *ʿulamāʾ* in China'.[5]

After a massacre of Hui Muslims by local Han (non-Muslim Chinese) officials working in Yunnan, Ma Dexin led a rebellion against the Qing dynasty that lasted from 1857 to 1862. When Yunnan Muslims rose in self-defence, the antagonism between the Hui and Han peoples intensified, leading to a deterioration of conditions for the former. This state of affairs appears partly to explain Ma Dexin's surrender to the Qing government in 1862, as well as his turn against another rebel leader, Du Wenxiu, who continued to resist the Qing army until his death in 1872. Ma Dexin seems to have assumed that the rebellion would eventually collapse, harming the Hui Muslims.[6] In response, he argued for the categorisation of China as *dār al-ḥarb* not to incite rebellion, but rather to encourage compliance with both divine Islamic commands and Chinese regulations. He thus sought to reconcile them with the Han majority and the Qing government. This line of thought was transmitted by Ma Dexin to his student Ma Lianyuan, and thence to Ma Lianyuan's son, Ma Anyi.

After his pilgrimage to Mecca in the early twentieth century, Ma Anyi taught Islamic sciences at the mosques on Hainan Island in Guangzhou, in Shanghai and (after 1936) in various places in Yunnan such as Kunming and Yuxi. In 1905 (*Dhū'l-ḥijja*, 1322 H.), he wrote an Arabic work titled *Taḥqīq al-īmān*. It is composed of three sections, each of which explicates the articles of Islamic belief under the rubric of the six pillars of belief (*arkān al-īmān*), the six conditions of belief (*sharāʾiṭ al-īmān*) and the six regulations of belief (*aḥkām al-īmān*). The last section, and especially the explication of its second article, is remarkable in its elaboration of China's location within the *dār al-ḥarb* and the implications of this designation for the everyday lives of Muslims residing there.

China as dār al-ḥarb

Ma Anyi asserts that China was *dār al-ḥarb*,[7] and that Muslims in that country had the legal status of *musta'min*, or those of the *dār al-Islām* who entered the *dār al-ḥarb* with a guarantee of security from its rulers (*amān*).[8] He also claims that it was wrong of some Chinese *'ulamā* to regard non-Muslim Chinese as *dhimmī* (those protected by the Islamic *umma* on condition of their accepting the political authority of Muslims and paying the *jizya*, or head tax) or to classify China as belonging to a third category that was neither *dār al-Islām* nor *dār al-ḥarb* but rather *dār al-amān*; that is, an area where non-Muslim rulers guarantee the security of Muslims.[9]

Why did Ma Anyi argue counter to the position of some other Hui scholars to characterise China as *dār al-ḥarb*? He supported his argument with reference to three particular pieces of evidence.[10] First, in China, Muslims never levied the *jizya*. Second, in that country, a form of non-Islamic law was in force (although some Islamic regulations were observed by Chinese Muslims within their own communities, this was not officially supported by the Chinese government). Third, according to the doctrine of the *Ḥanafī* legal school that Hui Muslims exclusively followed, only the categories of *dār al-ḥarb* and *dār al-Islām* were recognised, and there was no grounding within the tradition for the novel designation of *dār al-amān*.

Aside from these legal grounds for Ma Anyi's placing of China in the realm of *dār al-ḥarb*, the influence of precedent must also be considered. The first Hui Muslim work that explicitly identified China as in the *dār al-ḥarb* was probably Ma Dexin's Arabic work *Mushtāq*, in which he states, 'Between the *dār al-Islām* and *dār al-ḥarb*, there are great gaps in the law (*mu'āmalāt*), which depend on differences in their words and terms. For this reason, the Qur'ān does not contain regulations corresponding to some matters that are allowed in this country.'[11]

From the theoretical viewpoint of Islamic jurisprudence, Ma Dexin's labelling of China as *dār al-ḥarb* potentially legitimised the attack of Muslims against the Qing Empire, at least under specific conditions. Although he assumed the leadership of the Yunnan Muslim rebellion his intent was not to engage in an offensive *jihād* against the Han people. Ma Dexin tried to evade the great devastation that the rebellion would bring to the Yunnan Muslim community. The purpose of his audacious labelling of China was to draw the attention of Hui Muslims to the reality of Qing rule, where non-Islamic laws were in force, and to have them practise Islam in compliance with both divine commands and Chinese regulations.

Ma Dexin's text then goes on to discuss discrepancies between the *sharīʿa* and Qing law on divorce, and argues for a means of resolving its contradictions. According to Islamic law, the words of a husband pronouncing divorce, regardless of whether his wife is at fault, establish the legal dissolution of a marriage. However, Qing law punished husbands for unlawful divorces, including Islamic ones that occurred without a wife's fault. Consequently, the cautious scholar, following the Qurʾān, argued that if a Muslim husband let the word of divorce slip in a quarrel with his wife, he has to divorce her, even though he had no intention of doing so. However, he would be punished in China for such an action according to the Qing code, or the *Da Qing lüli*.[12] Ma Dexin thus proposes the following loophole: 'Oh husbands, be careful not to blurt any word of divorce. Rather, choose beating as a countermeasure against the disobedience of your wife!'[13] Of course, given our contemporary values, we cannot agree with this opinion. However, in its historical context it is indisputable that his recommendation of domestic violence can be seen as a rather extreme attempt to reconcile the lived realities of *sharīʿa*-observant Muslims living under the non-Islamic law of the Chinese state. By instructing husbands to avoid words of divorce, which forced Chinese Muslims to choose between two laws, he was clearly grasping for a way to observe the demands of both legal orders simultaneously.[14]

Ma Dexin's admonishment and proposal about divorce is also cited in his disciple Ma Lianyuan's Arabic work, *Tawḍīḥ*.[15] The latter also seems to have shared with the master a determination to adapt Islam to the Chinese legal environment through recourse to the designation of China as *dār al-ḥarb*. These writers, in turn, must have inspired subsequent Muslim intellectuals such as Ma Anyi.

Being Muslim Outside the dār al-Islām

By setting China outside the *dār al-Islām*, Ma Anyi aimed to emancipate Hui Muslims from the contradiction between the commands of Allah and those of China's rulers. In the *Taḥqīq al-īmān*, this approach is found in his discussion of the second article of the six regulations of belief (*aḥkām al-īmān*), that is, the prohibition against taking the property of Muslims and infidels without their agreement, as in kinds of theft, robbery or swindling.[16] The author argues that according to the *sharīʿa*, Chinese Muslims, defined as *mustaʾmin*, are not permitted to disobey the '*sulṭān* of China', that is, the emperors of the Qing dynasty.[17]

In which provisions of Islamic law did Ma Anyi find the prohibition against Chinese Muslims' disobedience to the Qing Chinese state? In other words, how does he legitimise the former's obedience to the latter? The key-word for him here is 'betrayal' (*ghadr*). Ma Anyi regards any disobedience of Chinese Muslims to the Qing emperor as a betrayal of *mustaʾmin* against the guarantor of his security, by virtue of which Muslims are obligated to observe the legal injunctions of their host society.[18] In short, Ma Anyi argues here for the legitimacy of the Hui Muslims' obedience to the '*sulṭān* of China', based upon a doctrinal position that:

> When entering their territory [the *dār al-ḥarb*], a Muslim is obligated not to betray them . . . We, the people of Islām (*ahl al-Islām*) in China, are not allowed to escape from obedience to the *sulṭān* of China or put pressure on him, even though he is an unjust infidel, since we are *mustaʾmin* under his reign, administration, and guarantee of security. If a person among us puts pressure on the *sulṭān* of China, this person is considered to be a betrayer. Betrayal is forbidden (*ḥarām*).[19]

Elsewhere in the same text, Ma Anyi further elaborates this point:

> A Muslim, when entering China from the *dār al-Islām*, becomes one who implores them [i.e., the Chinese people] to guarantee his security (*mustaʾmin*). Undoubtedly, the people of Islam in China were previously ones who entered their territory from our own. They were among our ancestors. They were *mustaʾmin*. We, or the ones who are here now, are

> Muslims of *dār al-ḥarb*, not *musta'min*, but rather subjects of their king. For, he is an impartial *sulṭān* who does not discriminate between them and us. However, the regulation that applies to us as to our ancestors is that of *musta'min*. It is similar to the case that the regulation of *dhimmī* applies to the *musta'min* in our territory [i.e., those of *dār al-ḥarb* who entered the *dār al-Islām* with its ruler's guarantee of security], before becoming *dhimmī*, according to *Shāmī* [i.e., Ibn 'Ābidīn's *Radd al-Muḥtār*].[20] Therefore, we are forbidden to interfere with their [i.e., the Chinese people's] properties, blood, and women.[21]

Ma Anyi, however, qualifies this position in the light of particular contexts of political tensions to argue that: 'However, this shall not be applied when their king (*mālik*) betrays, as was the case in Dali-fu (*Buzurg li fu*) during the age of Du Wenxiu (*Du wun su*). At that time, the infidels determined to exterminate the Muslims of Yunnan, therefore we were allowed to interfere with their properties and bloods, except for their women.'[22] The loyalty demanded and the prohibition of betrayal was thus, for Ma Anyi, clearly not universal or irreversible. Indeed, he justified the Yunnan Muslim rebellion, which his father's master first led and then opposed, on the grounds that the avoidance of the betrayal is a mutual obligation for all parties involved.

Carefully, he confirms the illegality of betrayal (*ghadr*) in the *sharī'a* through examples of Islamic rulings. For example, he introduces the legal opinions of some authoritative juristic works that Muslims may engage in some non-Islamic business transactions as non-equivalent exchange, including lending with interest and the trade in liquor, pork or non-*ḥalāl* meat with non-Muslims in the *dār al-ḥarb*, on condition that the latter agree. Muslims are, however, forbidden if these transactions involve taking the property of non-Muslims without their agreement.[23] The point at issue here in defining betrayal was the existence or non-existence of an agreement. It was thus not the transactions themselves that were forbidden, but the lack of a proper agreement.

In this way, by utilising the concept of betrayal, Ma Anyi successfully argues that Allah allows Hui Muslims to follow Chinese rulers and their orders and laws, along with Chinese commercial practices. This marked a new discourse on the six regulations of belief that were previously expounded by his father Ma Lianyuan in his Arabic work, *Tafṣīl al-īmān*[24] or his Persian work, *Muhimmāt al-muslimīn*.[25] Moreover, similar explanations of the six regulations of belief are found in other writings by Hui Muslims.[26] Except for *Tafṣīl al-īmān*, these works do not treat the prohibition against the killing and seizure of the properties of infidels by Muslims, and none of them – including *Tafṣīl al-īmān* – discuss the concept of betrayal in relation to obligations of obedience upon Chinese Muslims to the guarantor of their security. Ma Anyi's originality lies in his taking up these subjects,[27] bringing into the discussion related accounts in the juristic work of the Syrian *Ḥanafī* scholar Ibn 'Ābidīn (d. 1836), *Radd al-muḥtār fī Durr al-mukhtār*.[28] By engaging with such authoritative juristic works, this enterprising Hui scholar refined his father's six regulations of belief, thus legitimising the obedience of Chinese Muslims to non-Islamic rulers.

At the same time that Ma Anyi acknowledged the theoretical right of Muslims in the *dār al-ḥarb* to defend themselves against various depredations, he did not seem to think that China should be 'restored' to *dār al-Islām*. If the premise of China's location in the *dār al-ḥarb* was not accepted, his elaborate justification of Hui Muslims living according to non-Islamic regulations would collapse. Indeed, if China were to be classified as *dār al-Islām*, Hui Muslims might become obligated to fight against non-Muslim Chinese rulers and their subjects. In light of this perspective, Ma Anyi's placement of China in the *dār al-ḥarb* justified Hui Muslims' avoidance of Islamic martial obligation along with their acceptance of non-Islamic rule.

He cites the following passage from a *Ḥanafī* juristic work, *Ḥāshiyya al-Ṭaḥṭāwī 'alā al-Durr al-mukhtār*:[29] 'When people of the *dār al-ḥarb*, where Muslims of *musta'min* exist, raid a group of Muslims, take their women and children (*dharārī*) prisoner, the Muslims [those of *musta'min*] must act against them [the raiders], if possible, even though they [the raided Muslims] are people of *khawārij*.'[30] However, Ma Anyi never notes whether Chinese Muslims had to engage in *jihād* for the defence of the Islamic land. This silence suggests that he did not approve of their involvement in it. Such an involvement would have resulted in Chinese Muslims' conflict with Qing rulers and the Han people. Such conflict could, potentially, prove altogether disastrous for the Muslim minority. Like Ma Dexin, the author of *Taḥqīq al-īmān* also shared such fears, reflecting the tragic end of the Yunnan

Muslim rebellion and the reality of non-Muslim dominance in China. Ma Anyi held that maintaining peaceful relationships with their Chinese hosts would allow Muslims to both survive and fulfil their religious obligations.

It seems safe to say that Ma Anyi decided to situate China in the *dār al-ḥarb* as a means to lawfully exempt Hui Muslims from the universal conscription of the *umma*, while still retaining their identity as Muslims. In this, he can be seen as proposing another, more pluralistic version of 'Islamic military cosmopolitanism' – one in which Muslims could coexist with their non-Muslim neighbours by regarding them neither as invaders nor oppressors in the *dār al-Islām*, but rather, as the guarantors of the security of Muslims in the *dār al-ḥarb*.

'Islamic Military Cosmopolitanism' and Chinese Nationalism

Anti-Japanese Resistance and Defensive Jihād

Ma Anyi's *Taḥqīq al-īmān* presents a sophisticated legal jurisprudential undertaking to negotiate between the requirements of Islamic law and the realities of political subordination to the non-Muslim Qing state. Later Hui writings, however, tended towards a more pronounced nationalist perspective on the question of designating China as either *dār al-ḥarb* or *dār al-Islām*.

Modern Muslim intellectuals often appealed to the dictum that 'loving the fatherland is a part of belief' ('*Ḥubb al-waṭan min al-īmān*'), which they believed as one of the Prophetic traditions. By reading 'loving the fatherland' (*ḥubb al-waṭan*) as patriotic, they sanctioned their allegiance to the Chinese nation. This modern Muslim political rhetoric arose in Arabic discourse from the Middle East, especially as circulated through new periodicals, including the famous Egyptian *al-Manār*. That nationalistic interpretation of 'the tradition' was introduced to China in 1930 by Wang Jingzhai (1879–1949), who had studied at al-Azhar University in Egypt.[31]

Wang Jingzhai, one of the most prominent Hui Muslim intellectuals of the modern period, argued that Muslims are not only obliged to follow Islamic teachings but also to defend their nation, while identifying the Chinese state as the fatherland of Chinese Muslims. Indeed, his nationalist framework is even reflected in his Chinese annotated translation of the Qurʾān, which omits any references to a conception of trans-national

Muslim community that might provide an alternative to Hui identity as Chinese. Thus, for example, he resorted to this omission in his translation of a verse of Qur'ān 23:52, the original text of which is as follows: 'Verily, this is your *umma*, which is a united *umma*' (*Inna hādhihi ummatu-kum ummatan wāḥidatan*). Wang Jingzhai, in the first version of his annotated translation of the Qur'ān,[32] glossed this same verse as 'Verily, this <the Islamic road of recognising God's uniqueness> is your <apostles'> road of teaching (*jiaodao*) <which is unchanging forever>.'[33] In later revisions for the second and third editions, he modified the verse to read, 'Verily, this is your road (*dao*), which is the sole road of teaching,'[34] and 'Verily, this is your road, which is the road of unification,' respectively.[35]

Here, Wang Jingzhai renders '*umma*' as 'road,' notwithstanding the fact that the standard Arabic works of Qur'ānic exegesis that he consulted interpret the term not only as 'road' but also as 'community'. For example, *Tafsīr al-Bayḍāwī* interprets the '*ummatu-kum ummatan wāḥidatan*' of 23:52 as 'your religion (*milla*), which is single religion, that is, one united in the theology and principles of law; or your community (*jamā'a*), which is a single community, that is, one unanimous in the belief and recognition of the divine uniqueness (*tawḥīd*) in the devotional service'.[36] Wang Jingzhai's Chinese interpretation of the verse is thus somewhat contrived, and he translates '*umma*' in other verses as 'a group' (*yihuo*) or 'a crowd of people' (*qunzhong*). It is almost certain that he was reluctant to depict the '*umma*' as a community of identity.[37]

A similar manipulation is found in his translation of Q3:110, that is, of the phrase 'You are the best *umma* produced for humankind.' The first and second versions of his translation rendered '*umma*' of this phrase as 'nation' (*minzu*).[38] However, he changes it to 'a crowd of people' (*qunzhong*) in the third version.[39] This occurred, most likely, because the term 'nation' recalled the concept of 'the Islamic nation' in which all Muslims or the *umma* constitute a single nation.[40] The concept was apt to contradict or undermine the loyalty of Hui Muslims to the Chinese nation. This sense of divided loyalty was regarded as dangerous by Chiang Kai-shek, the president of the Republic of China in the period when the third edition of Wang Jingzhai's text was written.

At the same time, however, Wang Jingzhai incorporated China into the *dār al-Islām*, or the territory of the ideal universal Muslim community, notwithstanding that such an incorporation might be seen by some as being in tension with their position in relation to the Chinese nation. In the second and third version of the aforementioned Qur'ānic translation, Wang Jingzhai writes:

> If Muslims live in a place where they cannot perform religious duties, it means that they live in a hostile district, and they must migrate to other place in accordance with the Qur'ān . . . [However,] we have freely observed Islamic teachings and performed religious duties in China without any interference from the government. Thus, we cannot regard this country as a hostile country but rather similar to an Islamic country (*huijiaoguo*).[41]

This passage is not found in the first edition of his text, which was written before the Second Sino-Japanese War. It did, however, suit well the needs of those Hui Muslim intellectuals who, as we will see later, characterised the armed support of Chinese Muslims for China as a holy war to liberate 'the Islamic nation' from colonisation.[42] These intellectuals attempted to reinforce their co-religionists' patriotic feelings towards China and involvement in the anti-Japanese resistance. Wang Jingzhai seems to have agreed partially with them, although he was cautious about assuming the characterisation of Chinese Muslims as an 'Islamic nation'.

Wang Jingzhai's apparently ambivalent attitude might, however, be read as consistent with his intention to reinforce the national identity of Chinese Muslims. In considering China '*dār al-Islām*', he aimed to rouse their attachment to China and the Chinese nation as opposed to some universal Islamic entity. That is why Wang Jingzhai in the passage above suggests that there is no need for the *hijra*, or the migration of Hui Muslims from China to an 'Islamic country'.

Population movement is often discussed as an important aspect informing the constitution of cosmopolitan visions. The intermingling of Hui Muslims with non-Muslim Chinese people originated with the migration of Muslims from the Islamic world to China since the Tang period. Wang Jingzhai, however, was also critical of other vectors of mobility – particularly calls for Hui Muslims' emigration from China – as such rhetoric threatened the dissolution of the harmonious relationships between the Hui and the Han, or perhaps even between the Hui who emigrated and those who chose to stay.[43] Conversely, non-movement, or Hui Muslims staying in China, accompanied the amicable relationship between the Hui and the Han, although the former had to make a great effort to sustain it. This position also facilitated a particular modality of 'Islamic military cosmopolitanism' – one in which Muslims were not globally united against the rule of non-Muslim infidels, but rather one in which Islamic law was read in terms that justified Muslim military support of the non-Islamic Chinese state.

Hui Muslim intellectuals during the modern period, like Wang Jingzhai, opted for this sedentary – rather than mobile – model of Islamic cosmopolitanism. As Chinese nationalism became dominant, Chinese-speaking Muslims who had already put down roots in Chinese society came to imagine no other fatherland but China. Consequently, Wang Jingzhai developed Islamic legal frameworks that facilitated their continued presence in China and the maintenance of harmonious coexistence with their non-Muslim neighbours, without any contradiction to the *sharīʿa*. However, it is certain that he did not intend to promote the assimilation of Muslim to non-Islamic Chinese society. But, rather, his assertion that China was an Islamic country was probably also an encouragement to deepen their ethnic identity as a particular constituent of the Chinese nation.

During the Second Sino-Japanese War (1937–45), many Hui Muslim intellectuals described Chinese Muslims fighting against Japan as a defensive *jihād* and proclaimed that they had no fatherland but China.[44] These intellectuals attempted to encourage their co-religionists to participate in the anti-Japanese resistance, induce foreign Muslims to support it, and thereby demonstrate that Chinese Muslims held allegiance and made a contribution to 'the Chinese nation' (*Zhonghua minzu*).[45] Here, we see a vision of 'Islamic military cosmopolitanism' that was in harmony with a Chinese nationalism that appears to have developed gradually according to shifting historical conditions. Although previous studies have not paid sufficient attention to these shifting contingencies, a thorough inquiry into this issue will help to illuminate the role of coercion and state-building underlying such ideas of cosmopolitanism.

The gradual evolution of Chinese models of 'Islamic military cosmopolitanism' is particularly noteworthy, especially in *Yuehua*, one of the most influential modern Chinese periodicals issued by Hui intellectuals.[46] Many Hui writers in this journal have argued that Chinese Muslims joining the Chinese national struggle against Japan was consistent with the teachings of the Qur'ān on defensive *jihād*. However, in the beginning, none among them identified the patriotic fight with a 'defensive *jihād*' that the global *umma* had to wage for the defence of *dār al-Islām*.

For example, 'An Announcement Letter to Islamic Companions all over the world', published in *Yuehua* (vol. 11, Nos. 4–6) on 25 February 1939, stressed that Chinese Muslims resisted Japan in order to maintain both the state and their religion in accordance with teachings on the 'defensive *jihād*' in Qur'ān 2:190. Nevertheless, the anti-Japanese resistance is not described as a defensive *jihād* or as a mobilisation of the *umma* in the name of a unified Muslim political idea, but rather as an anti-imperialism struggle of the Chinese nation in which Muslims played an important but only supporting role. The articles in *Yuehua* before volume 11 take the same position. For example, 'An Announcement Letter to the Islamic People in Near East', volume 10, No. 18, published on 25 September 1938, requested that the 'Islamic people in Near East' boycott Japanese commodities to help China, since 'the Chinese nation and every nation in Near East' shared interests about security and stood on the same front.

However, the Hui writers of *Yuehua* soon raised the issue of the defensive *jihād* as a concern for the broader global community of Muslims, declaring themselves in favour of the immediate solidarity between Chinese Muslims and foreign co-religionists, along with the liberation of 'the Islamic nation' as the final goal, in which Muslims would assume the leading role and to which the anti-Japanese resistance was simply one stage. This position appears faintly in 'A Diary of the Pilgrimage to Mecca' (vol. 11, Nos. 7–9), published on 25 March 1939, which contains the following passage:

> God said, 'In the way of justice, kill the one who aggresses against you . . .' [2:190?] He also said, 'You need not be afraid of them [plunderers]. You, fear us [God]!' [9:13] . . . Islam is universal and one. Islam in China is a part of the universal Islam. We must shoulder the blame for the stagnation of Islam. We must, in accordance with the divine instruction, stand together with our compatriots all over China, stake our lives in battles against the

> aggressors, and expel the ferocious Japanese invaders from our national borders. Then, we will found an independent and powerful state. Furthermore, by our power, we will help our co-religionists trampled by the horseshoe of imperialism to be released from their shackles and to obtain the freedom of their religion, state, and nation. In this way, when the divine justice is manifested and realized in the world, the Islamic nation will be restored to its past power.

Here, 'the Islamic nation' is imagined as a single universal Muslim community transcending established political boundaries. The passage thus suggests that Allah had instructed Chinese Muslims to struggle against the Japanese invaders as a step towards the triumph of the global Muslim community against imperialist aggressors. However, in this article, 'our power' in the phrase 'by our power, we will help our co-religionists . . .' implies the power of the non-Muslim Chinese state, and the 'we' implies the Chinese Muslims as citizens of that state. The writer thus portrays the salvation of the Islamic nation as the mission of the Chinese state or nation more than as the martial obligation of Muslims beyond its borders.

Chinese Muslims as Members of the Umma

The participation of Chinese Muslims in the united front of the *umma* was increasingly emphasised in subsequent articles. For example, in '10 Years of *Yuehua* and the Islamic World' (vol. 11, Nos. 31–3), published on 25 November 1939, Xue Wenbo writes:

> Tentatively looking around the Islamic world, everywhere, the atmosphere of complaint has matured gradually, and the scream of indignation has been heard. They [Muslims] try to take advantage of the opportunity offered by the competition of many aggressors which brings about the situation that loot is distributed unequally among them; thereby [Muslims] prepare to kill them and struggle against them [aggressors] so that [Muslims] win the freedom and liberation of all the Islamic nation. [As a part of this struggle], 50 million co-religionist brothers [i.e., Chinese Muslims] have already staked their lives in battles against aggressors for more than two years.

Here, the battle of Chinese Muslims is clearly seen as part of the liberation war of the Islamic nation, whose goal was to drive away colonialists. Although its accordance with divine instruction is not explained anew, it appears to have been taken as self-evident as Xue Wenbo imagined the Chinese Muslims as constituents of the Islamic nation.[47] Furthermore, in an article titled 'The Anti-Aggression Movement and the Contact with Near Eastern Islamic States' that appeared in *Yuehua* (vol. 11, Nos. 34–6), 25 December 1939, Tang Kesan, the president of the Chengda Normal School that published the journal, urged, 'We hope that our religious companions all over China and the Islamic nation all over the world together join the anti-aggression movement.' The writer boldly expresses the immediate solidarity of the Muslims in China and those of other states, although he does not forget to state the solidarity of the Chinese nation, including Chinese Muslims, and foreign Muslims; remarking specifically that he follows Sun Yat-sen's testament that expresses the hope of 'the collaborative struggle in alliance with nations which treat with us evenly'. Tang Kesan's support for the unity of the global *umma* resonates with the tone of another article carried at the top of the same issue of *Yuehua*, 'Welcoming the Envoy of Turkey, Dr. Xibaxi'.[48] This piece argues that it was not until Islamic culture had diffused among the Muslim masses that 'the consciousness of the Islamic nation was unified, its power was concentrated, and the goal of the simultaneous liberation [of the Islamic nation] was accomplished'.

In 'Discussing Enemies, Us, and the Islamic World in the Upheaval of European Situation', published by *Yuehua* (vol. 12, Nos. 13–18), on 25 June 1940, the author, who calls himself Zhisheng (perhaps a pseudonym meaning 'immature student'), notes the following:

> The Islamic world is a group constructed by the same religion and culture. It is a group oppressed in the world. It includes various people who believe in Islam, such as Arabs, Turks, Persians, Indians, people of the South Seas, Africans, and Europeans. This group is organized around the core of Islam and Islamic culture. Their races are varied, but they form a group united fast like an iron through the same religious belief.

After noting that 'China has 50 million Muslims', the author concludes that 'Muslims all over the world form a family.' 'Muslims are just brothers' (Qur'ān 49:10). 'It is unbearable for companions in the Islamic world to neglect their Muslim brothers [in China], who are plundered and slaughtered.'

After March 1939, Hui writers in *Yuehua* began to relate Chinese Muslims to 'Islamic military cosmopolitanism' in the sense of the joint struggle of the *umma* against aggression, by characterising the anti-Japanese resistance as the defensive *jihād*. The turning point was probably the assimilation policy of Chiang Kai-shek, who believed that the solidarity of the Chinese nation was crucial for winning the anti-Japanese war. This drove him as far as to deny acknowledging Hui Muslims any distinct identity as an ethnic group, and in July 1939 he prohibited the use of the designation 'Islamic ethnic group' or 'Islamic nation' (*Huizu*), even going so far as to reject any acknowledgement of the Hui people as distinct from the Han people or the Chinese nation itself.[49] Some Hui intellectuals responded to this by emphasising their association with the global Muslim community.[50] By such a strategy, they seem to have tried to establish the Hui people's ethnic particularity within the Chinese nation.

At the same time, however, they never denied the Hui Muslims' Chineseness. Rather, their belonging in the Islamic nation, or the global *umma*, sustained their patriotic contribution to the Chinese nation. For example, the opening article of *Yuehua* (vol. 11, Nos. 28–30), 25 October 1939, argues that Chinese Muslims could play a positive role in mediating between the Chinese government and West Asian states, thus contributing to the Chinese state. Furthermore, Zhisheng in the article above maintains that overthrowing empires and restoring the Chinese nation could not be accomplished without the participation and unification of the Islamic nation (*Huizu*). In other words, he stresses that it was indispensable for the Chinese state to appreciate the Hui Muslims' affiliation with the universal Muslim community, which attracted sympathy and support from abroad that could be beneficial to the Chinese state. This means that he justified the Hui Muslims' ethnic particularity and membership in a global *umma*, through which they could contribute to the Chinese state and express their allegiance to the Chinese nation. In short, forming a united front with the *umma* functioned as a tool by which the Hui people simultaneously proved their loyalty to the Chinese nation and maintained their distinct Hui.

Conclusion

During the modern period, Hui Muslims have devised various forms of 'Islamic cosmopolitanism' and negotiation with non-Muslims through the Islamic legal reaction to non-Islamic political dominance and authority. In doing so, they have striven to both survive as religiously observant Muslims and as ethnically distinct among non-Muslim Chinese, while at the same time thriving within Chinese society and maintaining a status of loyal citizens to a non-Islamic state.

Ma Anyi situated Chinese Muslims outside the territory that the global *umma* had to defend, and by categorising China as *dār al-ḥarb* he protected the religious status and personal security of Muslims under the Qing rule and its non-Islamic regulations. In this case, his refusal of a border-crossing 'Islamic military cosmopolitanism' or enlistment in the ideological allied forces against invaders to the *dār al-Islām* allowed Muslims to exist peacefully and piously in China.

Wang Jingzhai directed attention away from discourses of a global *umma* to argue for China to be considered as an Islamic country. This assertion would render the call to *hijra* as irrelevant to Hui Muslims and better adapt them to contemporary contexts of rising Chinese nationalism. In this case, his abandonment of 'Islamic military cosmopolitanism' for *hijra* was followed by a call for Chinese Muslims to become conscious of their Muslim-ness and Chinese-ness at the same time.

Hui writers in the modern journal *Yuehua* have advocated the unity of the cosmopolitan Muslim community in the defensive *jihād* against the Japanese in order to make Chinese nationality and Hui ethnicity compatible, while opposing Chiang Kai-shek's homogenisation policy. In this case, 'Islamic military cosmopolitanism', oriented against 'infidel imperialists' served to harmonise their status as Muslims with their loyalty to the Chinese state. Tracing this history, we can see the ways in which evolving forms of Islamic cosmopolitanism reflected at every turn tensions and power dynamics such as majority pressures on minority communities and the friction between different religious values and legal orders.

Notes

1. For example, in his work on Ḥanafite jurisprudence the *Radd al-Muḥtār*, Ibn ʿĀbidīn (d. 1836) interprets Qur'ān 9:123 as a source for the doctrine of *jihād* imposed as a 'collective obligation' (*farḍ kifāya*) on Muslims living adjacent to the lands of 'infidels' (*kuffār*). As long as sufficient numbers of Muslim facing the frontier take up this responsibility, other Muslims are not universally obliged to do so as well. However, 'If the enemies assault one of the borders of Islam (*thaghr min thughūr al-Islām*), then *jihād* becomes an individual obligation (*farḍ ʿayn*).' Muḥammad Amīn al-shahīr bi-Ibn ʿĀbidīn, *Radd al-Muḥtār ʿalā al-Durr al-Mukhtār Sharḥ Tanwīr al-Abṣār fī Fiqh Madhhab al-Imām al-Aʿẓam Abī Ḥanīfa al-Nuʿmān*, vol. 3 (n.p.): Shirka-yi Saḥāfiyya-yi ʿUthmāniyya, H.1307, pp. 303–4.
2. For example, see Hanley, Will, 'Grieving Cosmopolitanism in Middle East Studies', *History Compass* 6(5) (2008): 1346–67. In this article he says, 'Reference to cosmopolitanism consistently entails nostalgia for a more tolerant past, along with grief over modern-day Middle Eastern states and societies' (p. 1346). Simpson and Kresse criticise the use of 'the adjective "cosmopolitan" as an epithet in relation to the Indian Ocean, often in a somewhat lazy sense to suggest population movement and the sharing and inter-mingling of cultural values' (p. 2). Simpson, Edward and Kai Kresse, 'Cosmopolitanism Contested: Anthropology and History in the Western Indian Ocean', in Edward Simpson and Kai Kresse (eds), *Struggling with History: Islam and Cosmopolitanism in the Western Indian Ocean* (London: Hurst, 2007), pp. 1–41.
3. The Hui people have for centuries lived as committed Muslims while also pursuing harmonious coexistence with the broader Chinese society. In light of this, an ambitious project of Li Huanyi, which J. Lilu Chen discusses in Chapter 6, this volume, can be seen as a striking example of this. Chen demonstrates how this Hui scholar attempted to secure Chinese Muslims' 'centrality' to both Islamic and Chinese histories, as well as to the history of humankind as a whole. For a pioneering discussion of the simultaneity between Muslim-ness and Chinese-ness in Hui Muslims in pre-modern times, see also Benite, Zvi Ben-Dor, *The Dao of Muhammad: a Cultural History of Muslims in Late Imperial China* (Cambridge, MA: Harvard University Asia Center, 2005).
4. On Mạ Anyi, see Yao, Jide, Rongkun Li and Zuo Zhang, *Yunnan Yisilanjiao shi* (Kunming: Yunnan daxue chubanshe, 2005), p. 230.
5. On Ma Dexin and Ma Lianyuan, see Lin, Chang-Kuan, 'Three Eminent Chinese

ʻulamāʼ of Yunnanʼ, *Journal of the Institute of Muslim Minority Affairs* 11(1) (1990): 100–17.

6. Atwill, David G., *The Chinese Sultanate: Islam, Ethnicity, and the Panthay Rebellion in Southwest China (1856–1873)* (Stanford, CA: Stanford University Press, 2005), pp. 124–6, 128, 154.
7. Muḥammad al-Ḥasan Ḍiyāʼ al-Dīn b. al-Shaykh al-Ḥājj Muḥammad Nūr al-Ḥaqq [i.e., Ma Anyi], *Taḥqīq al-īmān* (n.p., H. 1322 [1905]), p. 142.
8. al-Ḥaqq, *Taḥqīq*, p. 146.
9. al-Ḥaqq, *Taḥqīq*, pp. 150–1. The Indian Islamic modernist Sayyid Aḥmad Khān (d. 1898) identified India as *dār al-amān* to counter arguments that Indian Muslims would be justified in rebelling against British rule. See Verskin, Alan, *Oppressed in the Land?: Fatwās on Muslims Living under Non-Muslim Rule from the Middle Ages to the Present* (Princeton, NJ: Markus Wiener, 2013), p. 80; Jalal, Ayesha, *Partisans of Allah: Jihad in South Asia* (Cambridge, MA: Harvard University Press, 2010), p. 135.
10. al-Ḥaqq, *Taḥqīq*, pp. 151–8.
11. [Ma Dexin] *Mushtāq* (n.p., n.d.), f. 25a. This version can be found in the collections of the Tōyō bunko in Japan, and is included among some Arabic works in a box with shelf-mark [III-14-B-41].
12. According to *Da Qing lüli* (Hulü, Hunyin, Chuqi), if a husband divorced his wife unilaterally without specific reasons, he was flogged eighty times with a heavy stick.
13. *Mushtāq*, ff. 25b–26a. According to *Da Qing lüli* (Xinglü, Douou xia, Qiqie oufu), when a husband had beaten his wife, if she was not injured, he was not punished; even if she was injured, his penalty was reduced two grades less than the ordinary punishments for inflicting bodily injury.
14. See Nakanishi, Tatsuya, *Chūka to Taiwa suru Isurāmu: 17–19 seiki Chūgoku Musurimu no shisōteki eii* (Kyōto: Kyōto daigaku shuppankai, 2013), pp. 183–92.
15. Al-Ḥājj al-Sayyid Muḥammad Nūr al-Ḥaqq b. al-Sayyid Luqmān al-Ṣīnī al-Yunnānnī al-Sihīnnī [i.e., Ma Lianyuan], *Tawḍīḥ*, Kānbūr: Maḥmūd al-Maṭābiʻ, H. 1321 [1903], pp. 290–1.
16. al-Ḥaqq, *Taḥqīq*, pp. 143–4.
17. Ibid., pp. 145–50.
18. Ibid., p. 146.
19. Ibid., pp. 145–6.
20. ʻĀbidīn, *Radd*, vol. 3, p. 344.

21. al-Ḥaqq, *Taḥqīq*, p. 148.
22. Ibid., pp. 148–9. In addition, Ma Anyi did not wish the blind obedience of Chinese Muslims to the Qing emperors. He writes, 'Our ancestral *'ulamā'* concealed their queues under turbans completely in the *ẓuhr* prayer, following the apostle's *sunna*, because he had his head shaved entirely after his pilgrimage of separation. We have our queues hanging down our back, except in prayers', al-Ḥaqq, *Taḥqīq*, p. 150.
23. Ibid., pp. 144–5. According to Gaborieau, Marc, *Le Mahdi incompris Sayyid Ahmad Barelwî (1786–1831) et le millénarisme en Inde* (Paris: CNRS Éditions, 2010), p. 44, Shāh 'Abd al-'Azīz (d. 1824) also declared that loans with interest were permitted in India, since the area became *dār al-ḥarb*. Also see Jalal, *Partisans of Allah*, p. 68.
24. Muḥammad Nūr al-Ḥaqq b. Luqmān [i.e., Ma Lianyuan], *Tafṣīl al-īmān: Faṣl a-arba' fī sabīl Allāh: Tianfangfenxinbian – Sibianyaodao: Bosiwen Zhongwen duizhao*, revised and translated into Chinese by Yousufu Wang Peishan (Kunming: n.p., 2003), pp. 17–18, 20. This version and probably the original version, *Tafṣīl al-īmān* was written in Arabic, while *Faṣl a-arba'* was written in Persian. I was able to consult an older version of *Tafṣīl al-īmān*, probably published in 1914 (ff. 9a–10b), by the grace of Mr Zhu Weiyong, who was the *imām* of the Xiaoweigeng mosque in Yunnan province. He permitted me to see the version which his ancestor had used. I express my sincere gratitude for his kindness.
25. Muḥammad Nūr al-Ḥaqq b. Luqmān [i.e., Ma Lianyuan], *Muhimmāt al-Muslimīn: Jiaokuanjieyao (Muxinmetai) Bosiwen Hanwen duizhao*, revised and translated into Chinese by Yousufu Wang Peishan (Kunming: n.p., 2002), pp. 14, 16. I have also seen an older version of *Muhimmāt al-Muslimīn* published in 1894 (ff. 8b–10a). Again, I deeply thank Mr Zhu Weiyong who let me see the version which his ancestor had used.
26. Ma, Boliang, *Jiaokuanjieyao* (Guangdong: Yuedong qingzhensi, Tongzhi 6 [1867]), ch. 3 (Zhuming īmān de duanfa liujian), in Zhongguo zongjiao lishi wenxian jicheng bianzuan weiyuanhui (eds), *Qingzhen dadian*, vol. 15 (Hefei: Huangshan shushe, 2005), pp. 198–9 [*Jiaokuanjieyao* was completed in 1678]. Yu, Haozhou, *Zhengongfawei* (Chengdu: Baozhentang, Guangxu 10 [1884]), vol. 2, Chapter of Renshi men, section 5 (Yimana duanfa liushi), in *Qingzhen dadian*, vol. 15, p. 318 (*Zhengongfawei* was first published in 1793–5, see Nakanishi, *Chūka to Taiwa suru Isurāmu*, pp. 109–10, n. 12). Ma, Liangjun, *Qingzhenzuiyaozhi* or *Kitāb ahamm muhimmāt al-masā'il al-Islāmiyya*, 3rd ver-

sion (Urmuqi: Shanxi dasi, 1949), in Haiying Wu et al. (eds), *Huizu dianzang quanshu*, vol. 42 (Lanzhou: Gansu wenhua chubanshe, 2008), pp. 387–8 (*Qingzhenzuiyaozhi* was first published in 1928, see Hu, Long and Xianxi Ma, 'Bisheng jiangxue chuanjiao zhushu dengshen yijing xuanjing hongyang minzu wenhua: jinian Ma Liangjun ahong guizhen 50 zhounian', *Huizu yanjiu* 67 (2007): 121–8).

27. Nakanishi, Tatsuya, 'Kindai Chūgoku Musurimu no Isrāmu hō kaishaku: Hi Musurimu tono kyōsei wo megutte', *Tōyōshi Kenkyū* 74(4) (2016): 1–35 (esp. pp. 2–19).
28. For example, we find the following passage as the original text of al-Ḥaṣkafī's *al-Durr al-Mukhtār*, on which *Radd* (vol. 3, p. 341) was a commentary: 'When a Muslim enters *dār al-ḥarb* with the guarantee of security (*amān*), he is prohibited to interfere with any of their properties, blood, and women [i.e., properties, blood, and women owned by people of *dār al-ḥarb*], since the Muslim is under their regulations.' The *Radd* further comments on it, saying, '[he is prohibited to interfere with any of properties, blood, and women owned by People of *dār al-ḥarb*] because he is given security at his request (*isti'mān*), if he does not stand against them. Betrayal was forbidden, except in the case that their king betrays him.' These passages are cited in the *Taḥqīq*, pp. 146–7.
29. Ṭaḥṭāwī, *Ḥāshiyya Ṭaḥṭāwī ʿalā al-Durr al-mukhtār sharḥ Tanwīr al-Abṣār fī madhhab al-Imām Abī Ḥanīfa al-Nuʿmān*, vol. 2 (Būlāq: al-Maṭbaʿa al-ʿĀmira, H. 1282), p. 457.
30. al-Ḥaqq, *Taḥqīq*, p. 149.
31. Matsumoto, Masumi, 'Chūgoku Isurāmu shin bunka undō to nashonaru aidentiti', in Shigeo Nishimura (ed.), *Nashonarizumu: rekishi kara no sekkin (Gendai Chūgoku no kōzō hendō 3)* (Tōkyō: Tōkyō daigaku shuppankai, 2000), pp. 99–125 (esp. pp. 111–12); Matsumoto, Masumi, 'Rationalizing Patriotism among Muslim Chinese: the Impact of the Middle East on the Yuehua Journal', in Stéphane A. Dudoignon, Hisao Komatsu and Yasushi Kosugi (eds), *Intellectuals in the Modern Islamic World: Transmission, Transformation, Communication* (London: Routledge, 2006), pp. 117–42.
32. He revised this first version of 1926, first from 1937 to 1942, and then from 1938 to 1946. Wang, Jingzhai, 'Wo zhi yijing xiaoshi', *Yiguang* 101 (1939): 6–13, in Saibei, Ma (ed.), Wang, Jingzhai, *Xianyi xiangjie Weigaye (Zhongguo huizu guji congshu)* (Tianjin: Tianjin guji chubanshe, 1986), pp. 363–73.
33. Wang, Wenqing [i.e., Wang Jingzhai], *Gulan yijie* (Beiping: Huijiao Jujinhui, 1932), vol. 18, p. 4, in Zhongguo, *Qingzhen dadian*, vol. 8, p. 365.

34. Wang, Jingzhai, *Baihua yijie gulan tianjing* (Ningxia: Ningxia huijiao xiehui, 1942), vol. 18, f.4b, in Zhongguo, *Qingzhen dadian*, vol. 10, p. 95.
35. Wang, Jingzhai, *Gulanjing yijie* (Shanghai: Yongxiang yinshuguan, 1946), vol. 18, p. 5, in Zhongguo, *Qingzhen dadian*, vol. 11, p. 488.
36. Nāṣir al-Dīn ʿAbdullāh b. ʿUmar al-Bayḍāwī, *Anwār al-tanzīl wa asrār al-taʾwīl al-maʿrūf biʾl-tafsīr al-Bayḍāwī*, vol. 3 (Dehlī: al-Maṭbaʿ al-Mujtabāʾī, H. 1343), p. 66.
37. This reluctance is also found in an anonymous article, titled 'Can Three-Principles of the People Substitute for Religious Belief?', carried in *Yiguang* No. 97, 1938 (October), which says as follows: 'The meaning of *momin* (*muʾmin*) is one having orthodox belief, but not people of Muḥammad. We just call ourselves Muḥammadan disciples. We are not subjects of Muḥammad.' This view surely was shared by Wang Jingzhai, because he was the chief editor of a periodical *Yiguang*.
38. Wang, *Gulan yijie,* vol. 4, p. 3, in Zhongguo, *Qingzhen dadian*, vol. 8, p. 88; Wang, *Baihua yijie gulan tianjing*, vol. 4, f. 4a, in Zhongguo, *Qingzhen dadian*, vol. 9, p. 188. Translating '*umma*' of Q3:110 as 'nation' was Wang Jingzhai's original idea. The previous Chinese translations of the Qurʾān by Tie Zheng (published 1927) and Ji Juemi (published 1931) translates the same part as 'the best people of religion' and 'the excellent and distinguished disciples of religion', respectively.
39. Wang, *Gulanjing yijie*, vol. 4, p. 4, in Zhongguo, *Qingzhen dadian*, vol. 11, p. 98.
40. As for the Islamic nation, see Zhao, Zhewu, 'Interpretation of Four Characters, Hui Jiao Min Zu', *Yuehua*, vol. 1, No. 5, 1929 (December 15), and Wu, Jianli, 'Current Situation and Future of the Islamic Nation', *Yuehua*, vol. 2, No. 1, 1930 (January 5). Zhao and Wu define Muslims all over the world as a united nation, while calling it '*Huijiao minzu*' or '*Yisilan minzu*' (the Islamic nation), based on Sun Yat-sen's definition that a nation has a common blood, life, language, religion and customs.
41. Wang, *Baihua yijie gulan tianjing*, vol. 5, ff.15b–16a, in Zhongguo, *Qingzhen dadian*, vol. 9, pp. 254–5; Wang, *Gulanjing yijie*, vol. 5, p. 20, in Zhongguo, *Qingzhen dadian*, vol. 11, p. 139.
42. If China were considered *dār al-ḥarb*, Muslims there could not fight against non-Muslim Japanese invaders, according to *Fatḥ al-qādir*, a *Ḥanafī* work which is one of reference books of Wang Jingzhai's Chinese commentary on *Sharḥ al-wiqāya* written by Ṣadr al-Sharīʿa the second. It stipulates as follows: 'If

people of *dār al-ḥarb* attack people of the same area including a Muslim who is *musta'min*, he is not permitted to fight against those infidels (attackers) except for the case in which he is afraid of his life [because of his not fighting].' (Kamāl al-Dīn Muḥammad b. ʿAbd al-Wāḥid al-Sīwāsī, thumma al-Sikandarī al-maʿrūf bi-Ibn al-Hammām al-Ḥanafī. *Fatḥ al-qadīr li'l-ʿāziz al-faqīr, maʿa takmilati-hi Natā'ij al-afkār fī kashf al-rumūz wa al-asrār, li-Shams al-Dīn Aḥmad al-maʿrūf bi-Qāḍī Zāda, ʿalā al-Hidāya sharḥ Bidāya al-Mubtadi', ta'līf Burhān al-Dīn ʿAlī b. Abī Bakr al-Marghīnānī, wa bi-hāmishi-hi Sharḥ al-ʿināya ʿalā al-Hidāya, li-Akmal al-Dīn Muḥammad b. Maḥmūd al-Bābartī wa Ḥāshiyya Saʿd Allāh b. ʿĪsā al-Muftī al-shahīr bi-Saʿdī Chalabi wa bi-Saʿdī Afandī ʿalā Sharḥ al-ʿināya*, vol. 4 (Būlāq (Miṣr): al-Maṭbaʿa al-Kubrā al-Amīriyya, 1316 AH), p. 348.

43. Simpson and Kresse, 'Cosmopolitanism Contested', pp. 17–19, point out the following comparable cases: when those whose ancestors had emigrated returned to their homeland, they noticed differences in practices between themselves and descendants of those who had stayed there.
44. Matsumoto, Masumi, 'Sino-Muslims' Identity and Thoughts during the Anti-Japanese War: Impact of the Middle East on Islamic Revival and Reform in China', *Nihon Chūtō Gakkai Nenpō (AJAMES)* 18 (2003): 39–54; Matsumoto, Masumi, 'Chūgoku no Isurāmu shin bunka undō: Musurimu mainoritī no iki-nokori senryaku', *Gendai isurāmu shisō undō to seiji undō (Isurāmu chiiki kenkyū sōsho 2)* (Tōkyō: Tōkyō daigaku shuppan kai, 2003), pp. 141–65 (esp. p. 159); Yakubo, Noriyoshi, 'Chūgoku Musurimu dantai ni totte no shūkyō to "kōsen": Chūgoku kaikyō kyōkai to sono rinen wo chūshin ni', *Shichō* 74 (2013): 37–51.
45. Sun Yat-sen and Chiang Kai-shek envisaged that Manchurians, Mongolians, Uighurs and Tibetans had been, or would eventually be, assimilated into the Han people (including the Hui Muslims as 'Muslim Han', or the Han people that believed in Islam) and unified into the Chinese nation. See Nakata, Yoshinobu, *Kaikai minzoku no shomondai* (Tōkyō: Asia keizai kenkyūsho, 1971), p. 142; Gladney, Dru. C., *Muslim Chinese: Ethnic Nationalism in the People's Republic* (Cambridge, MA: Harvard University Press, 1996), pp. 83–5; Wang, Ke, *20 seiki Chūgoku no kokka kensetsu to 'minzoku'* (Tōkyō: Tōkyō daigaku shup-pankai, 2006), pp. 95–100.
46. Matsumoto, 'Rationalizing Patriotism', pp. 123–36.
47. From the early 1930s, Xue Wenbo strongly insisted that Hui Muslims were not Han people who believed in Islam, but rather another 'nation (*minzu*), the 'Hui nation' (*Huizu*); however, he agreed that the Hui nation was a part of the Chinese nation (*Zhonghua minzu*). On his advocation of 'Huizu', see Andō,

Junichirō, '"Kaizoku" aidentiti to Chūgoku kokka: 1932 nen ni okeru "kyōan" no jirei kara', *Shigaku zasshi* 105(12) (1996): 67–96 (esp. pp. 83–4); Yamazaki, Noriko, 'Kindai Chūgoku ni okeru "kanjin kaikyōto" setsu no tenkai: 1930 nendai no Musurimu erīto ni yoru gensetsu wo tegakari ni', *Nenpō chiiki bunka kenkyū* 17 (2014): 136–56 (esp. p. 143). Xue Wenbo seems to have believed that the global 'Islamic nation' was composed of various 'Islamic nations' of each country, including 'Huizu', and Huizu belonged to both the Islamic nation and Chinese nation.

48. Xibaxi was probably Sipahi. 'The Republic of Turkey assigned the reputable diplomat Mr Emin Ali Sipahi to Chongqing in December 1939 as its envoy', [interview with Ambassador Muzaffer Eröktem, 'Turkey and Taiwan Complement Each Other on the Opposite Corners of Asia', 11 December 2013 on the Ulusulararası Stratejik Araştırmalar Kurumu website, available at: http://www.usak.org.tr/usak_det.php?id=3&cat=840&dil=ing#.VIE0UsmE2IN.
49. At the first congress of Chinese Islamic Association for the Salvation of the Nation (*Zhongguo Huijiao Qiuguo Xiehui Diyijue Quanti Huiyuan Daibiao Dahui*), 26 July 1939, Chiang Kai-shek proclaimed that he hoped comrades would recognise that it is impossible to call Islamic believers '*Huizu*' (Islamic ethnic group, or Islamic nation). See Xue, Wenbo (recording), 'The President Chiang's Instruction at the Ceremony', *Zhongguo Huijiao Qiuguo Xiehui Diyijue Quanti Huiyuan Daibiao Dahui TeKan* (the commemoration issue in memory of the first congress), 10 August 1939. Also see Nakata, Yoshinobu, *Kaikai minzoku no shomondai*, p. 143; Gladney, *Muslim Chinese*, p. 84; Yu, Zhengui, *Zhongguo lidai zhengquan yü yisilanjiao* (Yinchuan: Ningxia renmin chubanshe, 1996), p. 314.
50. It is remarkable that Xue Wenbo recorded Chiang Kai-shek's instruction about '*Huizu*' at the first congress of the Chinese Islamic Association for the Salvation of the Nation, and then, in *Yuehua* on 25 November 1939, identified the anti-Japanese war with a part of the defensive *jihād*, as mentioned above.

6

Writing Cosmopolitan History in Nineteenth-century China: Li Huanyi's *Words and Deeds of Islamic Exemplars*

J. Lilu Chen

In 1874, the Chinese author Li Huanyi published a biographical compendium titled *Words and Deeds of Islamic Exemplars* (*Qingzhen xianzheng yanxing lüe*). In this collection, Li argued that Hui Muslims like himself had always been loyal supporters of the Chinese state, showing how this tradition was inaugurated during Muhammad's lifetime by the Prophet's Companion Saʿd b. Abī Waqqāṣ.[1] Waqqāṣ connects the figures in Li's compendium with a larger world history featuring China and Arabia and stretching back to the origins of humanity with Adam. For Li, the Hui are not an ethnic or religious minority on the fringes of the Chinese and Islamic empires. Rather, they are central to both histories and to the history of humankind as a whole.

Li's cosmopolitanism lies in his ability to situate the Hui in relation to both Chinese and Islamic history. He proposes a simultaneous, interactive past between China and Arabia. Indeed, his text supports Edward Simpson and Kai Kresse's claim that history writing can participate in achieving a cosmopolitan ideal through its 'conglomeration of pasts held in common'.[2] Yet what is interesting about Li's collection is that even as the author establishes historical connections between China and Arabia, his overall message is to emphasise the long-standing devotion of the Hui to the Chinese state. In other words, rather than transgressing ethnic and national confines as Simpson and Kresse's definition of cosmopolitanism would suggest, Li depicts a shared history only to reach a definitive end-point in China. In this respect, the kind of universal history found within this biographical compendium invites us to consider how cosmopolitan worldviews are used in the service of particular political and patriotic agendas.

This chapter introduces Li's text and explores the temporal framework in *Words and Deeds*. I examine the author's use of the word *Hui* and the polemical investment behind it. Li situates the Hui in a larger world history featuring China and Arabia and dating back to the first human being, Adam. This is followed by a discussion of the figure of Saʿd b. Abī Waqqāṣ. I show how Li's text emerges from a background of traditions affirming the dual authorities of the Chinese emperor and Muḥammad in establishing the first Muslim presence in China. The figure of Saʿd b. Abī Waqqāṣ appears in these origin tales as mediator between two sovereigns. He is depicted as undertaking multiple journeys between Medina and the Chinese court in Chang'an, during which he facilitates the transfer of important Islamic knowledge, scriptures and people to China. Li's compendium features a distinctive interpretation of Waqqāṣ' place in history. As the first biography in the collection, Li presents Waqqāṣ as the founder of Hui loyalty to the Chinese state that continues until his day.

The last section of this chapter will then take up the tradition of Hui service initiated by Waqqāṣ through three selected biographies from Li's collection: an Opium War hero, a cannibal military general; and an elusive immortal. Each of these lives epitomises Li's central message that the Hui throughout the dynasties have proved to be invaluable to the empire. I argue that this message was especially pertinent during the years that Li composed the text. As Hui rebellions broke out in northern and southwestern China, Li tells a different story. His work affirms a sacred tie between the Hui and the state. It is a cosmopolitan history written in support of the empire.

Outlining Universal History

Of the author Li Huanyi, we know that he passed the county-level imperial exams and made a modest living as a teacher in Tang prefecture of Henan Province. As a scholar Li was relatively unknown, even among Hui Muslims. He did not hold a high rank in the Chinese bureaucratic system like his contemporary Lan Xu, nor did his texts enjoy the wide circulation of Liu Zhi's canonical works.[3] *Words and Deeds* had limited distribution in Li's home prefecture, though mention is also made of prints made in Jiangnan and Guangdong provinces.[4] The content and language of Li's writing, moreover, suggests that it was not intended to be read outside the Hui community. Indeed, the use of Islamic figures and landmarks would have dumbfounded non-Muslim readers. On the other hand, Muslim readers unfamiliar with Chinese classics, mythological figures and imperial history would have, likewise, found it impenetrable. Li's collection was written for readers invested in both of these traditions – it was written for the Hui.

Yet many Hui would have objected to Li's patriotic, pro-state agenda.[5] Indeed, in his day some Hui were taking up arms against the Qing. Approximately one year before Li completed his biographical collection, Qing forces executed the rebel leader Du Wenxiu in Yunnan Province, who had successfully led local Hui in establishing an Islamic state known as the 'Panthay Sultanate'.[6] At the same time in the northwestern provinces of Shaanxi, Gansu and Ningxia, a long spell of violence erupted between Hui and Han groups as well as amongst different Hui factions, causing even more strain on Qing control.[7] Li is notably silent about these events and does not include biographies of any Hui associated with the rebellions in his collection.

Completed during this volatile time, *Words and Deeds* focuses instead on unearthing and narrating a long tradition of loyal Hui servants to the state. Li's son claims that his father spent more than ten years working on the project, consulting hundreds of historical works in order to consolidate the records of learned and high-ranking Hui throughout imperial history.[8] The text is comprised of two volumes, with biographies organised according to dynasty. Li's coverage begins in the Sui dynasty with the entry of Muḥammad's companion Saʿd b. Abī Waqqāṣ into China. The collection then continues through the Chinese dynasties until the Qing dynasty, covering a total of ninety-five Islamic exemplars. Waqqāṣ is the only figure from the Sui dynasty (581–618), followed by twenty-two figures in the Tang dynasty section (618–907), eleven in the Song (960–1279), eleven in the Yuan (1271–1368), twenty-eight in the Ming (1368–1644) and twenty-two in the Qing (1644–1912).

The majority of exemplars unearthed by Li are state officials – bureaucrats and more often military heroes like the famous Turkic Tang general Han Geshu. In recounting their lives, Li relies on Chinese dynastic histories, often reproducing extracts from official state biographies. Li also includes Islamic religious scholars in his collection, beginning with Wang Daiyu's biography in the Ming dynasty section, and followed by notable Hui scholars such as Ma Zhu, Liu Zhi, She Qiyun and Jin Tianzhu. The collection also introduces a few holy men presented in the style of the Chinese immortal – idiosyncratic recluses who escape or elude death as evidence of their great powers. The last section of this chapter explores these biographies in greater detail.

Words and Deeds of Islamic Exemplars is a carefully constructed, self-conscious reflection on the Hui past in China. Not only does Li offer a collection of Hui heroes, but the author also situates their history within the development of Islam, Chinese civilisation and human civilisation as a whole. Muḥammad's companion Saʿd b. Abī Waqqāṣ becomes the progenitor of the Hui people, even as the teachings of these people stretch back even further in time. For Li, *Hui* refers to people originating from lands west of China – specifically the region encompassing Arabia, Persia and Central Asia. In the Tang dynasty, most of these westerners were of Turkic descent and followers of Mani, a prophet from the Persian Sasanian Empire who founded Manichaeism.[9] This is why the majority of Li's Tang dynasty figures and many of his Song and Yuan dynasty figures are described as being Uighur (*huihe*, *huihu*), and Li includes the construction of a Manichean temple in 807 alongside a lineage of famous Islamic buildings in China. Li integrates these details about Uighurs and Manichaeism into his collection because he wants to date the compendium all the way back to Waqqāṣ and the Prophet Muḥammad's lifetime in the Sui dynasty. He expands the term *Hui* to encompass all those with western origins dating back to the Sui dynasty – Manicheans included – who settled in China.

In the preface to his work, Li situates his biographical compendium within a grand overview of human history. He summarises human civilisation in Arabia and China by allocating his attention to each respective site by time period. Arabia holds a monopoly on antiquity, and human origins are better understood through Islamic narratives. However, following the flood and the dispersal of Noah's sons across the world, a parallel history emerges chronicling the development of the Arabian and Chinese empires. These two empires meet in the Sui and Tang dynasties with the arrival of Muslim emissaries to China. Afterwards, the only history that matters is the history rooted in China.

Li's treatment of antiquity employs many of the same themes used by other Sino-Muslim authors. He combines the Islamic figure Japheth with the Chinese sage Fu Xi. He also identifies Adam with the Chinese mythical figure Pan Gu. Li writes:

> When the universe opened up, Adam was born in Arabia. Just as the Hui scriptures call him Adam, the Confucian scriptures call him Pan Gu. He was also known as 'Ya Dan'. They were probably the same person with different names.
>
> When Adam's tenth generation descendant Noah quieted the flood-waters and set right the path, he enlightened people as to the correct way to conduct themselves. Noah had three sons. The oldest was called San Mu [Shem]. He spent his life watching over the middle lands, which is present-day Arabia. The second was called Han Mu [Ham]. He was given governance of the western lands, which are the present-day countries of Europe. The third was called Ya Fu Xi [Japheth]. He was given governance of the eastern lands, which is present-day *Chi ni*. *Chi ni* refers to the 'middle country', China.[10]
>
> The 'Chronicle of Arabian Generations' [*Tianfang Shiji*][11] says that Fu Xi [son of Noah] is the same as Fu Xi [Chinese mythological sage]. He is the eleventh generation descendent of the ancestor of human beings Adam. From Arabia he crossed the desert and cultivated the fertile farmlands. He was the first to go east and set up his capital there.[12]

Li equates the Islamic Adam with Pan Gu, who appears in Chinese myths as the first living being. He notes that this figure goes by different names in Chinese and Hui (Islamic) texts but is essentially the same person. Later, following the Islamic tradition of ten generations separating Adam and Noah, Li presents a division of the post-flood world between Noah's three sons as consisting of Europe to the west, Arabia in the middle and China to the east. Noah's sons become the progenitors of each of these civilisations. Like Hui authors before him, Li makes the connection between Noah's youngest son Japheth, who is purported to have travelled east in the Islamic traditions and the Chinese flood figure Fu Xi, who has a strikingly similar sounding name. The effect of equating Fu Xi with the Islamic Japheth is that the birth of Chinese civilisation becomes linked to an even earlier origin of human beings in Arabia.

Li emphasises that these connections make sense given that Chinese historical accounts of what happened between Pan Gu and Fu Xi are vague if not missing altogether:

> When you examine the history after Pan Gu and before Fu Xi, they all remained in Arabia. And that is why the records of Shu Yi and Xun Fei[13] are muddled and without solid evidence. The episodes of Nüwa patching up the sky and Yi shooting down the ten suns are preposterous, fabricated tales. Because of this, the Grand Historian says: 'The historian should begin with Fu Xi'[14] . . . Moreover, Confucius left out the *Shang Shu*, only starting with the dynasties of Yao and Shun. For how could he speak of these things without a foundation?[15]

If Fu Xi were indeed Noah's son, then the details of human history predating him would have been virtually unknown in China since human beings between Pan Gu and Fu Xi actually 'remained in Arabia'. Thus, Li argues that the true history of this early time lies in the Islamic sources. Other Chinese tales of this period involving Nüwa patching up the sky and Yi shooting down the suns are 'preposterous and fabricated'. Only the histories rooted in Arabia – the Islamic ones – have authority over what really happened before Fu Xi came to China. Li points out that other Chinese historians have agreed with him on the weakness of Chinese sources for this period. The Grand Historian Sima Qian and Confucius all began their histories after Fu Xi. Arabia, therefore, becomes the cradle of human civilisation. Chinese history begins only after the dispersal of Noah's sons.

For Li, Noah marks the transition from one unified world history to multiple histories. From Fu Xi onwards, Li paints two parallel timelines between the Chinese civilisation descended from Fu Xi and the 'Hui religion' upheld by San Mu's descendants in Arabia. On the Chinese side, the original religious lineage (*dao tong*) traced back to Fu Xi and even further to Adam diverges after the Qin and Han dynasties. China thereafter witnesses the rise of Buddhism, Daoism and other teachings deviant from the true root in Arabia. Concurrently, the Hui religion is in turmoil in Arabia and almost vanishes. However, it ascends again during China's Liang (502–57) and Chen (557–89) dynasties of the North–South era. This would have been concurrent with the lifetime of the Prophet Muḥammad, according to Li's calculations.

Li's narrative arrives, finally, at the Chinese Sui and Tang dynasties, during which China encounters the Hui religion via the first Sui emperor's 'invitation to the west for a scholar to fix the calendar' and Tang emperor Taizong's edict sanctioning mosque construction in the capital. Following this, each successive Chinese dynasty is summarised with a defining characteristic in relation to the Hui. 'The Song age held the Hui customs in esteem. The Yuan hired Hui talent. The Ming ancestors praised Hui knowledge. This sagely dynasty [the Qing] emphasises Hui works.'[16]

Li's preface outlines a history of the world that defines Chinese history as a subset of a larger history rooted in Arabia. He presents a parallel timeline chronicling the development of Chinese civilisation and the Hui religion, which meet during the Sui and Tang era. From this time forward, the author makes the case that the state enjoyed a long history of contributions from the Hui. Yet despite this long history, Li believes that there has not been significant inquiry into the Hui as a whole or celebration of their achievements within Chinese historical texts. Li writes, 'The honour of the emperors and wise gentlemen and the wisdom of the great ministers of the court have already been praised and rewarded. But the following individuals, whose luminosity is like a consuming fire and cries are like an earthenware kettle, how can one not inquire about them?'[17] The biographies that follow in his collection, then, are presented as a new grouping of famed Hui from the state's history, a grouping that has previously been overlooked in the general acknowledgement of notable Chinese such as emperors and ministers.

By outlining a lineage of human history from his Qing dynasty back to Noah and Adam in Arabia, Li positions the Hui in a particularly meaningful place. The Hui join together the two lineages of China and Arabia, which date back to the first human being Adam. Yet as Li notes, the achievements of the Hui as a group have not been given sufficient attention in Chinese history. The rest of the collection is devoted to 'uncovering' these virtuous life stories as they have been scattered in various Chinese imperial sources and reintegrating them into a new lineage. This lineage connects eminent Hui back to Arabia and the time of Muḥammad through the origin figure of Saʿd b. Abī Waqqāṣ.

Saʿd b. Abī Waqqāṣ between Two Empires

For Li Huanyi, the figure of Saʿd b. Abī Waqqāṣ encapsulates all of Hui history dating back to the lifetime of the Prophet. Li's interpretation of Waqqāṣ as the link joining the Chinese and Islamic civilisations builds upon origin narratives circulating among nineteenth-century Hui. In his own rendition of Waqqāṣ' life, Li uses the figure to initiate a lineage of Hui loyal to the state – something I argue is the true focal point of Li's collection. Through analysis of the biographies that follow that of Waqqāṣ, I demonstrate how Li defines the Hui not so much in terms of ethnic or religious characteristics, but rather through their loyalty to the Chinese empire.

Waqqāṣ in Nineteenth-century Lore

The figure of Saʿd b. Abī Waqqāṣ is situated at the centre of narratives about Hui origins circulating in nineteenth-century China.[18] These stories reveal a certain fascination with documenting imperial involvement behind the transfer of Hui to China. On the one hand, the stories highlight the Chinese emperor's need for Muslim assistance and his affirmation of Hui teachings. On the other hand, the dating of these origin stories to the lifetime of the Prophet and the details given about Waqqāṣ' relationship to Muḥammad belie an investment as well in Islamic imperial authority.[19] This is evident through Muḥammad's appearance in the stories as the Islamic head of state and the details provided on the excellences of his rule in Arabia. In the origin stories, Waqqāṣ' multiple journeys from Muḥammad's kingdom in Medina to the Chinese court in Chang'an provide the crucial temporal and spatial link joining these two poles of authority. The narratives therefore lend valuable insight into the subtle ways in which cosmopolitan affiliations with different empires were negotiated by nineteenth-century Hui.

Many Hui sources survive from Li's time and earlier concerning the origin of Muslims in China. While these traditions share a great deal in common, they are not all consistent with each other. Some date the earliest arrival of Muslims to the Sui dynasty and others to the Tang dynasty. Yet all agree that the first entry was during the lifetime of Muḥammad. The 1724 biography of the Prophet, 'The Utmost Sage of Arabia' (*Tianfang Zhisheng Shilu*) by the famous scholar Liu Zhi, which enjoyed wide circulation among Hui into the nineteenth century, assesses the multiple dating and settles in favour of the Sui dynasty. Liu Zhi writes:

> The account of the entry of the religion of the Prophet into China in the seventh year of Wendi of the Sui dynasty [587], following the sending of an envoy to the West, is given in detail in several Chinese histories, so it can be proved . . . The old statement that it was in the reign of Xuanzong of the Tang dynasty [713] that the entry occurred is an error. That period was over one hundred and fifty years separated from the advent of the Prophet, so the time does not tally nor do the circumstances agree.[20]

While Liu Zhi rules in favour of the Sui dynasty dating, the most elaborate versions of the origin tale feature Tang emperor Taizong. Taizong is prompted by a dream in which his palace is under assault from a hideous monster. Just in time, a turbaned man emerges to vanquish the monster and save the palace from disaster. When the emperor recounts his dream to the Imperial Astronomer, the astronomer confirms that on the previous night when he was observing the sky, he noticed a strange appearance among the stars and a felicitous light appearing in the west. The astronomer concludes that there is impending danger but a sage from the west can save the kingdom. The emperor decides to send a messenger to the west to inquire about this man. This marks the first invitation for a Muslim to appear at the Chinese court.[21]

In almost all the versions, the man from the west dispatched by the Prophet to China is identified by the name Waqqāṣ. Waqqāṣ is said to have made multiple journeys to China. Liu Zhi recounts how Muḥammad was urged to send Waqqāṣ one last time when he encountered an envoy from Sui emperor Yangdi scouting out the western lands. The Prophet surmises correctly that Emperor Yangdi is being remiss in his governing duties at home and obsessing over western expansion. He thus decides to send Waqqāṣ to help guide Emperor Yangdi and also to look after the increasing numbers of Muslims in China. The Prophet is reported to have instructed Waqqāṣ:

> If the Emperor of China asks you what I am doing, tell him that I am engaged in the work of transformation at the command of Heaven, promoting the correct and destroying the false, abolishing idols and images and leading to the worship of the True God; I am daily busy with the affairs of the people, denying myself in every way for the general good.
>
> If he should ask you about the duties of an emperor tell him to act in accordance with the will of Heaven and to follow the examples of the prophets and pay due respect to worthies; be as a parent to the people, exercise wide benevolence, and let laws be correct and forbearing; but let the wicked be sought out and admonished; there should be daily self-examination, and also investigation into the misfortunes of the people; there should be no covetousness or oppression, power and position should be lightly regarded in comparison to the importance of the welfare of the empire; let all selfishness be set aside, and follow that which is virtuous and good.[22]

This lengthy oration on the proper duties of a ruler casts the Prophet in an ideal light epitomising how rulers should behave. Muhammad shares this wisdom with Emperor Yangdi through his envoy Waqqāṣ, who acts as an intermediary conveying the lesson on how to rule. In this episode, the transmission between Chang'an and Medina is prompted by the Prophet, who sees that the Chinese ruler is in need of support to better govern his kingdom, and that the Muslims in China are in need of additional guidance. In the previous episode involving Tang Taizong's dream, it is the Chinese emperor who initiates the contact with Muḥammad, forewarned by various signs that his kingdom is in need of help from the west. Underlying both these episodes, however, is the interest in presenting Muslim origins in China as something sanctioned by both imperial heads, who legitimate the exchange as something much needed for the welfare of the Chinese state.

Waqqāṣ in Li Huanyi's Collection

Building upon these narrative traditions, Li's presentation of Waqqāṣ emphasises the many assets he brings to the Chinese emperor. I demonstrate below how Li uses Waqqāṣ' biography to initiate a lineage of Hui service to the Chinese state. As the first and longest in the entire collection, Waqqāṣ' life story is easily the focal point. Unlike the other biographies that follow, which are limited to the lifetimes of the individuals in question, Waqqāṣ' biography extends from his life all the way to Li's Qing dynasty. This extended temporal frame emphasises his special position as founder of the lineage and representative of the Hui. For Li, Waqqāṣ' biography is an occasion to encapsulate all of Hui history, beginning with its origins in the Sui dynasty.

Li commences the biography by describing Waqqāṣ as an official serving as a messenger from Arabia, highly skilled in both civil and military affairs with a special gift for calendric calculations. Waqqāṣ hails from a country, Arabia, which is presented in the most ideal light. Li notes:

> One name for Arabia is the 'western lands' [*xi yu*], another name for it is the country of Persia [*da shi*],[23] and yet another name for it is *Tianfang*. There is pleasant scenery and a mild, temperate climate. The people there have upright customs. From the officials to the lowly masses, all worship God and they take it as the religion of the realm.
>
> If you examine those books that are profound and authentic, you will find that the laws of the country prohibit alcohol, dogs and pigs. Their customs place great emphasis on the method of slaughter, and they do not eat things that have been slaughtered by others. The people and their customs are genial, and there are no impoverished households. The officials impose neither taxes nor corvée labour, and they also do not deal out punishments. All honour the religious regulations and naturally manage themselves. They do not steal or engage in other inappropriate conduct.[24]

Li idealises Arabia, emphasising how upright the people are, referring specifically to Islamic law forbidding intoxication and labelling dogs and pigs as unclean. He also touches upon Muslim *ḥalāl* practices and the importance of ritually slaughtered meat. For Li, the inhabitants of Arabia all follow these practices. In fact, the people there are so pious and law-abiding, that the government does not need to impose taxes or corvée labour since 'all honour the religious regulations and naturally manage themselves'. There is neither law enforcement nor poverty since the place is so harmonious and prosperous. Arabia emerges as a land China could only aspire to emulate in terms of how upright its people and officials are.

Furthermore, Arabia possesses crucial knowledge of calendric calculations that China lacks. The first appearance of Muslims at the Chinese court is presented in Waqqāṣ' biography as arising from a need to correct the Chinese calendric records, which had become muddled in the chaos of the North–South era (420–589). The founding emperor of the Sui dynasty, Wendi (r. 581–600), decides to dispatch a messenger to the west upon hearing that Arabia possesses an extraordinary person who 'writes scriptures containing everything' and is 'skilled in his calendric calculations'. This 'extraordinary person' arrives in the person of the Prophet. In the following paragraph of Waqqāṣ' biography, Li writes:

> In the Dingwei year, that is the seventh year of the Kaihuang era [of Emperor Wendi, 587], the sage of the nation Muhammad commanded his official Sayyid Waqqāṣ and others to follow the emissary and pay tribute to the Chinese emperor. They brought with them thirty volumes of heavenly scripture for presentation to the emperor. They reached Guangzhou via the southern seas. The first thing they did was to build the Huaisheng Si ['Prophet Remembrance Mosque'] in Guangzhou.[25]
>
> They reached Chang'an where they reported to the emperor. The emperor read the scriptures and liked them immensely. He allowed them to build mosques in China and transmit the teachings. He also allowed them to stay and reside in the eastern lands [*dong tu*] and to revise the calendar. It was completed in the Yiwei year of the Kaihuang era [599]. This is how China came to have the Huihui calendar system.[26]

The association of the Hui with the imperial calendar is taken up again later in Li's collection within Wang Daiyu's biography, whose ancestors are described as coming from Arabia to the court in Nanjing during the fourteenth-century founding of the Ming dynasty.

> With the emperor, they established the intricacies of the astronomical calendar. They corrected the errors in the calendric system, surpassing the knowledge of the ancients with extreme subtlety and not a single error. The great emperor was delighted. He concluded that they must have legitimate transmission of orthodox teachings in order to arrive at such accurate calculations. Therefore, he endowed them with the position of Directorate of Astronomy. They were granted residency in the capital and were exempt from corvée labour.[27]

Waqqāṣ' biography is an occasion for Li to project the themes of Hui history he wishes to highlight back onto an individual who lived during the Prophet's lifetime. Waqqāṣ legitimates Hui history in China precisely through his proximity to Muḥammad. As Li puts it, it is Muḥammad who first commanded that Waqqāṣ pay tribute to the Chinese emperor, sending him off with Islamic knowledge in the scriptures and the astronomical calendar. Furthermore, Waqqāṣ receives affirmation from the Prophet's contemporary ruler in China – the founding Sui emperor Wendi – who 'read the scriptures and liked them immensely', leading to the bestowal of Muslim residences and mosques in China. In this way, Waqqāṣ' story enables the Hui to trace their origins back to two authoritative poles in Medina and Chang'an.

The Chinese emperor's good impression of the Hui, beginning with Waqqāṣ and the corresponding bestowal of imperial favour, is a theme that echoes through Waqqāṣ' biography and throughout the collection. Li ends Waqqāṣ' biography with an overview of ancient mosques in China and the dynasties that bestowed them. His historical work forefronts a long tradition of imperial legitimation of Islam from the Sui dynasty to his present Qing.

Li begins with the Huaisheng Si ['Prophet Remembrance Mosque' in Guangzhou], which he calls 'the origin of Hui mosque construction in the east'. This mosque was supposedly built by Waqqāṣ upon his first arrival in China via the southern seas.[28] The next oldest Islamic structures in China, the Tang mosques in Chang'an, are also linked to Waqqāṣ through the men who accompanied him to China. Li writes that during Waqqāṣ' last journey to China, Muḥammad selected teachers to spread Islamic doctrine in China and dispatched them with Waqqāṣ. In the following Tang dynasty, these Muslim teachers were summoned to Emperor Taizong to respond to hundreds of questions about Islam. The emperor was impressed by their responses and exclaimed, 'This only has minor differences with the Confucian path and is largely similar. The two paths of the Hui and Han can be undertaken simultaneously without any risk.' Thereupon he issues an edict for the construction of mosques in Chang'an.[29] Here the emperor's approval of the teachings transmitted by Waqqāṣ' travelling companions corresponds with the appearance of mosques in Chang'an.

Li's overview continues with the Tangming Si, which he dates to the first year of the Tianbao reign of Emperor Xuanzong (742). This emperor is purported to have 'taken the dao of the sage from the western regions to be the same as that of China'. Therefore, he commanded his supervisor of the Ministry of Works to oversee the construction of this mosque in Chang'an.[30] In the following section, I analyse another biography in Li's collection of the Tang dynasty, holy man Tao Baba, who assumes Waqqāṣ' role in expounding the virtues of Islam to the emperor, leading to the imperial construction of this mosque.

Li continues Waqqāṣ' biography with accounts of other mosques constructed and renovated in the Song, Yuan and Ming dynasties along with their corresponding imperial patrons. He interweaves quotes from various Chinese rulers assessing the Hui religion. The last emperor mentioned is the Ming dynasty Wanli emperor, Shenzong (r. 1572–1620). Linking all these developments with the Qing dynasty of his day, Li writes in conclusion to this section and Waqqāṣ' biography as a whole, 'Now we reach this current dynasty, whose benevolence is deep and profound, whose grace tumbles forward like a wagon wheel, mosques proliferating all over.'[31]

Through Waqqāṣ' biography, Li outlines the history of imperial favour towards the Hui, as evidenced by the bestowal of mosques from various emperors throughout the dynasties. Waqqāṣ initiates this partnership between the Hui and Chinese state by being the first westerner with Islamic affiliation to cement ties with the emperor. This tradition is then continued by others of western origin who subsequently come to China and whose descendants also serve the empire. Li's promotion of the Hui and their western teachings is accomplished by focusing on a long line of contributions to the state and the corresponding affirmation of value by emperors throughout history.

Servants of the State

After Waqqāṣ, the subsequent biographies in Li's collection all focus on Hui in relation to the Chinese state. In the 1860s and 1870s when Li was composing *Words and Deeds*, the Hui occupied a precarious position within the Chinese empire. The Tongzhi era (1862–75) witnessed widespread violence involving Hui in Shaanxi and Gansu provinces, many of whom were taking up arms against each other, neighbouring Han and the state. Displaced Hui refugees were fleeing the empire to Xinjiang and neighbouring Central Asia.

Just a year before the completion of Li's text in 1874, Qing forces put an end to the Islamic sultanate in Yunnan and executed its leader Du Wenxiu. Hui throughout the province were being systematically massacred.

There is a remarkable silence in Li's text about all of these events. Certainly, none of the Hui involved with these rebellions are mentioned in his history. Rather, Li's focus is on past events as if the present is too volatile to speak of. In the section that follows, I explore the lives of three Hui in the collection: the Qing dynasty hero Sha Chunyuan, the Ming dynasty martyr Tie Xuan and the Tang dynasty holy man Tao Baba. The Hui in Li's history are nothing like the dangerous upstarts in contemporary Yunnan, Shaanxi and Gansu provinces. Rather, they appear throughout this work as subjects loyal to the state whose virtues are continuously affirmed by the imperial centre. The biographies below point to how Li's cosmopolitan vision of Hui history is built upon an inseparable devotion to the Chinese state.

Sha Chunyuan

Among the most dramatic life stories in Li Huanyi's collection are those of the two martyrs Sha Chunyuan and Tie Xuan. Both heroes were natives of Henan, the same province that Li hailed from.[32] Li himself had met Chunyuan in the years before the hero's epic death in the Second Opium War. Li describes Chunyuan as having a 'dignified and grave appearance' as well as a 'lively manner of conversation'. The author notes, 'I recognised that he was an extraordinary person and I felt reverence towards him.'[33]

Li introduces Chunyuan as someone who succeeded in the imperial exam system, eventually earning a military *jinshi*. After moving through various posts as a junior guardsman and then brigade officer, Chunyuan commanded Emperor Xianfeng's army against the 1852 Taiping Rebellion in Anhui province. Li credits him with effectively blocking the Taiping expansion northwards into Henan province, and notes of Chunyuan's performance on the battlefield that, 'he always placed himself in front of the foot soldiers. Because of this, he won all his battles. The number of traitors he wiped out completely was beyond count.'[34]

Eventually, Chunyuan was promoted to brigade commander and, in 1858, acted as the regional vice commander for the Tianjin brigade. He was responsible for protecting the port against the Anglo-French invasion of the

Second Opium War. Li chronicles the epic end to Chunyuan's life in the midst of cannon fire between the British and Chinese. After mounting the cannon deck and shattering two foreign ships with his 'calm and collected' aim, Chunyuan was close to weakening the enemy. When his fellow Chinese soldiers were fleeing their positions, urging him to leave as well, Chunyuan reportedly rebuked them saying, 'If you give up land, the army is lost. I can only repay my country with death. This is the spot where I will die.' Chunyuan refused to desert his position, remaining on the cannon deck until eventually, he was fatally hit by cannon-fire, fulfilling his wish to repay his country.

Li notes that martyrdom for the state had been a life-long ambition of Chunyuan's:

> Even though Chunyuan did not habitually read, he enjoyed being in the company of learned and cultivated officials. He often commanded others to expound on and discuss the official histories. He would quietly listen to them. Whenever he heard of an especially loyal or outstanding official, he would earnestly wish to be like them in his heart. When the port fell, the old men of his town said to each other: 'Alas, Chunyuan must have died with the port.' And in fact that is what happened. Probably they understood for a long time his longstanding ambition to die in battle.[35]

It is emphasised that Chunyuan's bravery in battle exceeded that of his non-Muslim compatriots, who were all fleeing the port. Li emphasises how Chunyuan's exceptional devotion to the state was recognised by the emperor. Upon hearing of Chunyuan's virtuous conduct, the emperor granted him imperial burial rites. His body was returned to his ancestral home and re-interred in the cemetery for war heroes.[36] Chunyuan also earned a place in the temple for those who had exhibited the utmost loyalty. His descendants were awarded the hereditary title 'Commandant of Fleet-as-Clouds Cavalry'. In the conclusion to this biography, Li offers his own reflections on Chunyuan's death and composes a eulogy in praise of his martyrdom.

> When I heard that Chunyuan had died in Tianjin sacrificing himself for the country, I was both pleased and full of grief. I grieved that he lost his life before the enemy was entirely extinguished. I was pleased that while

> his physical body had been killed, he was able to sacrifice himself for a just cause . . . Alas! In order for a great man to repay the great benevolence of his ruler, he must die on the battlefield. This is a worthy death. This poem can serve as a eulogy for Master Sha:
>
> Even today when passing the Tianjin shore
> I mount the platform of combat
> And gaze outwards, recalling the brave warrior.
> Who could not refrain from admiring
> Those who step forward in moments of great crisis
> While dead, he is as if alive.[37]

Sha Chunyuan and the following Ming dynasty figure Tie Xuan epitomise for Li the apex of loyalty to the Chinese sovereign. Chunyuan gave up his life battling the British and French. Tie Xuan defends Emperor Jianwen against Zhu Di. Both men are lauded for their successful careers in the imperial military, culminating in epic deaths displaying their valiant devotion to the state.

Tie Xuan

Tie Xuan's biography is one of the most grotesque in the collection, with an account of Xuan's cannibalism of his own body parts that attests to this hero's extreme loyalty. This hero died in the aftermath of the Ming civil war (1402), during which he sided with the reigning Emperor Jianwen against Zhu Di, the Prince of Yan and future Yongle emperor. Li's life account presents an upright and steadfast government servant whose loyalty to the Ming emperor extended into the very last moments of his life. [38]

After graduating from the Imperial Academy, Xuan served as Administration Vice Commissioner of Shandong. Li notes that he 'inspected the water transportation of grain and not once did anything go missing'.[39] Xuan's integrity as a government servant is further complemented by his loyalty to Emperor Jianwen, sustained even in the face of crisis. After Jianwen's imperial troops lost to the Prince of Yan and fled south, Xuan continued to recruit soldiers for the emperor's cause, urging them to swear vows and pledge their lives.

Li describes one incident during the second year of the civil war when Xuan worked with the Commissioner in Chief of Jinan, Sheng Yong, to successfully protect the city from Zhu Di's invading forces. After an initial plan to feign surrender and ambush Zhu Di failed due to the fumbling of his men, Xuan came up with an even better scheme. He engraved the name of Ming dynasty founding emperor Taizong on a stele and suspended it from atop the city. Upon seeing this, the commanding generals of Zhu Di's army dared not attack. Xuan then ordered the Commissioner in Chief to send his troops undercover in the darkness of night to attack Zhu Di. The Prince of Yan lost in 'a great defeat' and Emperor Jianwen took back Dezhou. Xuan was credited with the success of this campaign and promoted to various posts within Shandong.

Despite Xuan's clever efforts on the battlefield, Emperor Jianwen eventually lost the civil war. Xuan, however, remained loyal to him. Even when the emperor was deposed and Zhu Di became established as the new Yongle emperor, Xuan kept his remaining troops stationed in Huainan with plans to march to Jianwen's rescue. Xuan was eventually captured and brought before the Yongle emperor in a climactic end to his life in which Li recounts how even Xuan's corpse testified to his unwavering loyalty.

> Xuan sat with his back turned to the throne. The emperor [Yongle] commanded that they cut off his nose and ears. Yet he did not turn around. They cut off his flesh and made him eat it. When asked if it was sweet or not, he replied in a stern voice, 'How could the flesh of a loyal official and righteous man be anything but sweet.'
>
> It was commanded that they ladle oil into a big cauldron and throw his corpse inside to cook. They adjusted his corpse to face north [towards the Yongle emperor]. Yet it tossed around and faced outwards. Then it was commanded that the eunuchs use iron rods to rotate the corpse to face north. Chengzu [temple name of the Yongle emperor] laughed and said, 'Now you have to pay homage to me.' Before his words were finished, the oil in the cauldron boiled over, scorching the hands of the eunuchs, who had to drop their rods and flee. The bones still faced outwards. The emperor was greatly astonished. He ordered that the corpse be buried. At that time Xuan was thirty-seven years old.[40]

In this last episode of Xuan's life, his loyalty to Jianwen extended even to the bodily mutilation and self-cannibalism to which he was subjugated. Not only is the flesh of Xuan's body 'sweet' to the taste due to his lifelong loyalty and righteousness, but the bones of his body also testify to his character. After death, his corpse staunchly refuses to pay respect to the Yongle emperor by facing him. Xuan's biography ends with an astonished Yongle who at last recognises the power of Xuan's loyalty and righteousness. Yongle gives up on his operation to force Xuan to pay homage to him. In an action indicating his newfound fear and respect, he orders that Xuan's corpse be buried. The fact that even Emperor Jianwen's usurper to the throne comes to begrudgingly recognise the power of Xuan's virtue is the crowning achievement in Li's biography of this remarkable Ming official.

Li celebrates Tie Xuan's loyalty to the emperor. *Words and Deeds* is not a history critical of the Chinese state or the decisions and weaknesses of its leaders. Emperor Jianwen is not passed over in favour of the victorious Zhu Di. No mention is made in Sha Chunyuan's biography of the various blunders on the part of the Qing court that led to the Second Opium War. The heroes in Li's collection pledge their military allegiance to a single ruler and state, never wavering in their devotion. Further examples of this in the Chinese case is offered by Tatsuya Nakanishi are in Chapter 5 of this volume.[41] Nakanishi refers to an 'Islamic military cosmopolitanism' in which the security of Chinese Muslims always comes first. In this, Hui authors continually negotiate strategies for survival in China, re-evaluating how to classify the nation so that they can live harmoniously within it. For Chinese Muslims, the endeavour to unify nations, cultures and people is inextricable from state involvement.

Tao Baba

Tao Baba's biography is the exception that proves the rule in Li's collection. While *Words and Deeds of Islamic Exemplars* is primarily focused on the lives of civil and military officials, Tao Baba is presented in the image of the holy man – a reclusive immortal (*xian*) more likely sighted on mountain tops than on battlefields. Yet even the legitimacy of this unearthly figure relies upon endorsement from the Chinese court.

Li notes at the beginning of the biography that 'baba' is what those of the Hui religion call elderly people. Tao Baba was 'originally a person of the west' who journeyed to Chang'an during the Tang dynasty. He was learned, having 'mastered the classics and calendar systems of all the various nations of Arabia'. Li writes that Emperor Xuanzong heard of Tao Baba and summoned him to court. After listening to him discuss the Hui scriptures, the emperor decided that even though people in the east (China) have generally not heard of them before, they contain valuable teachings about 'ethics, diet, and customs of daily life'. He thereupon issues an edict for the construction of the Tangming Si mosque in Chang'an and allowed the Hui to spread their western teachings widely.[42]

Li depicts Tao Baba in many of the same ways as Waqqāṣ. Like Waqqāṣ, Tao Baba comes from the west and arrives at the Chinese court in Chang'an. Like Waqqāṣ, he imparts Islamic knowledge to the emperor and earns imperial recognition for Islam. This enables the construction of Islamic buildings and the proliferation of Islamic teachings, just as Waqqāṣ had done earlier in the Sui dynasty.

Yet quite differently from Waqqāṣ, Li characterises Tao Baba in the tradition of a Chinese immortal. Tao Baba's white hair, ruddy complexion and child-like face match the standard appearance of Daoist masters of the internal arts, who sit on mountains cultivating immortality.[43] Li notes that Tao Baba's life was full of strange occurrences. 'Once when he was crossing the water his boat overturned. Tao was the only one to stand on top of the water and his clothes were still dry. Whenever he walked in the mountains, tigers and wolves would all become tame and obedient to him.'[44] While other characters in Li's collection like Sha Chunyuan and Tie Xuan are known for their epic deaths, 'the details of Tao Baba's death are not known'.[45]

Instead, it seems, Tao Baba influenced the death – or lack thereof – of another famous figure in Chinese history. A large portion of the biography focuses on the Tang calligrapher and imperial officer Yan Zhenqing (709–84), who appears as Tao Baba's friend and student. Yan Zhenqing recounts how he learned the arts of immortality from Tao Baba. He is quoted saying, 'In the past, I encountered an ascetic of the path [*daoshi*] in Jiangnan named Tao Baba. He gave me the jade cloud medicine spoon pellet, which can prevent death. Up until today, my health has not waned.' The biography then describes various miracles Tao Baba performed in front of Yan Zhenqing, such as predicting correctly where they would meet each other again. Upon seeing Yan in the aforementioned location, Tao Baba pointed his finger towards a nearby mountain and vanished into thin air.

An anecdote at the end of Tao Baba's biography illustrates just how effectively his lessons in immortality served Yan. Tao Baba predicted that after the age of seventy, Yan would encounter 'a great calamity' in Luofu. This came to pass, and Yan is buried on the northern mountain of Yanshi. Afterwards though, a curious incident occurred.

> There was a merchant who journeyed to the Southern Sea [*Nanhai*]. He saw an ascetic of the path playing chess. This ascetic of the path asked him to bring a letter to the Yan family home in Yanshi. When the merchant arrived there he realised it was a grave. The tomb-keeper was an old man with ashen-grey hair. He jumped in fright when he recognised the lord's [Yan Zhenqing's] handwriting in the letter. The family members decided to open up the grave at once that very day. They found that the coffin had already been emptied.[46]

Yan's empty coffin substitutes for Tao Baba's empty coffin, as the abandoned grave is a standard way to end biographies of Chinese immortals. Yet the value of this last anecdote in the biography is to show that Tao Baba had effectively taught Yan how to elude death. In other words, Tao Baba's importance is built upon his transmission to Yan Zhenqing.

In Li's biographies, the power and legitimacy of Hui figures is brokered through their interactions with the Chinese court. The presentation of Tao Baba in the mode of a Daoist immortal points to the indigenous Chinese tropes with which Li depicts Hui heroes. The endorsement by Yan Zhenqing and the account of his death suggests that despite the avowedly 'Islamic' title in *Words and Deeds*, Tao Baba's legitimacy is built upon the fame of this Tang official and calligrapher. Indeed, Yan Zhenqing performs the same role as Emperor Xuanzong and Emperor Yongle in the biographies of She Chunyuan and Tie Xuan. He affirms Tao Baba's power and virtue.

Throughout *Words and Deeds*, Li co-opts well-known figures in Chinese history and inserts them into the biographies of lesser-known Hui. His collection creates a new centre, one in which the Hui serve as nexus between the ancient Islamic portion of history and the contemporary Chinese period. To do this, legitimacy for the Hui must come from both temporal poles of authority. The earliest figure in this collection, Saʿd b. Abī Waqqāṣ, receives affirmation from the Prophet Muḥammad and the Sui emperor. Subsequent figures like Tao Baba continue to be recognised by imperial authorities.

Conclusion

To what extent can we can call *Words and Deeds* a cosmopolitan history? On the one hand, the biographies following Waqqāṣ are all focused on China, where the figures are presented in light of legitimation and praise by members of the Chinese ruling elite. Furthermore, Li describes the Hui in the language of Chinese 'types'. Tao Baba fits the standard description of Chinese immortals. The heroes Tie Xuan and Sha Chunyuan are martyrs for the sovereign and nation. The prevailing theme in all these biographies is that Hui have been consistently valuable to the empire. This message would have been particularly pertinent during the late Qing dynasty, which witnessed a series of revolts associated with Hui in the southwest and northwest frontiers of China and a proliferation of imperial writing and law-making concerning how to tell treacherous Hui from peaceful ones. In this respect, Li's account joins the state dialogue by identifying 'good Hui' in Chinese history and bringing them to light.

Yet Li's ability to package all these loyal heroes – from Tang Uighurs to Yuan Bukharans and Qing domestic Hui – within a single collection relies precisely on a cosmopolitan imagination linking the Chinese and Arabian past. Li's collection is headed by a Sui dynasty Arab by the name of Waqqāṣ, within whose biography he encapsulates all of Hui history in China from the Sui to the Qing dynasty. Li's preface situates Waqqāṣ' involvement with the transmission of Islam into China in the context of a broader, universal narrative. This narrative goes from Adam, to the division of the world between Noah's three sons, to the developments of the Chinese dynasties and Hui religion, until their encounter in the Sui and Tang dynasties. Waqqāṣ' role in the collection is to take the succeeding biographies of Hui individuals out of a purely Chinese context and position them in a history harking back to the very first interchange between the Chinese and Islamic states.

Waqqāṣ himself epitomises the story of the subsequent Hui featured. He comes from the west and dies in China after offering valuable contributions to the Chinese state. In this way, Li reconciles Chinese and Islamic history by relegating each to temporal limits. The featured figures in Li's collection all originate from the west, the land of Islam from which Muḥammad hails. Yet they ultimately live and die in China, after offering themselves in service to the Chinese empire. Likewise Li's overview of human history as a whole from Adam onwards stresses that Arabia has a monopoly over the ancient past. The Chinese records are insubstantial before the time of Fu Xi. Yet after Fu Xi, and especially after the transmission of Islam into China during the Sui and Tang dynasties, the defining framework for Hui Muslim identity in this text is Chinese imperial history. The present is rooted in China, yet the past must not be forgotten regarding how these westerners first arrived there sanctioned by both the Prophet and the Chinese emperor.

Li's vision of cosmopolitanism relies upon deep investments in imperial authority and state power. Rather than transgressing various kingdoms, the Hui in Li's history uphold the authority of imperial regimes grounded in both Arabia and China. This endorsement begins with Waqqāṣ' biography in which Muhammad is presented as head of state. It continues in the subsequent biographies with the appearance of Chinese emperors. Li's history presents a Sino-Islamic past that testifies to Hui loyalty to the Chinese state – a message countering the image of Muslim rebels against the empire prevalent during his day.

Notes

1. My use of the term Hui follows Dru Gladney's definition: 'The people now known as the Hui are descended from Persian, Arab, Mongolian, and Turkish Muslim merchants, soldiers, and officials who settled in China from the seventh to fourteenth centuries and intermarried with local non-Muslim women. Largely living in isolated communities, the only thing that some but not all had in common was a belief in Islam.' Gladney, Dru, *Muslim Chinese: Ethnic Nationalism in the People's Republic* (Cambridge, MA: Harvard University Press, 1991), p. 97.
2. Simpson, Edward and Kai Kresse (eds), *Struggling with History: Islam and Cosmopolitanism in the Western Indian Ocean* (New York: Columbia University Press, 2008), p. 3.
3. Contemporaneous Hui scholar Lan Xu served as district magistrate of Xingzi district in Jiangxi Province. Among his works, see Xu, Lan, 'Tianfang zhengxue', in Wu, Haiying et al. (eds), *Huizu diancang quanshu*, vol. 35 (Lanzhou: Gansu wenhua chubanshe, 2008). Several English-language analyses of Liu Zhi's works

exist. For an overview of Liu Zhi's significance in the context of the Hui education system, see Ben-Dor Benite, Zvi Aziz, *The Dao of Muhammad* (Cambridge, MA: Harvard University Press, 2005), pp. 144–153.

4. For evidence of other publication sites for this text, see Li, Huanyi, 'Qingzhen xianzheng yanxing lüe', in Haiying Wu et al. (eds), *Huizu diancang quanshu*, vol. 105 (Lanzhou: Gansu wenhua chubanshe, 2008), p. 237. For more on the distribution and history of this text, see Lu, Fenglin, *Nanyang Shigu* (Beijing: Zhongguo wenhua chubanshe, 2005). According to Lu, the 1917 woodblocks were destroyed in the Cultural Revolution. The current surviving prints are from the personal collection of Li Huanyi's descendant Li Guanglu. Li Guanglu gave them to a relative by marriage, a doctor named Gong Kebing, for safekeeping.
5. I am not aware of any surviving evidence of opposition to *Words and Deeds*. More likely, the text's limited distribution among Li's family members and wider social network would have meant that it was only disseminated privately among educated Hui who, like Li, were invested in the Chinese state.
6. For a look at the intricate factors supporting Du Wenxiu's rebellion, see Atwill, David, *The Chinese Sultanate: Islam, Ethnicity, and the Panthay Rebellion in Southwest China, 1856–1873* (Stanford, CA: Stanford University Press, 2005).
7. See discussion in Lipman, Jonathan, *Familiar Strangers: a History of Muslims in Northwest China* (Seattle, WA: University of Washington Press, 1997), pp. 115–29.
8. See Li Zumian's preface in Li, 'Qingzhen xianzheng yanxing lüe', pp. 233–4.
9. The prophet Mani lived during the Persian Sasanian Empire. He founded Manichaeism, which spread into Central Asia and China.
10. Li, 'Qingzhen xianzheng yanxing lüe', pp. 229–30. *Chi ni* is a transliteration of the Persian word for China *chīn.*
11. This is a highly generic title. Li is likely referring here to a section of Liu Zhi's *Tianfang Zhisheng Shilu*, which contains a section chronicling the generations after Adam. In Noah's biography, Liu Zhi makes the connection between Noah's youngest son Japheth and rulership over China. See Zhi, Liu, 'Tianfang Zhisheng Shilu Nianpu', in Zhou, Xiefan and Qiuzhen Sha (eds), *Zhongguo Zongjiao Lishi Wenxian Jicheng*, vol. 89 (Hefei Shi: Huangshan shushe, 2005), p. 69.
12. Li, 'Qingzhen xianzheng yanxing lüe', pp. 229–30.
13. Shu Yi and Xun Fei are segment number ten and number seven, respectively, of the *Shi ji* text. The *Shi ji* divides into ten segments the 2,760,000 years spanning

the opening of heaven and earth and coming of the human emperor (*ren huang*) to the Spring and Autumn period of ancient Chinese history.

14. The Grand Historian (*tai shi gong*) here refers to the Han dynasty holder of this position, Sima Qian, who wrote the famous *Shi Ji*, a monumental history of China up to the Han dynasty, on which all subsequent imperial histories are based.
15. Li, 'Qingzhen xianzheng yanxing lüe', pp. 229–30.
16. Ibid.
17. Ibid.
18. Saʿd b. Abī Waqqāṣ was a companion of the Prophet Muḥammad and an Arab military commander. For his place in Islamic traditions outside of China, see Hawting, G. R., 'Saʿd b. Abī Waqqāṣ', in *Encyclopedia of Islam*, 2nd edn (Brill Online), available at: http://www.referenceworks.brillonline.com/entries/encyclopaedia-of-islam-2, last accessed 15 December 2014. For an investigation into the historical veracity of Waqqāṣ visiting China and theories as to how he came to be associated with Chinese Muslim origin stories, see Leslie, Donald Daniel, 'The Sahaba Saʿd Ibn Abī Waqqāṣ in China', in *The Legacy of Islam in China: An International Symposium in Memory of Joseph Fletcher, Harvard University, 14–16 April 1989* (Cambridge, MA: John King Fairbank Center for East Asian Research, 1989), pp. 1–32.
19. This Islamic imperial authority, however, is limited to the Muslim state under Muḥammad, and does not concern the future caliphal states (Umayyad, ʿAbbāsid, etc.), which govern Muslims after Muḥammad's death. No mention is made of the caliphates in the Chinese sources I consulted.
20. Liu, 'Tianfang Zhisheng Shilu'. This translation is taken from Isaac Mason's English translation of the text. See Mason, Isaac, *The Arabian Prophet: a Life of Mohammed from Chinese and Arabic Sources* (Shanghai: Commercial Press, 1921), p. 94. Mason's use of Wade–Giles transliteration has been changed here and elsewhere into the Hanyu Pinyin system for consistency.
21. This tradition of the emperor's dream and the stars appears in Liu Zhi's *sira* as well as the *Huihui Yuanlai* and the *Xilai Zongpu*. The *Huihui Yuanlai* ('The Origins of the Hui Hui') dates as early as 1712. Partial translations of this text can be found in Broomhall, Marshall, *Islam in China: a Neglected Problem* (London: Morgan & Scott, 1910), pp. 62–8. For analysis of these two works, see Ben-Dor, Zvi Aziz, '"Even unto China": Displacement and Chinese Muslim Myths of Origin', *Bulletin of the Royal Institute of Inter-faith Studies* 4(2) (2002): 93–114.

22. English translation of Liu Zhi from Mason, pp. 246–7. This episode involving Muḥammad sending an envoy to China after encountering a scout from a land-lusting Emperor Yangdi is also mentioned in another nineteenth-century biographical compendium featuring Waqqāṣ. See Lan, 'Tianfang Zhengxue', pp. 376–82.
23. *Da shi* originally designated the Sasanian Persian-speaking empire. Since the Tang dynasty it has been used in reference to the Islamic lands.
24. Li, 'Qingzhen xianzheng yanxing lüe', p. 244.
25. Li cites that this episode is recorded in the 'outer lands treatise' (*Shu yu zhi*) of the imperial Sui Annals (*Sui Shu*).
26. Li, 'Qingzhen xianzheng yanxing lüe', pp. 244–5.
27. Ibid., p. 400.
28. Ibid., pp. 250–1. Here Li cites the Ming dynasty text *Shu yu zhou zi lu* as his source.
29. Ibid.
30. Ibid., pp. 250–1. Li cites his source here as Liu Zhi's *sira* 'Tianfang Zhisheng Shilu'. Most likely this is taken from fascicle twenty of the text, which contains stele inscriptions.
31. Ibid.
32. The collection, however, is not limited to Henan. The Ming and Qing sections also include figures from the northwestern provinces of Shaanxi, Gansu and Ningxia, as well as the southern provinces of Jiangnan and Yunnan.
33. Li, 'Qingzhen xianzheng yanxing lüe', pp. 451–2.
34. Ibid.
35. Ibid.
36. No mention is made in Li's biography of any tension between this method of burial and Islamic rites.
37. Li, 'Qingzhen xianzheng yanxing lüe', pp. 451–2.
38. It is remarkable that the Hui eunuch Zheng He, who served Emperor Yongle, is absent from Li's collection. Li covers twenty-eight figures from the Ming dynasty. Based on my examination of these biographies, Zheng He is not among them. It is possible Li consciously chose to omit him or more likely was not aware of Zheng He. Either way, Zheng He's absence suggests that his contemporary fame as an iconic Hui figure in Chinese history did not come about until the twentieth century, long after Li's death.
39. Li, 'Qingzhen xianzheng yanxing lüe', pp. 372–4.
40. Ibid.

41. See Tatusya Nakanishi, 'Variations of "Islamic Military Cosmopolitanism": the Survival Strategies of Hui Muslims during the Modern Period', Chapter 5, this volume.
42. Li, 'Qingzhen xianzheng yanxing lüe', pp. 266–7. *Tangming Si* is another name for *Da xuexi xiang qingzhen si* in Xi'an. The current name of the mosque comes from the lane on which it is located, *da xue xi xiang*, the very lane that Tao Baba is noted in Li's biography as having dwelt in. This mosque currently contains a plaque dating it to the eighth century, though the authenticity of the inscription is questionable.
43. For more tropes involving the *xian*, see Campany, Robert, *Making Transcendents: Ascetics and Social Memory in Early Medieval China* (Honolulu, HI: University of Hawai'i Press, 2009).
44. Li, 'Qingzhen xianzheng yanxing lüe', pp. 266–7.
45. Ibid.
46. Ibid. Here Li cites the Qing dynasty Kangxi era text, *Zengding Guangyu Ji* by Cai Fangbing, also known as *Cai Jiuxia* (1626–1709). This appears to be a geographic text of Chinese areas. Most likely, Li culled this miracle story concerning Yan Zhenqing's grave and incorporated it into his biography of Tao Baba.

7

The 'Shaykh al-Islām of the Philippines' and Coercive Cosmopolitanism in an Age of Global Empire

Joshua Gedacht

In 1912, an American military officer, Major John P. Finley, departed from his post in a remote corner of the US Empire, in the 'Moroland Province' of Mindanao and Sulu, a predominantly Muslim stretch of the southern Philippines. By this time, Finley had already logged nearly ten years in the troubled region.[1] During his tenure, ongoing US military campaigns visited significant violence upon the local Muslim 'Moro' population, killing between 600 and 1,000 people in a single battle alone.[2] Yet, by 1913, American rulers had committed themselves to a transition from a military regime towards nominally civilian rule. The new pro-consul in Mindanao and future Commander of the Allied Forces in the First World War, General John J. Pershing, sought to remove all army officers from district governorships and to replace them with civilians. Major John Finley's departure thus appeared to herald the end of his Moroland service.[3]

Yet John Finley did not consider his mission to be complete. Once the major returned to the United States, he did not abandon plans to return to the Philippines. Quite to the contrary, his own personal writings and his subsequent actions make it clear that the major still believed he had more work to do, that he needed to help rid Mindanao of the scourge of violent resistance, ensure the consolidation of law and order and, perhaps most importantly, help to solve the intractable 'Mohammedan Problem'.[4] Finley believed that if only he could defuse the local tendency towards rebelliousness by demonstrating 'respect' for Islam, American rule could finally be secure.[5] And the most critical step on this path to completing colonial hegemony lay neither in the Philippines nor the United States nor even somewhere nearby in Southeast Asia. This path instead took Finley from Zamboanga to Washington and onward to the cosmopolitan, if distant, capital of the most influential Muslim kingdom on earth: the city of Istanbul in the Ottoman Empire.

Two years earlier, a Mindanaoan Muslim and a close ally of Major Finley, Ḥaji Abdullah Nuño, had helped to draft a petition in the local language of Tausug directed to the Ottoman sultan with a request for assistance in the affairs of Islam.[6] Finley bore this petition, signed by fifty-eight local leaders, with him on his visit to Istanbul. The major then negotiated with the Ottoman government to arrange for the dispatch of a teacher from the office of the Shaykh al-Islām, the state bureaucracy responsible for administering *'ulamā'* and issuing *fatwa* legal rulings.[7] This educator, Shaykh Wajīh al-Kilānī, hailed from a prominent family in the Palestinian city of Nablus, had proven himself a talented student of Islamic studies, and, in 1906, travelled to Istanbul to work for the correspondence section of the Shaykh al-Islām.[8] In 1913, this ministry identified Shaykh Wajīh as a suitable candidate for the mission to the Philippines.

Major Finley's 1913 transit through Istanbul sparked a series of reactions that would reverberate near and far through the coiled circuitry of global empire, generating alternating feelings of hope and dread, possibility and disenchantment, in the highly charged atmosphere of imperial–Islamic encounters. Travelling separately from Finley between Turkey and Mindanao, Shaykh Wajīh charted a cosmopolitan Indian Ocean course, meeting with the nominal Muslim ruler of Egypt in Cairo, ministering to over 100 Filipino *ḥajis* in Jeddah, and greeting large crowds in Singapore.[9] This oceanic procession garnered exuberant reporting in Islamic newspapers from the British-controlled Malay Peninsula to the Dutch island of Sumatra in present-day Indonesia. At the same time, however, this sojourn alarmed Finley's American colleagues in the Philippines as well as competing European empires. These critics believed that this alliance of an American junior officer with a Muslim shaykh would not secure the pacification of Mindanao but unleash a dangerous threat to empire across Asia.

This chapter will examine this wide-ranging series of transnational entanglements and contestations that marked Shaykh Wajīh's voyage to the Philippines. In particular, it will apply a frame provisionally denoted as 'coercive cosmopolitanism' to make sense of this moment of heightened possibility and peril. On the one hand, the imperial world of cosmopolitan circulations and imbrications appeared to bring the colonial project of fashioning 'modern Mohammedan' subjects into a fortuitous, if contingent, synchronicity with the growing reformist impulse to pursue the 'True' Path to Islam. Such a cosmopolitan world, however imperial, seemed capable of nurturing genuine affinities between Muslims and non-Muslims. Yet this chapter will also contend that Shaykh Wajīh's peregrinations through the knotted pathways of transnational empire could not escape their origins in coercion and conquest, as decades of pacification freighted his journey with a heavy weight of mistrust and mistranslation, engendering accusations of naiveté, treachery and nefarious plotting. This coercive provenance would ultimately scuttle this dream of cosmopolitan opportunity, making Major Finley and Shaykh Wajīh's moment just that: an evanescent moment that could not survive the asymmetries of power separating non-Muslim coloniser from Muslim colonised.

Islam and Coercive Cosmopolitanism

The case of Major John Finley, Abdullah Nuño and Shaykh Wajīh, in many respects, distils the paradoxes at the core of Islamic–imperial encounters in the early twentieth century. In particular, the peregrinations of these two individuals from cosmopolitan capitals to colonial frontiers bring into stark relief the catalytic power of coercion and warfare. The very same forces of military power that visited such devastation on Muslim bodies in Mindanao also reinvigorated long-standing patterns of Muslim trade, re-connecting travellers with their far-flung co-religionists and encouraging them to think in terms of a broader Islamic world.

In an influential 2000 article, one of the leading theorists of cosmopolitanism, Sheldon Pollock, addresses this seeming paradox. In his seminal formulation of 'cosmopolitanism' as 'unbounded spatiotemporal circulation', a form of contact 'that travels far, indeed, without obstruction from any boundaries at all, and, more important, that thinks of itself as unbounded, unobstructed, unlocated', Pollock recognises that such limitless horizons did not emanate from goodwill alone.[10] Violence and force also played a constitutive role. For example, the widespread dissemination of Latin as a common medium for communication across the Euro-Mediterranean world resulted from the brute fact of conquest and the 'obliteration' of all other competing vernacular languages. This forcible dimension inspired Pollock to ever so briefly sketch a concept of 'coercive cosmopolitanism' as a process in which 'participation in larger . . . worlds is compelled by the state'.[11]

In spite of the provocative paradox suggested by Pollock, few have revisited 'coercive cosmopolitanism' as a conceptual tool for elucidating the place of war-making in the movement of Muslim peoples, texts and ideas across borders and space. This absence is especially acute in the extant literature on Islamic mobilities. To some extent, the seminal statements on Muslim travel do acknowledge, albeit obliquely, forms of power that underpinned motion. In their ground-breaking 2005 introduction to religious networks, for instance, miriam cooke and Bruce Lawrence allude to the soldiers who enabled the constitution of courtly power that in turn, also 'facilitated the travel and residence of [Muslim] writers and artists'. In the case of China, Cooke and Lawrence note, Muslim soldiers even served non-Muslim emperors in pre-modern China, helping 'to quell local rebellions while they [also] strengthened existing commercial and cultural ties'.[12] Such movements of soldiers, in turn, shaped the gradients of power that brought *ʿulamāʾ* from imperial centres to 'frontier kingdoms in need of jurists' – a historical template that informed al-Kilānī's transit from Istanbul to the distant shores of Muslim Mindanao.

Despite tacit acknowledgements of the role that state and military power can play in constituting cosmopolitan circulations, the entanglements of such relationships have yet to receive sufficient scholarly attention. This lacuna is particularly pronounced in Indian Ocean world and Southeast Asian studies. In his superb study of refugee flows in the Pakistan, Afghanistan and Tajikistan borderlands region in Central Asia, for example, Magnus Marsden draws a stark contrast between his own 'violent' case study in the mountainous interior and other expressions of cosmopolitanism among the 'coastal

Muslims' of 'the expansive Indian Ocean region'.[13] Ronit Ricci similarly affirms this bracketing of violence from the development of the 'Arabic Cosmopolis of South and Southeast Asia' when she notes that 'no organized political power, colonial enterprise, military conquest, or large migration was involved' in 'the diffusion' of Arabic to the larger Southeast Asia region.[14] While clearly referring to the earlier pre-colonial age, this broad assertion nonetheless discourages attempts at understanding how Euro-American colonial armies may have unintentionally amplified the resonances and salience of the Arabic cosmopolis in later periods.[15]

This chapter seeks to further develop Pollock's concept of 'coercive cosmopolitanism' through the prism of Shaykh Wajīh al-Kilānī's transit from Istanbul to Mindanao to Washington. What happened when Euro-American empires attempted to discipline Muslim networks and to put them into the service of military conquest? A prominent early twentieth-century American educational reformer, John Dewey, encapsulates the view that war could in fact compress the distance between peoples and impart a cosmopolitan education of sorts:

> Every expansive era in the history of mankind has coincided with . . . factors which have tended to eliminate distance between peoples and classes previously hemmed off from one another. Even the alleged benefits of war . . . spring from the fact that conflict of peoples at least enforces intercourse between them and thus accidentally enables them to learn from one another, and thereby to expand their horizons.[16]

While we must be careful to renounce the idea of war as some sort of benevolent enterprise, an opportunity to bring superior Western learning and civilization to benighted Muslims, Dewey nonetheless touches upon a crucial reality: war could have an inadvertently productive capacity. Indeed, as will be seen, John Finley and Shaykh Wajīh's mission to the Philippine could not be understood apart from the context of prolonged pacification. Could colonial warfare thus compel the Muslims of Southeast Asia to 'participate in larger. . .worlds,' as Pollock put it?[17] And could that wider world even be an Islamic one?

This concept of 'coercive cosmopolitanism' might invite scepticism. In her thoughtful study titled *Thinking Differently about Cosmopolitanism*,

Marianna Papastephanou inveighs against the 'celebration of unbounded movement and unconditional border crossing' as little more than apologetics for colonialism, an attempt to cloak empire in the sanitizing gloss of universality.[18] Indeed, by arguing that the most brutal aspect of colonialism – warfare – provided opportunities for connectedness to Southeast Asian Muslims, the framework of 'coercive cosmopolitanism' might appear to fall into this trap of exculpation. However, while Papastephanou anticipates a legitimate pitfall, if taken to its logical extreme, her criticism would occlude many historical developments and leave us little room to explore the tensions and ambiguities of the collaboration between Major Finley and Shaykh Wajīh. To disregard such phenomena for fear of valorising colonial rule would, ironically, deny important agency within the history of Southeast Asian Muslims. Only by examining the coercive underpinnings of Muslim mobility can scholars grasp what Papastephanou regards as the true locus of cosmopolitanism: 'the intellectual, emotional, and ethico-political . . . significance of spatiotemporal border crossing'.[19] In sum, the conjunction of 'coercive' with 'cosmopolitan' can help to locate Muslim movement, border-crossing and ethics in the context of conquest.

John P. Finley, *Juramentado* Holy War and the Search for 'Modern Mohammedanism'

To understand the precarious synchronicity between colonial conquest and Muslim mobility characteristic of 'coercive cosmopolitanism', it is helpful to return to the origins of the 'Shaykh al-Islām of the Philippines' episode. Ultimately, the main catalyst for the sojourns of Shaykh Wajīh al-Kilānī from Istanbul, through Egypt and Arabia, the Malay Peninsula and onward to Manila and Mindanao, was an obscure American military figure, Major John Park Finley. The distinguished SOAS historian William Clarence-Smith has done critical work identifying the full name of the oft-mentioned 'Sheik ul-Islam of the Philippines' as Sayyid Muḥammad Wāji b. Munīb Zayd al-Kilānī al-Nāblusī, a 'distinguished clerk' in the Ottoman office of the Shaykh al-Islām in Istanbul originally from a prominent family in Nablus, Palestine.[20] In his writings, Clarence-Smith has also outlined the broad strokes of John Park Finley's role in bringing Shaykh Wajīh to the Philippines, noting the US major's distinctive interest in the 'purification' of Islam as the best path to peace in Mindanao; the appointment of Finley as '*vekïl-i- mutlak*', or special envoy, of Haji Nuño and other Moros to the Ottoman sultanate; and Finley's audience with the Ottoman Sultan Mehmed V in the Royal Hall of Ambassadors in May 1912.[21] The passion that Finley, an otherwise unremarkable American military officer, developed for promoting the 'purification of Islam' can perhaps be instructive in understanding not only the coercive dimensions of cosmopolitanism, but also how states came to collectively discipline and constitute the category of 'religion' in the high colonial age.

Finley's early career might seem to offer little inkling of his travels to Istanbul. Born in 1854 to a prominent farming family from the state of Michigan, the young Finley pursued an education in science and soon enlisted in the US Army Signal Service, where he received instruction in meteorology. The budding army scientist rose through the ranks with his study of tornadoes, travelling throughout the American Great Plains to catalogue severe weather and acquiring a reputation as the 'First Severe Storms Forecaster'.[22]

When the project of empire and conquest thrust the long-time military scientist to the distant outpost of Mindanao in 1903, it is likely that he possessed little knowledge of the Philippines, the Ottoman Empire or the Islamic World in between. Yet Finley's experiences in studying, and hence containing, the natural world perhaps furnished apt training for the crucible of colonialism. When the major arrived in the Moroland capital city of Zamboanga, he did not confine himself to the standard tasks of military planning or bureaucratic administration. Finley instead dived into the work of ethnology, cataloguing the peoples, cultures and landscapes of the Zamboanga Peninsula in exacting detail, while eventually publishing a book on one specific local community, the animist 'Subanos' peoples, for the Carnegie Institution of Washington.[23] This ethnological inclination and intellectual curiosity, however, also propelled Finley to look beyond specifically local practices and rituals to a consideration of significant world-historical force in the region: the religion of Islam.

Upon first inspection, John Finley's views with respect to the Muslim subject population did not deviate appreciably from the mainstream of the US military establishment in Mindanao. Like most of his peers, Finley sought to balance a ruthless determination to eradicate opposition against American rule with a profession of respect and tolerance for the religion of its peoples. Finley expressed little compunction about the employment of military means against Muslim malcontents. In particular, 'priests' and purveyors of 'fanatical' doctrines who preyed 'upon the superstitious and credulous masses, justifying all manner of excesses', must be extirpated.[24]

One of the worst excesses, Finley believed, was the *juramentado* or *magsabil* attack, a local variant of the Islamic theological injunction to *perang sabil*, or 'holy war'. According to colonial discourse, the *juramentado* featured a Muslim assailant who literally swore an oath to God – hence *juramentado* in Spanish – and performed a ritual act of purification before ambushing soldiers or colonial civilians with a wavy blade known as the *kris*.[25] This *juramentado* would then kill as many Americans as possible before attaining his final martyrdom in a hail of bullets. This image informed a pronounced trope or discourse on Islam during the colonial period that shares resonances with the construction of the suicide bomber in our own age.[26] Only by isolating 'fanatics' and by promoting a more congenial type of Islam, Finley believed, would Americans succeed in quelling the scourge of 'holy war' in their Southeast Asian colony.[27]

It was in his proposed solution to the problem of *juramentado* that Finley distinguished himself. The Americans, Finley believed, could not simply defer to local religious authorities on domestic issues such as marriage and inheritance while focusing on pacification. They could not leave Islam to the local Muslims. Rather, 'to campaign successfully against these insidious and very serious evils among the Moros', declaimed Finley, 'requires intervention by the government through the instrumentality of modern Mohammedanism'.[28]

Much of what Finley conceived of as 'the instrumentality of modern Mohammedanism' bore little direct relationship to religion per se. Being a modern 'Mohammedan' often meant conforming to behaviours that could just as easily obtain in the case of non-Muslims. In a 1915 letter, Finley declared that modernity could be achieved only when locals acted to 'surrender their weapons as instruments for piratical gain of livelihood, to liberate their slaves, and to accept an industrial scheme organized under the name of the Moro Exchange System of markets and stores'.[29] Through such exertions, Mindanaoans could make 'an honest and progressive effort to better themselves according to modern ideas'. Beyond such bromides, Finley also believed that 'modern Mohammedanism' might conform to a cosmopolitan ethos of mutual respect, emphasising the 'importance of friendly intercourse among the various non-Christian tribes' and of seeking a common ground of 'religious toleration'.[30]

Nonetheless, the US governor of Zamboanga also interpreted 'modern Mohammedanism' as something more than Muslims compartmentalising their faith within the strictly private realm of individual belief, as Americans or Europeans might view it. In his study of colonial cosmopolitanism, Peter van der Veer observes that within liberalism, the idea prevails that 'religious people can be cosmopolitans, but they have to become modern Christians, modern Hindus, or modern Muslims, that is to say, progressive liberals with private, religious world-views'.[31] John Finley was not immune from such concerns, taking pains to argue that cooperation with Muslims did not imply an 'endorsement of the Mohammedan religion' or any sort of 'special privilege and protection'.[32] However, the governor did insist that the United States must act through, rather than against, the Islamic faith. Indeed, he noted the 'special form of government was devised by Governor Taft, not because the people concerned are of Malay extraction, but from the fact that they are and always have been Mohammedans'.[33]

In many senses, the vision articulated by Finley for a cosmopolitan brand of 'modern Mohammedanism' comprised both more and less than standard, perhaps simplistic notions of secularisation as relegating religion to the private sphere; it involved the veneration of 'sacred' dimensions of Islam alongside the strict delineation and compartmentalisation of what could count as sacred.[34] In his seminal work on the anthropology of the secular, Talal Asad argues that the move towards 'secular' modes of thought in nineteenth-century Europe entailed the transformation of 'a variety of overlapping social usages rooted in changing and heterogeneous forms of life into a single immutable essence . . . the object of a universal human experience called "religious."'[35] Intimately intertwined with this 'essentialisation of the "sacred" as an external, transcendent power' was the concomitant idea that such sacred domains 'must never, under threat of dire consequence, be violated – that is profaned'.[36] Such a 'profanation', in turn, argues Asad, dictated that the authorities respond with 'a forcible emancipation from error and despotism . . . reason requires that false things be either proscribed and eliminated'.[37] For John Finley, the Moros of the Philippines comprised just such a profanation, a 'degraded form of Mohammedanism'.[38] Indeed, almost the entirety of local Moro custom and culture, with its 'vicious habits', its system of slavery, its 'piratical' tendencies and, most problematic of all, its commitment to *juramentado*, constituted an impure deviation from the 'Koran', a manipulation of 'ignorant, fanatical native priests'.[39] Such profanation needed to be disciplined.

Finley thus undertook an effort to 'combat the vicious', profane habits of Moros not only through violence, although that was certainly a part of it, but also through the cultivation and restoration of the 'sacred' in Moro life.[40] The anthropologist Asad noted that upholding the sacred and counteracting the profane involved the management of 'everyday practices by which the subject's experience is disciplined'.[41] Brute, direct violence obviously comprised one such disciplinary tactic. Finley never foreswore military discipline or pacification, in consonance with Asad's description of the 'importance of violence . . . a readiness to cause pain' as an integral component of 'saving' the degraded. Such a fearful imperative is manifest in the destructive record of American warfare in Mindanao and Sulu, where estimates suggest that 10,000 Moros ultimately perished.[42] However, Finley also believed that military pacification alone would be insufficient and that the Americans needed to simultaneously cultivate his cosmopolitan brand of 'modern Mohammedanism'. This fashioning of 'modern Mohammedanism', perhaps unsurprisingly, turned upon concepts of a transcendent but strictly delimited sacredness. In contrast to the debased, profane everyday habits of the Moros, the United States instead needed to promote 'a better and truer Mohammedan faith' to help contribute to an appreciation for that sacred essence of Islam that local Muslims were somehow missing.[43]

Finley turned his attention to an aspect of belief that perhaps most resonated for a Michigander raised in a Protestant milieu: the text of the Qur'ān. In his article on the 'Moro Problem', Finley located the essence of Islamic sacredness in the texts of the Qur'ān. Those that 'know the Koran, the life and purposes of the Prophet, and are familiar with the sacred Arabic, the prayers and forms of worship,' in Finley's estimation, are those most obviously attuned with the essence of Islamic religiosity. Finley believed that knowledge of such fundamentals could help instil habits of discipline and self-restraint, arguing that the 'Koran teaches constant prayer, and inculcates abstinence from all intoxicants and temperance in all things. He lives by faith and his God is an Entity not a Person.' The more problematic aspects of Muslim religious practice like polygamy, in Finley's view, are not to be blamed 'on the creed of Islam . . . but [rather] . . . Oriental custom', on race and social custom. Thus, the primary remedy for solving the problems of wayward Muslims like the Moros rested in cultivating a proper appreciation of scripture. When writing about the Qur'ān, Finley frequently referred to 'Sacred Arabic' and sought ways to inculcate knowledge of it to the Muslims of America's Southeast Asian colony.[44]

In 1915, Finley wrote in an article that after a 'careful inspection of their teachers, we found that they were not being taught in accordance with the doctrines of their religion as laid down in the Koran'.[45] If only the United States could assist the Moros in arriving 'at a better and truer Mohammedan faith', it could neutralise those 'ignorant native priests [who] do not live by the Koran'.[46] The governor thereupon sought to find teachers who would 'know the Koran' and be 'familiar with the sacred Arabic, the prayers and forms of worship'.[47] While such sentiments reeked of paternalism, Finley's thinking also suggested a genuine interest in cultivating Muslim devotion. To enhance Islamic practice in Mindanao, Finley turned towards what he conceived of as the wellspring of the faith: the Middle East, and specifically, the Ottoman Empire. With its intermittent support of a global caliphate, its claims to modernity and its myriad educational institutions, Istanbul beckoned to Finley's scientific and ethnological mind-set. There, in one of the 'various institutes of learning at or near', the Americans might just find one of those 'accredited' teachers of Islamic faith for whom they were searching.[48] Indeed, Finley believed that an educator from the Ottoman Empire could provide a panacea for all that ailed Moroland:

> A modern Mohammedan from Constantinople, selected with due care and official approval, may be brought to the Moro Province to aid the government in successfully combatting the vicious habits of the Moros that now so seriously retard their progress.[49]

Once brought to Mindanao, this cosmopolitan, modern Mohammedan could thus 'instruct as to the provisions of Al Koran and the American laws

against vice, slavery, unlawful use of weapons, and of resistance to lawful authority'.[50] By inculcating 'loyalty to . . . the government', this Turkish teacher would help to fashion 'good Mohammedans'.[51]

The enthusiasm for Middle Eastern forms of Islam and its perceived tempering influence spilled beyond the governor's office to the larger colonial milieu of Zamboanga. The *Mindanao Herald*, the mouthpiece of the settler community and a one-time apologist for US Army massacres, held up the Muslims of the Middle East as an exemplar of proper behaviour. In one article titled 'The Folly of Juramentado', for example, the editorialist rhetorically queried local Moros, asking 'do you not know that Turkey, Persia, and other Muhammadan countries . . . live in peace with the surrounding nations, whether the latter are Muhammadan or non-Muhammadan?' The editorialist then argued that 'juramentado far from carrying out the precepts of the Koran violates its express commands'. The article concluded with a final invidious comparison between Moros and Muslims from the rest of the Islamic world:

> How can such an inconsiderable portion of the Islamic world . . . create the new religious doctrine of the juramentado which enjoins the taking of life and which is not practiced by the Arabs, nor Turks, nor Egyptians, nor Berbers, nor Persians, nor Indians, nor Malays, nor by anyone else on the face of the earth?

Although the *Mindanao Herald* invoked the 'Arabs' and the 'Turks' mostly as polemical foils, it still nonetheless attested to a willingness, however tentative, to enlist the larger Islamic world in their campaign to subdue resistance in Mindanao.[52]

The Ottoman Connection and Trans-imperial Synchronicity

Amid this curiosity and search for the sacred in the Middle East, Governor Finley embarked on his 1913 trip to Istanbul with the objective of recruiting a 'modern' Mohammedan official for service in Zamboanga. Among other things, the Turkish instructor 'should be recognized as an official of the Moro Province and to that extent given a title, such for example, as Moro Agent and Instructor, Traveling Moro Deputy, or Provincial Moro Advisor'. Finley also clarified that 'that he should be paid at least a nominal salary, under such official designation and permitted to occupy a desk in the Provincial Building at Zamboanga'.[53] Finley thus aspired to incorporate this new Ottoman official into the apparatus of the American colonial state and to imbue the colonial Moroland administration with the legitimacy of transnational Islamic connections.

The early 1910s marked a significant period of transition and transformation within the Ottoman Empire itself, a period of flux that perhaps provided an important opening to a figure like Major Finley. Indeed, the resonance of Finley's overtures in various Ottoman circles suggests that this American officer was not simply an idiosyncratic meteorologist turned autodidact Orientalist; his views conformed to cosmopolitan trends in the conceptualisation of religion, the 'sacred' and the power of the state that transcended national, imperial or even religious boundaries. On some level, of course, a passing Ottoman interest in the Philippines or John Finley's overtures should not be all that surprising.[54] The history of Ottoman interest in Southeast Asia extends back to a sixteenth-century age of empire and exploration across the vastness of the Indian Ocean, when merchants, travellers and even soldiers materialised on shores as distant as those of Sumatra.[55] While such connections abated in subsequent centuries, by the late nineteenth and early twentieth century, the Ottoman Sultan Abdülhamid II sought to retrieve these glories and to reassert the kingdom's role in the wider Islamic world as it jostled for influence among the European Great Powers. Indeed, as nationalist movements and Great Power rivals peeled off most of the old Ottoman territories in Europe and the Balkan Peninsula, Abdülhamid II turned to a specifically Islamic identity, or what some scholars have referred to as an 'Islamic *Osmanlılık*', to compensate for these losses. Increasingly, Abdülhamid II turned to Asia to reclaim lost glories and promote the idea of an Ottoman-led global caliphate.[56]

Beyond overarching histories and politics, it would also have made sense for the Turkish state to refer Finley to the bureaucracy of the Shaykh-al-Islām. The late Ottoman period witnessed the consolidation of this religious administrative body as the principal fulcrum of Islamic law in the wider empire, appointing judges (*qāḍīs*) and issuing *fatwa*s in the outlying provinces.[57] The preponderance of these *qāḍīs* circulated between surrounding Arabic provinces and Istanbul, as embodied by the history of the Palestinian-born

Wajīh Al-Kilānī, but it seems plausible that the Shaykh al-Islām administrators might come to see the dispatch of an Islamic religious scholar to an even more distant corner of the Islamic world as a natural extension of its pre-existing mission.

However, it is also important to note that by the time Finley arrived in Istanbul, Sultan Abdülhamid II no longer occupied the throne. In 1908, the Young Turk Revolution had forced the sovereign to abdicate and within the next few years, a new force, the Committee of Union and Progress (CUP), had emerged as the dominant Ottoman political power. While the sultanate survived Abdülhamid's abdication, with Mehmed V occupying the throne from 1909 to 1918, the monarch by this time constituted little more than a figurehead; genuine authority had passed to the CUP. It is not my purpose here to provide a thorough overview of the CUP ascendancy spearheaded by a triumvirate of CUP military leaders, Enver, Talat and Jamal Pasha. Of relevance to our story here, the Young Turks and the CUP can be seen in relation to an amalgam of competing and somewhat contradictory tendencies, of army officers and constitutionalists, parliamentarians and political activists jostling for power, simultaneously promoting reform and a more powerful, even authoritarian role for the state. CUP leaders and activists did not entirely repudiate the Islamic *Osmanlılık*, but they did generally advocate for a type of Ottomanism that featured Muslims, Jews and Christians as equal citizens. The role of Islam in statecraft, in the view of most CUP leaders, should be circumscribed. Thus, John Finley arrived in Istanbul at a moment of profound change.[58]

In spite of the turn away from an explicitly Islamic view of Ottoman nationalism, the emergence of arguably more 'reformist' factions within the CUP played a role in driving Ottoman enthusiasm for the Shaykh Wajīh mission and engendering a degree of synchronicity with an American like Major Finley around issues of state control and the cultivation of a specific, disciplined regime of the sacred. The historian William Clarence-Smith has highlighted the competing and somewhat opaque motivations of the CUP in supporting Shaykh Wajīh's travels, noting that one of the ruling CUP triumvirate, Ahmad Cemal Pasha, did take up Shaykh Wajīh's cause.[59] Another member of the governing Ottoman CUP troika, Ismail Enver Pasha, was identified in American diplomatic cables as a key catalyst for a subsequent trip that Wajīh undertook to the United States in 1915 after he left the Philippines. Ismail perhaps supported Wajīh as part of a larger ambition he had of sponsoring a *jihād* against Britain and other Allied Powers during the First World War.[60] Indeed, Clarence-Smith noted that Ismail funded Wajīh's trip specifically to spread information to the United States about *jihād* undertaken by various Muslim groups in the 'vicinity of Hindistan'.[61] Shaykh Wajīh, however, in the view of Clarence-Smith, appeared much more interested in promoting the case of Philippine Muslims to American rulers and securing passage back to Mindanao than furthering Ottoman imperial ambitions.[62] Before the Ottomans joined the war, however, why would certain factions of the government have expressed an interest in Finley's March 1913 visit to Istanbul? Several documents left behind in a Mindanoan library provide information on a possible conjuncture. Among these sources are 'Greetings to the Musselmen of the Philippine Islands',[63] a message from the Bab-i-Fetva Bureau of Correspondence in the ministry of the Shaykh al-Islām,[64] and a message from the Persian ambassador to Istanbul reflecting interest among both the Qajar Iranian and Egyptian royal families.[65] As English translations, these letters merit scepticism. However, they potentially illuminate an alignment of relatively 'progressive' interest in Istanbul and Mindanao around Shaykh Wajīh.

On the one hand, these three translated letters could be interpreted as a heavily embroidered or even invented fiction of the American authorities. Much of the language in the letter on progress, good government and Islam, sounds almost interchangeable with the sentiments expressed elsewhere by Finley. For example, the general 'Greetings to the Musselmen of the Philippines Islands' commended 'the tolerant spirit manifested by the United States toward all religions, and especially on behalf of Mohammedanism . . . by organizing for the Moslems of the Philippines a special form of government, which is adapted to their intelligence, customs, and religion'.[66] That same letter also emphasised economic progress, lecturing Muslim Filipinos that however 'faithful to Islam your prosperity must depend upon agricultural and commercial efficiency'. The Bab-i-Fetva letter echoed such preoccupations, instructing Filipino Muslims that 'vessels on the sea are going everywhere. Upon such vessels you must make commerce and go in search of food.'[67] In the Persian letter, meanwhile, enthusiasm for education assumed a scripturalist form, as the ambassador not only praised 'the even-handed Government of the United States', but also cited 'chapter 39 verse 13' to tell Muslim Filipinos to 'Seek knowledge from the cradle to the grave.'[68]

Furthermore, even injunctions against rebelliousness seemed to mimic the coercive proscriptions of Major Finley against *juramentado*, as when the Bab-i-Fetva letter warned that 'Moslems of the Philippines also should keep aloof from offenses and vices such as murder, gambling, drunkenness, prostitution, robbery', and other 'deeds' rendered by 'the Qur'ān absolutely forbidden'.[69] The greetings concluded with a paean to 'the liberal, humane, and progressive policy of the great American government', as well as the statement that 'we are happy to acknowledge and welcome you as our friends and co-religionists in the Faith and Virtues of Islam'.[70] Even accounting for the niceties of diplomacy, this celebration of the United States, with its pronounced echoes of Finley's own thought and ideals, strains the credibility of these letters.

However, even if one may dismiss these translations as little more than a projection of Finley's ideology onto a Muslim correspondent, certain aspects of these letters do suggest real engagement with Istanbul. First, the general address to the Muslims of the Philippines assigned Major Finley the honorific title of *vekïl-i-mutlak*, a term with long-standing resonance in the Ottoman court meaning 'absolute deputy' or 'main servant' of the sultan.[71] Given the fact that this term does not circulate widely outside Turkey, its deployment in this context hints at the possibility of a deeper alliance between Finley and his Ottoman interlocutors.

More convincing proof of an Ottoman–American alignment, however, arises in references to the liberal Turkish milieu. Specifically, the address to the Muslims of the Philippines endorsed 'the high conception and progressive views of the mission of your Vekil-i-Moutlac [sic] as expressed by Hallideh Hanoum in the Tanin, published at Constantinople on 9 April 1913'.[72] Halide Edib Hanoum, also known as Halide Edib Adıvar, was the daughter of an Ottoman palace official who attended Istanbul's American College for Girls and later emerged as a leading Turkish writer and feminist.[73] Indeed, Adivar is often hailed in historiographies of the Middle East as one of the cutting-edge feminists of her age.[74] Adıvar also retained the connections with the United States that she had developed at the American College, serving as a key American–Ottoman liaison during the First World War.[75] She also wrote a regular series of columns and articles for the *Tanin* newspaper, a leading and relatively reformist example of the profusion of newspapers that emerged during the heady days of the early CUP period.

While the interviewer is never clearly identified, the *Tanin* newspaper ran an extended question-and-answer piece between Major John Finley and an interlocutor who appears to be Halide Adıvar on 9 April 1913, a Q&A illustrative of a significant degree of imperial synchronicity. The Ottoman Turkish-language article, ran under the title 'An Appeal to the Seat of the Caliphate Concerning the Muslim Filipinos', contained a mixture of direct quotations attributed to Finley alongside a number of revealing interjections from his interlocutor (presumably Adıvar). Finley's responses by and large dovetailed with his English-language writings, perhaps even tilting even further in the direction of emphasising local Moro 'savagery' and the American–Ottoman role in promoting spiritual and sacral uplift. Indeed, Finley informed his interlocutor that 'the morals of these people have been spoiled through age-long wars and strife', and that 'they have become savage, neglecting entirely the fundamentals of Islam'. Only through the assistance of Ottoman collaborators, Finley asserted, could Moros come 'to know their faith' and, more fundamentally, 'make them live and be human'. Islam and Ottoman Islamic pedagogy would thus transform Muslim Filipinos from savagery to fully-fledged humanity.[76]

Much about Finley's venture, including both his civilising mission and approach to religion, resonated with Adıvar and in fact seemed to offer a template for remedying problems at home in the Ottoman territories of Anatolia. Finley's discussion of religion, in particular, would have appealed to those reformers most interested in promoting equal Ottoman citizenship among Christians, Jews and Muslims. Finley proclaimed that 'America accepts its own subjects' religion as an internal affair related to their consciences. Preferring or venerating this or that religion goes against the government's foundation.' However, this did not mean that Americans or Ottomans should not help to cultivate the sacred 'moral precepts' and 'commandments of Islam'.[77]

Such sentiments struck a chord with Adıvar. Writing poetically of

Finley's 'white hair crowning his beardless face like snow, his eyes sincere and kind like an old child', Adıvar presented Finley as 'thinking tolerantly and compassionately about his Muslim children in the Philippines'. Finley's experiences in the Philippines also echoed what Adıvar saw 'in poor and orphaned Anatolia that is Muslim and Turkish like us'. Indeed, Adıvar discerned here an opportunity for closing the 'civilizational gap' in a humane way and for promoting an 'Ottoman identity in the East' with its diversity of 'peoples and families'. For too long, in Adıvar's view, past Ottoman governments had perpetrated 'terrors and injustices' in the Balkan Peninsula, contributing to revolts and the eventual loss of those territories. However, she hoped that Finley, 'this great man who wants to build an edifice out of these . . . savage tribes with faith, morals, moderation, and civilization', would provide an example for a new generation of Turks to cultivate the sacred, to allow 'these new Turks, the self-sacrifice and intelligence to build a new and strong edifice, a government, and a life together with the compatriots of what little land remains to them'. The recurring possibility of violence against 'savage', rural Anatolians remained a strong undercurrent, but Adıvar, much like Finley, hoped that a 'new and strong' state could cultivate a proper appreciation of the bounded role of the sacred and thus promote 'respect' for 'its subjects' rights, lives, and consciences'.[78]

In sum, the nexus between John Finley, Halide Adıvar and the CUP reveals that the major's mission to Istanbul amounted to more than an imaginative act of projection by a colonial autodidact. It also attested to a genuine synchronicity of interests between muscular progressive factions in two empires, one non-Muslim and one Muslim, both seeking to bind the sacred as a means to discipline unruly subjects. The itinerary followed by Shaykh Wajīh al-Kilānī from Turkey to Mindanao thus represented imperatives of coercion as much it did cosmopolitanism, the desire of one power to reassert its imperial vigour and another to suppress *juramentado* attacks. But would the Muslims of Southeast Asia see this journey by Shaykh Wajīh as an imperial power grab, or as a new beginning on the straight Path of Islam?

Ḥaji Abdullah Nuño and the Reception of Shaykh Wajīh in the Philippines

After the long series of negotiations between John Finley and the Ottoman authorities, Shaykh Wajīh al-Kilānī finally departed from Istanbul in October 1913, wending his way through the Indian Ocean from Mecca to Singapore and boarding a German steamship for the last stage of his journey to the Moroland capital of Zamboanga, arriving in late January 1914.[79] In turn, John Finley travelled back to his erstwhile post in defiance of the Moroland Army brass, greeting al-Kilānī and pronouncing him the 'Shaykh al-Islām of the Philippines'. In addition to Finley, another important personage who greeted al-Kilānī and the 100 Muslim Filipino *ḥaji*s accompanying him from Mecca was Ḥaji Abdullah Nuño. This local Samal leader, arguably, played just as important a role as Finley in orchestrating the journey of Shaykh Wajīh through his initial petition to the Ottoman sultan.[80] Moreover, as we shall see, the life of Ḥaji Nuño reflected the imprint of conquest and coercive cosmopolitanism in all its myriad forms.

Ḥaji Abdullah Nuño's activities encapsulated the possibility that Finley's dream of 'modern Mohammedanism' might permeate the local population.[81] A victim of the Spanish expulsion of Sama Muslims from Balangingi Island in 1848, Nuño spent most of his childhood far from home, on the predominantly Catholic island of Luzon in the Philippine north. Once there, Nuño 'was used . . . as a houseboy and compelled to submit to Christian baptism', before being 'shipped to . . . [a] hacienda'.[82] Thus exiled into an alien environment, Nuño toiled along with his Samal peers on a tobacco plantation, one of the biggest profit generators for Spanish colonialism. While details of his youth in Luzon remain murky, historians do know that Nuño later carved out a position as the Samal leader and accumulated some wealth.[83]

The experiences of dispossession, of cosmopolitanism without a choice, however, did not sever young Abdullah's attachment to his religion, but instead enhanced it, propelling the exile to make the long journey to Mecca for *ḥajj* in the 1880s at a moment when few beyond the sultan of Sulu's retinue or a small circle of *datu* made the journey from Mindanao.[84] Through the pilgrimage, he acquired a religious legitimacy that would allow him to consolidate his leadership position. Nuño simultaneously cultivated a relationship with the Spanish authorities such that he 'secured permission from the Spanish Governor-General to return with some of his people to Zamboanga'.[85] Amid the searing crucible of exile, Nuño had thus proven to be adept at negotiating between the colonial Catholic and indigenous Muslim realms.

By all accounts, in the years following Ḥaji Nuño's return to the Zambaonga Peninsula, the Samal leader continued to balance a savvy ability to manoeuvre through colonial politics with a commitment to his community. For instance, as early as 1904, the US government assisted Nuño in brokering with the Spanish tobacco planter in Isabel to permit the remaining Samal exiles to return to Mindanao.[86] After this agreement, Nuño became a stalwart supporter of the US colonial regime and of John Finley. Assisting the Americans with the construction of a local government in Zamboanga, Nuño sat on the Zamboanga provincial board, participated in the colonial tribal ward system and helped police his community. The erstwhile exile embraced the coercive cosmopolitan ethos espoused by the Americans, observing that 'we all have an equal part [in local administration], Muslim, Filipino, and America'.[87]

At the same time that Nuño immersed himself in the colonial milieu, he continued to engage with currents of Islamic reformism that he likely encountered on his sojourn to the Middle East. Among other things, Nuño invited a range of religious scholars from around the wider Islamic world to his home district of Taluksangay, a small fishing village of Samal Muslims located on the outskirts the colonial capital of Zamboanga. The personages invited by Nuño included a Hadrami scholar named Shaykh Muḥammad Bahsuan, an Arab from Mecca named Shaykh Aḥmad Muṣṭafā, Sr and Shaykh ʿAbd al-Ghānī of Banjermas from Borneo. As a result, this once unassuming coastal district became a magnet for thousands of devout Muslims from Sulu, Lanao, Cotabato and the entire Mindanao–Sulu region.[88]

It was this context of cosmopolitan charisma, borne of coercion but re-shaped by Mindanaoan Muslims for their own purposes, which set the local stage for the arrival of John Finley and Shaykh Wajīh al-Kilānī. While information attesting to the local reception of Shaykh Wajīh is scarce, we do know that Ḥaji Nuño assisted Major Finley and mobilised thousands of locals for a grand welcome procession in Taluksangay. Indeed, the governor of Mindanao and Sulu from 1913 to 1920, Frank Carpenter, reported that al-Kilānī 'was met with great formality and introduced accordingly to a great concourse of Mohammedans from various parts of Mindanao–Sulu including all resident Turkish and Malay Mohammedan missionaries . . . which was . . . impressive'.[89] Furthermore, the governor reported that the Ottoman sojourner strove 'to purify Mohammedanism', a phrase then popular in reformist Muslim circles from Ottoman Istanbul and India to the Malay-speaking regions, perhaps suggesting that Ḥaji Nuño transmitted some of the spirit of religious renovation back to the Philippines. This event seemed to signal an end to the battles of pacification and the start of a newfound moment of Islamic cosmopolitanism inadvertently borne from the coercive workings of two empires, one Muslim and one non-Muslim.

Shaykh Wajīh in Southeast Asia: Cosmopolitan Currents and the True Path of Islam

The enthusiasm that permeated Taluksangay and Zamboanga, moreover, spilled beyond Mindanao's shores throughout the Indo-Malay Archipelago. Shaykh Wajīh had passed through key regional hubs of reformist Islam like Penang and Singapore. On his journey to Mindanao, the people he had encountered, as well as the 'resident Turkish and Malay missionaries' in the Philippines, appeared to provide a highly efficient conduit for the transmission of information back through the Muslim 'Lands below the Winds' of Southeast Asia. Events in Zamboanga, Taluksangay and later in Manila reverberated back to the Straits Settlements, generating newspaper articles in Jawi-language journals of Muslim reformers like *Neracha* in Penang, as well as in English-language standards like the *Singapore Free Press and Mercantile Advertiser*.[90] From these cosmopolitan hubs, the information then radiated outward to Sumatra in the Netherlands East Indies, catalysing coverage in the *Sinar Sumatra* and the well-known organ of religious reform in Padang, *al-Munīr*.[91] The odyssey of Shaykh Wajīh thus emerged as a region-wide sensation.

The coverage of Shaykh Wajīh's journey in one particular newspaper, *al-Munīr*, deserves special consideration for the way it accentuates a surprising synchronicity in the thought of colonial rulers and reformist Muslims, a synchronicity that shows how deeply modern disciplinary ideas of 'religion' had permeated Southeast Asian Muslim communities of the time. There was much in the two-page article, as reported and translated by the Dutch colonial expert on Islam, Ph. S. van Ronkel, that might conform to expectations of a leading journal of Islamic thought. The author extolled the capacity of Shaykh Wajīh to impart religious wisdom, to 'hold meetings with people every day after the midday and evening prayers', and to help point 'them toward the true teachings of the faith in addition to easing the path'. Van Ronkel further indicated in accordance with the *al-Munīr* article that before Shaykh Wajīh, there had been 'no Qadi in this Land' of the Philippines. The arrival of an Ottoman official with 'the title of Shaykh al-Islām' who served 'as a proxy to the caliph' and was 'entrusted . . . with control of all affairs having to do with religion' could thus only advance the cause of Islam in the Philippines and across Southeast Asia.[92]

The more surprising dimension of *al-Munīr* reportage, however, rested in its glowing assessment of American involvement. According to van Ronkel, the reformist journal betrayed little ambivalence over the fact that it was the US government that 'gave him [Wajīh] the title of Shaykh al-Islām', or that this religious official travelled 'aboard a warship'. Quite to the contrary, *al-Munīr* lauded the United States for conforming with the dictates 'of the holy law of the Prophet', and even cast it as an example worthy of emulation. Van Ronkel then reported that the Sumatran Muslim author of this *al-Munīr* article asked why the Dutch did not embrace a similar approach to the Muslims of Sumatra? Would the 'appointment of a religious official with government support also help control our land' in Indonesia much like it did in the Philippines? Echoing American and Ottoman rationales, moreover, the article argued that such an appointment ensured that 'religious affairs would be completely represented and promoted, and that there be no strife with respect to religion'. The writer even suggested that with a 'Shaykh al-Islām' in the East Indies, 'everything would be perfect, quiet, and orderly'.[93]

Muslim reformers in West Sumatra, in essence, reproduced the logic of colonial control expressed by John Finley and attempted to re-deploy it against the Dutch as a condition of possibility, as a means to extract concessions in the religious realm. Violence only persisted because of the disrespect evinced by administrators towards Islam. By contrast, if the Dutch regime heeded the American example of goodwill, facilitated the travel of learned *ʿulamāʾ*, and promoted 'religion' within a circumscribed but sacred sphere, peace would prevail. 'Agreement between us and the government,' argued *al-Munīr*, could then be reached. The promotion the 'true' path of Islam thus appeared to offer a cosmopolitan route beyond political antagonism, and the experiment of a relatively junior officer in the US military appeared to present an opportunity to the Dutch colonial regime – if only they would take it.

Conclusion: the Limits of Cosmopolitanism in a World of Coercion

The appropriation and re-deployment of Major Finley's language of colonial control by the *al-Munīr* writer, however, also contained a telling bit of irony that foretold the limitations of a cosmopolitanism borne of coercion. Originally, the American soldier had not disparaged his Dutch counterparts or imagined that his experiment might somehow sow political discord in neighbouring colonies. Quite to the contrary, Finley regarded the Dutch regime as a model that Moroland rulers should attempt to emulate. 'If the Moros' religion had been respected,' Finley contended, 'all else would have been easy. The Dutch in the East Indies, with their 35,000,000 of Mohammedans, know that.'[94] This assessment, of course, took little cognizance of the infamous, four decade-long Aceh war in Sumatra, where colonial powers displayed scant respect for Muslim religion and upwards of 15 per cent of the local population perished.[95] The Dutch model of tolerance inspiring Finley was mostly a fiction.

Perhaps, then, it is unsurprising that the Dutch responded to the news of John Finley's Shaykh Wajīh experiment with alarm rather than pleasure. Van Ronkel had noticed *al-Munīr*'s Philippine reporting in the course of a survey of the Islamic religious press in West Sumatra, and forwarded it to Snouck Hurgronje, the foremost Dutch expert on Islam and the architect of colonial counter-insurgency efforts in Aceh. On some level, Snouck's formulation of tolerance for Islam as religion but repression of Islam as political fanaticism seemed to dovetail with the thinking of Finley.[96] For all of his interest in respect, after all, the American major counselled military intervention against recalcitrant Muslims when necessary.

However, in his characteristically imperious way, Snouck expressed contempt for Finley's efforts to promote a cosmopolitan Muslim circuit from Istanbul to Mindanao. In a letter to the Netherlands Colonial Minister, Snouck described the travel of the 'so-called Shaykh-ul-Islam of the Philippines' and his attempts to convey 'friendship' to credulous colonial officials from Beirut to Manila. These professions of friendship, according to Snouck, constituted little more than a ruse to 'convey the impression to the native population' of the Philippines that he wielded great influence with the Americans and to disseminate the nefarious ideologies of pan-Islamism. Such 'trust' in the intentions of the Shaykh Wajīh was 'misplaced'. Cultivating a bounded sphere of sacred spirituality among Muslims, while perhaps part of the disciplinary logics of the march towards modernity described by anthropologists like Talal Asad, hardly comprised a seamless or frictionless process that colonial powers implemented without protest. Although Hurgronje never mentioned Major Finley by name, he obliquely disparaged him quipping that 'one does not only need to be naive, but also of the highest imprudence to act on such expressions in light of the unanimous hostility of the unofficial as well as the free pan-Islamic press' in Istanbul and Egypt. For Hurgronje, the imperative of coercion took precedence; to support 'pan-Islam' as embodied by Shaykh Wajīh was malfeasance of the highest order.[97]

Ultimately, it was not just Dutch scholars and administrators who recoiled against Shaykh Wajīh's journey, but also the American colonial establishment in Mindanao. Major Finley had framed his mission to find a 'modern Mohammedan' in terms of quelling *juramentado* resistance and realising conquest. However, for most of his counterparts, the arrival of Shaykh Wajīh al-Kilānī promised to amplify rather than ameliorate Muslim threats. While some American colonials praised Middle Easterners in the abstract, a real Ottoman Muslim religious scholar in their midst was quite another matter. The incoming governor of the Province of Mindanao and Sulu, Frank Carpenter, lamented the 'troublesome' impact of the 'so-called Sheik ul-Islam' upon the 'potentialities of public order'. Carpenter regarded Taluksangay not as a site of some cosmopolitan 'modern Mohammedanism', but as 'the great stronghold of Mohammedan religious fervor and propaganda in Mindanao-Sulu' and as 'a source of opposition to the good purposes of the government'.[98] Personal attitudes (and annoyances) towards Major

Finley also probably factored into Governor John J. Pershing's assessment of him as a 'pessimistic windbag of the most inflated variety'.[99]

The commotion over the arrival of al-Kilānī on Zamboanga's shores would, ultimately, scuttle the dreams of installing a permanent Shaykh al-Islām of the Philippines. Although Finley intended that al-Kilānī should serve a term of eighteen months, machinations for his removal began almost immediately. Frank Carpenter, in his capacity as the new Mindanao and Sulu governor, spearheaded this effort. Ruing the fact that 'a written contract appears to have been entered into by Finley' with the Ottoman scholar, Carpenter observed 'it was not an entirely simple matter to eliminate this distinguished individual from the Philippines'. However, the governor arranged just such an outcome, as a military transport spirited Shaykh Wajīh out of Mindanao to Manila and back to Istanbul. Although al-Kilānī would eventually go to the United States to 'appeal to the president', Carpenter reported, 'the matter settled itself by his timely death . . . near Washington'. This contingency helped to ensure that 'Mindanao–Sulu may be brought under effective Government control'. For all of Finley's grandiose rhetoric to engage with the Islamic world, the era of the Shaykh al-Islām of the Philippines would be abbreviated indeed.[100]

The ejection of Shaykh Wajīh from the Philippines reveals that for all the contradictions and inadvertent opportunities opened up by imperialism, colonised Muslim peoples could not easily outrun the long shadow of coercion as a framing factor in constructions of Islamic cosmopolitanism. Ottoman and American military officials might temporarily align around 'modern Mohammedanism', and *ʿulamāʾ* might traverse trans-imperial circuits to 'purify' Islam. Local Muslims might even secure prominent places in colonial administration while burnishing their status as religious leaders. However, as soon as the colonial version of 'modern' Islam began to morph into something broader, into an ethical project of commitment that transcended boundaries and promised religious community, imperial anxieties welled to the surface and the reflex to repress prevailed. Even the explicit mimesis of colonial narratives like those found in *al-Munīr* proved too much to bear when deployed against the short-term political interests of empire. Of course, none of this is to say that the contradictions and openings produced by colonial rule did not have important consequences. Possibility denied could well turn into movements of anti-colonial political consciousness and nationalism deferred. Yet the contingent and ultimately fleeting nature of alignments across colonial and religious boundaries exemplifies the limitations of coercive cosmopolitanism in practice. However important travel, mobility and the delineation of sacred spaces might be for constituting imperial state power, absent genuine ethical content commitment, such phenomena – what Bruce Lawrence refers to (Chapter 2, this volume) as 'counterfeit cosmopolitanism' – could prove ephemeral indeed.

Notes

1. Rogers, P. D., 'Major Finley and the Sheik Ul Islam: A Hitherto Unpublished Chapter of History', *Philippine Magazine* 36(1) (1939): 19.
2. Gedacht, Joshua, '"Mohammedan Religion made it Necessary to Fire": Massacres on the American Imperial Frontier from South Dakota to the Southern Philippines', in Alfred W. McCoy et al. (eds), *Colonial Crucible: Empire in the Making of the Modern American State* (Madison, WI: University of Wisconsin Press, 2009), p. 397.
3. Rogers, 'Major Finley and the Sheik Ul Islam', p. 19.
4. See Finley, John P., 'The Mohammedan Problem in the Philippines', *Journal of Race Development* 5(4) (1915): 353, 358.
5. Finley, 'The Mohammedan Problem in the Philippines', p. 359.
6. For the definitive analysis of this Tausug petition, see Kawashima, Midori, *The 'White Man's Burden' and the Islamic Movement in the Philippines: the Petition of the Zamboanga Muslim Leaders to the Ottoman Empire in 1912*, Monograph Series 17 (Tokyo: Institute of Asian Cultures, Sophia University, 2014).
7. Finley, John, 'A Review of the Moro Petition, its Origin, Scope and Purpose, and How its Object may be Realized in Aid of the American System of Control', p. 5, John P. Finley Papers, Military History Institute, Carlisle, PA, USA.
8. For Shaykh Wajīh al-Kilānī's Arab family background in Nablus, see Clarence-Smith, William, 'Wajīh al-Kilānī, Shaykh al-Islām of the Philippines and Notable of Nazareth, 1913–1916', in Mahmoud Yazbak et al. (eds), *Nazareth History and Cultural Heritage: Proceedings of the 2nd International Conference, Nazareth, July 2–5, 2012* (Nazareth: Municipality of Nazareth Academic Publications, 2013), pp. 173–4.
9. Clarence-Smith, 'Wajīh al-Kilānī, Shaykh al-Islām', p. 174.

10. Pollock, Sheldon I., 'Cosmopolitan and Vernacular in History', *Public Culture* 12(3) (2000): 599–600.
11. Ibid., pp. 600–1.
12. cooke, miriam and Bruce Lawrence, 'Introduction', in miriam cooke and Bruce B. Lawrence (eds), *Muslim Networks from Hajj to Hip Hop* (Chapel Hill, NC: University of North Carolina Press, 2005), p. 5.
13. Marsden, Magnus, 'Muslim Cosmopolitans? Transnational Life in Northern Pakistan', *Journal of Asian Studies* 67(1) (2008): 216.
14. Ricci, Ronit, *Islam Translated: Literature, Conversion, and the Arabic Cosmopolis of South and Southeast Asia* (Chicago, IL: University of Chicago Press, 2011), p. 15.
15. Ricci, *Islam Translated*, p. xx.
16. John Dewey, quoted in Papastephanou, Marianna, *Thinking Differently about Cosmopolitanism: Theory, Eccentricity and the Globalized World* (Boulder, CO: Paradigm, 2012), pp. 128–9.
17. Pollock, 'Cosmopolitan and Vernacular in History', p. 596.
18. Papastephanou, *Thinking Differently about Cosmopolitanism*, p. 21.
19. Ibid., p. 134.
20. Clarence-Smith, 'Wajīh al-Kilānī, Shaykh al-Islām', pp. 173–4.
21. Clarence-Smith, William G., 'Middle Eastern States and the Philippines under Early American Rule, 1899–1919', in Andrew Peacock and Annabel Teh Gallop (eds), *From Anatolia to Aceh: Ottomans, Turks, and Southeast Asia*, vol. 200, *Proceedings of the British Academy* (Oxford: Published for the British Academy by Oxford University Press, 2015), pp. 201–4.
22. Galway, Joseph G., 'J. P. Finley: the First Severe Storms Forecaster', *Bulletin American Meteorological Society* 66(1) (1985): 1389–95.
23. See, for example, John P. Finley's contribution to early Subanu ethnography: Churchill, William and John P. Finley, *The Subanu: Studies of a sub-Visayan Mountain Folk of Mindanao* (Washington, DC: Carnegie Institute of Washington, 1913).
24. Finley, 'A Review of the Moro Petition'.
25. For example, see Ugarte, Eduardo, 'Muslims and Madness in the Southern Philippines', *Pilipinas* 19(1/2) (1992): 20.
26. Dale, Stephen Frederic, 'Religious Suicide in Islamic Asia: Anticolonial Terrorism in India, Indonesia, and the Philippines', *Journal of Conflict Resolution* 32(1) (1988): 50–1.
27. Finley, 'A Review of the Moro Petition'.

28. Ibid. For discussion of the concept of 'modern Mohammedans', see Gedacht, Joshua, 'Holy War, Progress, and "Modern Mohammedans" in Colonial Southeast Asia', *The Muslim World* 100(4) (2015): 446–71.
29. Ibid.
30. Ibid.
31. Van der Veer, Peter, 'Colonial Cosmopolitanism', in Steven Vertovec and Robin Cohen (eds), *Conceiving Cosmopolitanism: Theory, Context, and Practice* (New York: Oxford University Press, 2002), p. 172.
32. Finley, 'A Review of the Moro Petition'.
33. Ibid.
34. This interest in delineating a sacred religious domain of 'inviolability' that was distinct from the messy realities of politics or nationalist thought was prominent in the thought of the foremost scholar of Islam (and colonial administrator), Snouck Hurgronje. Snouck cultivated Indonesian students, often known as '*ethici*' from the Dutch 'ethical policy', who could help to 'emancipate' local Muslims through their deep knowledge of the sacred dimensions of their religion and thus help deepen projects of colonial control. For this discussion of Snouck Hurgronje and the *ethici* , see Laffan, Michael, *Islamic Nationhood and Colonial Indonesia: the Umma below the Winds* (London: RoutledgeCurzon, 2003), p. 93.
35. Asad, Talal, *Formations of the Secular: Christianity, Islam, Modernity* (Stanford, CA: Stanford University Press, 2003), p. 33.
36. Ibid., pp. 34, 36.
37. Ibid., p. 36.
38. Finley, 'A Review of the Moro Petition'.
39. Ibid.
40. Ibid.
41. Asad, *Formations of the Secular*, p. 37.
42. Ibid., p.55; Walther, Karine, *Sacred Interests: The United States and the Islamic World, 1821–1921* (Chapel Hill: University of North Carolina Press, 2015), p. 167.
43. Finley, 'The Mohammedan Problem in the Philippines', p. 360.
44. Ibid.
45. Ibid.
46. Finley, 'A Review of the Moro Petition'.
47. Finley, 'The Mohammedan Problem in the Philippines', p. 362.
48. Finley, 'A Review of the Moro Petition'.

49. Ibid.
50. Ibid.
51. Ibid.
52. 'Folly of Juramentado', *Mindanao Herald*, 4 November 1911; Gedacht, 'Holy War, Progress, and "Modern Mohammedans"', pp. 159–60.
53. Finley, 'A Review of the Moro Petition'.
54. A. C. S. Peacock and Annabel Teh Gallop describe the enduring political, cultural and religious significance of the Ottoman Empire in both the imagination and actual diplomatic relations of a wide variety of Southeast Asian states, ranging from the Malay Peninsula to Sumatra to Mindanao. See Peacock, A. C. S. and Annabel Teh Gallop, 'Introduction. Islam, Trade, and Politics across the Indian Ocean: Imagination and Reality', in Andrew Peacock and Annabel Teh Gallop (eds), *From Anatolia to Aceh: Ottomans, Turks, and Southeast Asia* (Oxford: Oxford University Press, 2015), pp. 1–23. Isaac Donoso describes how various Philippine sultanates sought to contact the rulers of the Ottoman Empire, see Donoso, Isaac, 'The Ottoman Caliphate and Muslims of the Philippine Archipelago during the Early Modern Era', Andrew Peacock and Annabel Teh Gallop (eds), *From Anatolia to Aceh: Ottomans, Turks, and Southeast Asia* (Oxford: Oxford University Press, 2015), pp. 121–46.
55. Casale, Giancarlo, *The Ottoman Age of Exploration* (New York: Oxford University Press, 2010), pp. 4–5, 58.
56. For example, see Azmi Özcan, *Pan-Islamism: Indian Muslims, the Ottomans and Britain, 1877–1924* (Leiden, 1997).
57. Skovgaard-Peterson, Jakob, 'Levantine State Muftis: An Ottoman legacy?' in Elisabeth Özdalaga (ed.), *Late Ottoman Society: the Intellectual Legacy* (New York: RoutledgeCurzon, 2005), p. 279.
58. Ahmad, Feroz, *The Young Turks: the Committee of Union and Progress in Turkish Politics, 1908–1914* (New York: Oxford University Press, 1969), pp. 15–18; Psilos, Christopher, 'From Cooperation to Alienation: An Insight into Relations between the Serres Group and the Young Turks during the Years 1906–9', *European History Quarterly* 35(4) (2005): 547.
59. Clarence-Smith, 'Middle Eastern States and the Philippines', pp. 207–10
60. Ibid., pp. 210–11.
61. Ibid., p. 211.
62. Ibid., pp. 211–12.
63. 'Greetings to the Musselmen of the Philippine islands', n.d., Cameron Papers, Xavier University, Cagayan de Oro, Philippines.

64. 'Message to the Philippine Moslems, Bab-i-Fetva, Department of the Sheikh-Ul-Islmato, Bureau of Correspondence Constantinople', 1 June 1913, C-65.9-050-80, Cameron Papers, Xavier University, Cagayan de Oro, Philippines.
65. Ehtheshameh-Salaneh, 'Translation, Message of the Ambassador to our Dear Musulman Brethren in the Philippines', 8 June 1913, C-65-9-054-80, Cameron Papers, Xavier University, Cagayan de Oro, Philippines; Clarence-Smith, 'Middle Eastern States and the Philippines', pp. 205–7.
66. 'Greetings to the Musselmen of the Philippine Islands'.
67. 'Message to the Philippine Moslems, Bab-i-Fetva'.
68. Ehtheshameh-Salaneh, 'Translation, Message of the Ambassador'.
69. 'Message to the Philippine Moslems, Bab-i-Fetva'.
70. 'Greetings to the Musselmen of the Philippine Islands'.
71. Fodor, Pál, 'Sultan, Imperial Council, Grand Vizier: Changes in the Ottoman Ruling Elites and the Formation of the Grand Vizieral *Telḫī*', *Acta Orientalis Academia Scientiarum Hung. Tomus* 47(1/2) (1994): 74.
72. 'Greetings to the Musselmen of the Philippine Islands'.
73. Rappaport, Helen, *Encyclopedia of Women Social Reformers*, vol. 1 (Santa Barbara, CA: ABC-CLIO, 2001), p. 217.
74. Keddie, Nikki, *Women in the Middle East: Past and Present* (Princeton, NJ: Princeton University Press, 2007), p. 82.
75. Sonmez, Emel, 'The Novelist Halide Edib Adıvar and Turkish Feminism', *Die Welt des Islams* 14(1/4) (1973): 82, 88.
76. 'An Appeal to the Seat of the Caliphate concerning Muslim Filipinos', *Tanin*, 9 April 1913.
77. Ibid.
78. Ibid.
79. Kawashima, *The 'White Man's Burden'*, p. 11; Clarence-Smith, 'Wajīh al-Kilānī, Shaykh al-Islām', p. 174.
80. Kawashima, *The 'White Man's Burden'*, p. 8.
81. Mendoza, Helen N., 'The Moro Tapestry', in Antonio E. Orendain II (ed.), *Zamboanga Hermosa: Memories of the Old Town* (Manila: Filipinas Foundation, 1984), pp. 237–8.
82. Carpenter, F. W. to Carl Moore, Department Superintendent of Schools, 1 June 1918, Provincial Papers, Box 253: 'Manobos-Moros', Manuel L. Quezon Papers, Philippine National Library, Manila.
83. R. F. Wendover, 'The Balangingi Pirates', *Philippine Magazine* 38(8) (1941): 337.

84. Carpenter, 'Manobos-Moros'.
85. Ibid.
86. Wendover, 'The Balangingi Pirates', p. 337.
87. *Addresses on the Occasion of the Inauguration of Provincial Government at Zamboanga, September 1, 1914* (Zamboanga: s.n., 1914).
88. 'Taluksangay: The First Center of Islamic Propagation', *Zamboanga Today Online*, 13 June 2013, available at: http://www.zamboangatoday.ph/zamboangatoday/index.php/opinions/14211-taluksangay-the-first-center-of-islamic-propagation-hataman-a-new-breed-of-politician-basilan-has-ever-produced.html, last accessed 21 October 2013.
89. Carpenter, 'Manobos-Moros'.
90. Untitled, *Singapore Free Press and Mercantile Advertiser*, 21 April 1914, p. 6.
91. Van Ronkel, Ph. S. to the Director of Education and Worship, 11 September 1914, Bijlage [Appendix] X, pp. 32–33, in Mailrapporten [Mail Reports] bundle 4 April 1916, np. 54/670, het Archief van het Ministerie van Koloniën, 1900–1963: Openbaar Verbaal, 1901–1953, Invr. 1529, National Archives of the Netherlands, The Hague.
92. Van Ronkel to the Director of Education and Worship, 11 September 1914; *al-Munīr*, 11 March 1914.
93. Van Ronkel to the Director of Education and Worship, 11 September 1914; *al-Munīr*, 11 March 1914.
94. Finley, 'The Mohammedan Problem in the Philippines', p. 359.
95. Nordholt, Henk Schulte, 'A Genealogy of Violence', in Freek Colombijn and J. Thomas Lindblad (eds), *Roots of Violence in Indonesia: Contemporary Violence in Historical Perspective* (Leiden: Brill, 2002), p. 36.
96. Van Ronkel to Director of Education and Worship, 11 September 1914.
97. Hurgronje, Snouck to Minister of the Colonies, 12 March 1916, het archief van het Ministerie van Koloniën, 1900–1963: Openbaar Verbaal, 1901–1953, Invr. 1529, National Archives of the Netherlands, The Hague.
98. Carpenter, 'Manobos-Moros'.
99. John J. Pershing, quoted in Vandiver, Frank, *Black Jack: the Life and Times of John J. Pershing* (College Station, TX: Texas A&M University Press, 1977), pp. 1, 523.
100. Carpenter, 'Manobos-Moros'.

8

Bordering Malaya's 'Benighted Lands': Frontiers of Race and Colonialism on the Malay Peninsula, 1887–1902

Amrita Malhi[1]

Between 1891 and 1895, an armed uprising raged through the dense forest leading in and out of the hinterland of Pahang, a Malay Muslim polity on the east coast of the Malay Peninsula that had established its independence from Johor-Riau some three decades earlier. An offshoot and tributary of Melaka until its Portuguese conquest in 1511, Pahang's allegiance had followed the Melaka royal family to its new seat of power in Johor-Riau, which the Anglo-Dutch Treaty of 1824 later dismembered. Pahang, like Johor and the rest of the Peninsula, fell under Britain's sphere of influence, an assignation that – as Britain adopted a policy of 'forward movement' in the 1870s – ceased to operate as a passive British claim, becoming an active process of peninsular colonisation. In the late 1880s, after installing British Residents in Perak, Selangor and parts of Negeri Sembilan, Britain colonised Pahang, beginning with a treaty that installed a British Agent in 1887, followed by a Resident in 1888. This move 'consolidated British influence over the whole Peninsula east and west', as Frederick Weld, Governor of the Straits Settlements, stated in 1887,[2] with the additional effect that British territory now abutted Siamese tributaries across the width of the Peninsula.

This arrangement triggered a slow and subtle contest for these tributaries – polities where Britain recognised that Siam 'claim[ed] a right of interference' but not of sovereignty – the southernmost of which were Kedah, Kelantan and Terengganu.[3] Since leasing Penang Island from Kedah in 1786, the British had become amply familiar with Kedah's internal politics and relations with Siam, and now, from their new vantage point in Pahang, they had also gained an opportunity to observe Kelantan and Terengganu more closely than ever before. British officials worked to extend the reach of Pahang's new colonial state from its capital Pekan across its forested hinterland, whose extremities they aimed to secure, and whose human relationships they began to reshape. The new colonial state restructured local models of territoriality and practices of resource management, diverting the revenue streams of Pahang's hinterland chiefs, who had previously commanded access to land, cultivated goods, forest products and labour. In response to this intervention, in 1890 the district chief of Semantan, Dato' Bahaman, began to resist all cooperation with the British. He not only encouraged his followers to flout colonial laws, but also actively obstructed the establishment of a police station in his district. In 1891, he and his 700 followers killed three Sikh police officers and seized forty muskets, proceeding to sack Temerloh, the district capital.[4] In 1892, pursued by British troops, the rebels fled and sought refuge in Kelantan and Terengganu, from which they continued to launch raids on Pahang.

In recent historiography, discussions of this uprising refer to it as the 'Pahang War'. British officials of the time, however, preferred to refer to it only as a set of 'disturbances',[5] even though by 1892 it had already cost Britain $150,000 Straits dollars.[6] Its image refracted through an official, nationalist lens, the uprising is now usually imagined by Malaysians as a struggle for 'Malay tradition, Malay values, [and a] sense of Malay independence',[7] yet this view derives from the narrow, racial frame usually placed around the rebels' actions. This chapter expands this frame to include the wider context of the uprising, including larger, networked struggles set in concentric arenas of Islamic cosmopolitan political ferment. This context allowed Terengganu to become a centre of counter-colonial Islamisation to which the Pahang rebels turned to access resources to fuel their rebellion. The arenas in question consisted first of the Siamese tributaries, where a series of campaigns were waged by sultans, scholars, *ḥaji*s and chiefs against encroachments on their independence by both Siam and Britain – the two powers then enclosing them via 'competitive colonialisms'.[8] The second consisted of the dynamic, trans-local 'Muslim World', in which Muslims around the Indian Ocean littoral participated in a common project of counter-colonial world-making.[9] Late-nineteenth-century advances in European technologies and infrastructures fuelled faster, more frequent and more intense contacts between diverse Muslim communities even as they enabled British, French, Dutch and (in this region) Siamese colonial rule.[10] For some Muslims, such developments also fostered a new sense of shared space and subjectivity in which they could contest claims to superior civilisation made by their colonisers.[11]

Terengganu served as a channel for political developments across both these arenas between the outbreak of the Pahang War in 1891 and the production of the 1902 boundary separating Pahang from both Kelantan and Terengganu. Indeed, Terengganu became the central source of discursive and other political resources mobilised by the Pahang rebels, whose contact with its chief religious adviser, the Shaykh al-Islām Tokku Paloh (Sayyid ʿAbd al-Raḥmān b. Muḥammad al-ʿAydarūs), transformed their uprising. Under the shaykh's guidance, the Pahang rebels ceased narrating their actions in terms of lands and revenues and adopted a more universal language of *perang sabil* or 'holy war'. The shaykh – a scion of the prestigious al-ʿAydarūs line of Hadrami *sayyids* (descendants of the Prophet) – armed the rebels with *pelias* or amulets conferring invulnerability, swords traced with text from the Qurʾān and 100 new followers.[12] Bolstered by such contributions, the rebels returned to raid Pahang in 1894, killing the British Superintendent of Ulu Pahang district, E. A. Wise.[13] At this point, Acting British Resident Hugh Clifford determined he would pursue the rebels beyond Pahang's boundaries in case they continued to raid British positions with new followers mobilised by the shaykh.[14]

Clifford launched an expedition into Kelantan and Terengganu in 1895, only to find his efforts thwarted by locals, including Terengganu's royal establishment, and especially by Tokku Paloh. These figures' deftness in deflecting British inquiries was enabled by Terengganu's unique position, beyond the limits of Siam's southern reach, and of Britain's appetite for risk – it would not take Terengganu for fear of provoking a French countermove on Siam from Indochina. Unable to resolve such geopolitical concerns, Clifford and other British officials opted instead to tackle the immediate 'law and order' problem – by pressuring Siam to capture and kill the rebels. Britain also initiated a boundary between British territory and the rest of the Malay Peninsula, in which the nature of Siamese authority over its tributaries remained unresolved. The work of making this boundary, enacted in 1902, quickly accrued connotations of racial and civilisational hierarchy. In managing disruptive contagion from cosmopolitan Terengganu, the boundary upheld Britain's commitment to race as its preferred social technology for managing the political risks generated by its new and unruly Muslim subjects. It also allowed the British authorities to enclose and control emergent trans-local cosmopolitan formations, namely, by locating them outside their formal jurisdictional purview.

Framing the Pahang War

The Pahang War saw 500–700 rebels against the new colonial state, ranging with relative freedom between Pahang, on the one hand, and Kelantan and Terengganu, the 'free, wild places' to its north, on the other. These places, 'whither the law of the white men [had] not yet penetrated', were later dubbed the 'Benighted Lands' by Pahang's first British Agent (and later, its Resident) Hugh Clifford.[15] Yet Kelantan and Terengganu remained beyond the reach of 'white' law precisely because of the unresolved legal and geopolitical contests that surrounded them – contests that were underpinned by the very operation of European legal and territorial constructs. During this period, these constructs interacted with regional understandings of territory in ways that allowed these polities to retain a degree of autonomy, even while they became the subject of more frequent disputes between Britain and Siam.

First, their status as Siamese tributaries – which dated back to their distinct origins as polities in the 1700s – protected them from colonial encroachment by Britain, although Britain worked hard to be perceived as the coloniser of choice on the Peninsula.[16] Both Kelantan and Terengganu continued to pay regular tribute to Bangkok, at various times either accommodating or subverting regular attempts by Siam's ruler, King Chulalongkorn (Rama V, r. 1868–1910) to intervene in their domestic affairs. One such attempt had consisted of the publication in the 1869 Siamese government gazette of the title of the ruler of Terengganu, Sultan Zayn al-'Abidin III (r. 1881–1918), as 'governor' not 'sultan' following the king's visit to Terengganu in 1888. As Cecil Clementi Smith, Governor of the Straits Settlements, pointed out to the British Foreign Office, this was the 'appellation adopted by the Siamese Government in the case of the Rulers of States directly dependent on Siam'.[17] For Clementi Smith, such Siamese interventions were tantamount to sovereign claims on Terengganu, and Siam confirmed his suspicions in 1892 with an attempt to establish a post office in Terengganu's capital – which issued Siamese stamps.[18]

These moves, however, failed to achieve their desired outcome. Both Kelantan and Terengganu were arguably equally protected from Siam, this time by a second factor, the 1826 Burney Treaty, which listed them both as sites for free 'trade and intercourse' with Britain, which Siam was not permitted to 'obstruct or interrupt'.[19] This formulation placed them in an ambiguous and potentially different position from others it listed as specifically 'Siamese countries' – a status that nearby Kedah, another tributary, had been assigned. Kedah's treatment was a function of its occupation by Siam in 1821, although this occupation failed and Siam retreated in 1839 after the treaty was signed.[20] Kelantan and Terengganu were also protected from sharing the fate of Patani, further north, which Siam incorporated in 1785, partitioning it into seven smaller provinces in 1816 and successfully demoting its ruler from the rank of sultan to a governor.[21] Resulting from their dual status – protected by both Siam and Britain from each other's designs – Kelantan and Terengganu together were in effect a buffer zone, occupying a liminal frontier space between Britain and Siam.

This frontier space was, however, increasingly contested by both peninsular powers, and these polities' autonomy was becoming increasingly precarious as competition between Britain and Siam intensified. An 1888 letter by Governor Clementi Smith, which he wrote after King Chulalongkorn's visit to Terengganu, reflected his own determination to capture these tributaries instead, stating:

> there is no sort of doubt that the two States of Kelantan and Tringganu are independent of Siam. This being duly recognised, I see no reason why Tringganu should not, if the ruler wishes it, be placed under British protection, and yet at the same time the Treaty independence of Kelantan should

> be insisted upon by Her Majesty's Government. The encroachments of Siam should be resisted in every way . . .[22]

Such statements also reveal the motivations behind more frequent disputes between Britain and Siam during this period. On the one hand, Siam had already spent a century before the Pahang uprising consolidating its hold on Patani and its newer satellites, including Sai, Reman, Legeh and Setul, through its southern viceroyalty Ligor. [23] In response, British officials in Malaya attempted to push Siam back from what they feared was a continuing southern advance through a series of undermining measures, such as supporting a 'free' trade in muskets which was then transforming Terengganu into an arms bazaar.[24] In 1885, this support had resulted in the Siamese Consul approaching Clementi Smith's predecessor, Governor Weld, to request a restriction on British sales of 'gunpowder, arms and ammunition' to Terengganu, a request that Britain declined to entertain.[25] On the other hand, Siam perceived Britain's attitude as calculating, aimed at undermining its suzerainty over its tributaries – an assessment that was entirely correct. British officials and merchants hoped that Terengganu's guns, for example, might assist the frequent rebellions that the various tributaries were launching against the kingdom's southern outposts.[26]

Britain also waged a direct campaign against other Siamese claims as they came up from time to time, the most important case in the 1880s being that of Reman's – and therefore Siam's – claim to territory also claimed by British Perak.[27] British Consul-General in Siam Ernest Satow eventually intervened against the expansionist arguments made by officials in Malaya, aiming to defend Siam's territorial integrity for broader strategic purposes, namely, Britain's contest with France for Southeast Asian territory. In 1889, he used the Burney Treaty to argue that its text only prohibited obstructions to trade, and not assertions of political influence.[28] Meanwhile, Kelantan and Terengganu's own rulers remained alert throughout this period to both larger powers' strategies and tactics. For their part, they worked to complicate the contest as much as possible by further internationalising its dimensions – including by offering attractive land concessions to nationals from Britain's competitor powers, such as Germany. Such decisions were aimed at destabilising both their would-be colonisers even further still, and Terengganu, for example, issued its first such concession in 1889.[29] British officials in Malaya seized upon these concessions as still more evidence of the dangers Britain faced if it delayed colonising the entire Peninsula. Meanwhile, Terengganu's sultan continued to grant concessions over large areas of land, alienating much of its hinterland before his death in 1918.[30]

While legal constructs and diplomatic disputes provided cover for Kelantan and Terengganu's precarious, yet continued, autonomy, their densely forested landscapes were a physical screen for their function as 'free, wild places' and 'Benighted Lands'. A precursor to the idea of the 'ungoverned' space – a concept developed in the twenty-first century with the US RAND Corporation as an early pioneer[31] – the idea that Kelantan and Terengganu were 'wild' was a narrative device favoured by Clifford. The use of this device, however, foreclosed the possibility that important sections of these polities' populations were engaged in political activity aimed at thwarting British colonial power over them – activity that Clifford persistently failed to decode or understand. Even decades later, after much reflection over a long career in which he 'breathed frontier air, heard frontier talk, [and] dreamed frontier dreams',[32] Clifford continued to write works of creative non-fiction in which he dismissed the rebels' politics as mere 'fanaticism'. In his work, only fanaticism could explain the 'marvellous cohesion of the Muhamadans', and fuel their 'petty squabble' against British global paramountcy.[33] Further, just as the notion of ungoverned spaces now legitimises interventions in 'contested spaces within and between states where other types of actors rule',[34] so too did narratives of Kelantan and Terengganu's wildness prepare the ground for their future colonial conquest. These narratives therefore functioned to depoliticise cosmopolitan resistance by foreclosing the possibility that Muslim rebels might be capable of mobilising politically on their own terms, in spaces that only they could access or turn to such a purpose. Nevertheless, precisely the constraints then preventing British or Siamese officials from colonising these polities made their hinterland settlements – which were usually located next to rivers along the forest fringe – highly attractive to fugitive rebels. Conversely, the expansion of colonial government and governmentality was pushing these rebels out of Pahang, now within Britain's peninsular geo-body – or the 'operations of the technology of territoriality' then producing British Malaya as a spatial entity.[35]

The Pahang War was a revolt against precisely these operations, consisting of a series of mobile and violent hit-and-run raids on British colonial positions in which rebels moved between Pahang and the Benighted Lands via the Tembeling River and its tributaries. Their specific routes now lie submerged beneath Lake Kenyir – a hydroelectric dam completed on the Kenyir River, a tributary of the Terengganu River, in 1985.[36] In the 1890s, however, the Terengganu's tributaries were the means by which rebels could escape Britain's territorial reach. For example, when followed upstream from Pahang past a series of rapids, the Tembeling could lead travellers up the mountainous fold – 1,000 feet high in the Royal Asiatic Society's estimate – that separated its tributaries' watersheds from those of the Limau or Lebir rivers.[37] In any case, and further reflecting the paucity of colonial knowledge about this area, the published version of Clifford's expedition report lacks anything other than a rough sketch map. The original version, published in 1895, omitted his original 'Inclosure 1' – apparently a map he created and submitted with his report – and the map is therefore not present in the version republished by the Malaysian Branch of the Royal Asiatic Society.[38]

Tracking the Pahang Rebels

Most of Clifford's narrative descriptions of Kelantan and Terengganu deployed tropes of darkness and obscured vision to associate these polities' internal political lives with deception and intrigue. On the one hand, the Terengganu authorities were actively deceiving him, working to obscure the rebels' movements to preserve their capacity to destabilise the British and protect Terengganu's independence. On the other, Clifford's expedition had been joined by Siamese officials, who he argued were also duplicitous, working behind the scenes to prove to the Terengganu court that Siam would back its interests against the British, thereby seeming like a more desirable coloniser. Together, these layers of obfuscation prevented Clifford from 'seeing like a state'[39] – in this case by reading the rebels' movements and intentions so that he could apprehend them. Clifford's writing brims with metaphors depicting Terengganu's lack of visibility, for example, in his discussion of the sultan and Tokku Paloh working together to 'throw dust in [his] eyes'.[40] In his 1929 edition of *Bush-Whacking*, published thirty years later, Clifford stretches the metaphor of poor visibility even further still. For example, he wrote of his view being obscured by a 'cloak of mist',[41] while swirling, muddy rivers hid 'submerged' corpses.[42] These rivers flowed through an unmapped landscape, in which Clifford himself was forced to act as an eye,[43] even while his own eyes were still growing accustomed to the 'gloom' of the forest.[44] Illustrations depict Clifford scrabbling in the darkness, surrounded by a 'sea of forest almost black in colour'.[45] The effect of these metaphors was to justify the Pahang War, posing Terengganu as profoundly in need of illumination – through liberal colonial practices that Clifford valorised, such as gathering evidence, protecting property rights and issuing transparent justice.

Clifford's expedition report cast him as Terengganu's navigator, gradually uncovering the truth about the Pahang uprising by driving the rebels into the open, 'from the trickling waters to the breaking waves'.[46] Clifford's truth was that the rebels were supported by Terengganu, and to some extent Siam, as a destabilising factor on the Malay Peninsula. For example, Clifford discovered that Terengganu locals were actively covering the rebels' tracks, ultimately realising they had the sanction of the highest officials in the royal court, including the sultan himself. At one point, locals even told rebels to hide in the forest despite their 'famished' condition to avoid attracting punishment for sheltering them,[47] as Clifford carried with him a *chap* (authorisation) from the sultan to summarily punish anybody found to be protecting the rebels.[48] Clifford's response was to make forest life as risky as possible for the rebels, who in turn went to Tokku Paloh for assistance.[49] This decision exposed the relationship between the rebels and the *sayyid.* Clifford later discovered that 'the rebels lived for a considerable time' at Kuala Terengganu opposite the river from the sultan's own enclosure. The sultan himself had apparently discussed their presence with several of his advisers, after which he too 'decided to befriend his co-religionists', providing them with protection instead of offering them up to the British. From this location, the rebels 'had frequent interviews' with Tokku Paloh, who 'preached a Holy War to them', after which they travelled up-river to live in Kemuning, 'openly declaring their intention of waging a Holy War in Pahang, and being feasted by the people of Trengganu'.[50] On finding Kemuning unsatisfactory, the rebels later moved to the Kembiau River in the Besut district, 'with the full knowledge and approval of the Chiefs in charge of that district, and with the sanction of the Sultan'.[51] There, the sultan had forewarned them after hearing from the Siamese that Clifford's expedition was coming for them. When Clifford arrived, the rebels visited Tokku Paloh once more, receiving further assurances of protection.[52] As he went on, Clifford discovered that the *chap* he carried was worthless – in fact, the sultan had issued two *chap*s – one which he gave Clifford, calling on locals to assist him in any way they could, and another, with the opposite aim. This one was sent first to Setiu and Besut instructing people not to cooperate with Clifford at all, and if by some chance Clifford should catch them, the people of Terengganu should join the rebels in a '*sabil Allah* [*perang sabil*] or Holy War against the infidels'. According to Clifford, the locals were also informed that the later *chap*, which he would bring with him, was to be viewed as a 'dead letter'.[53]

Clifford had a difficult time determining where power truly resided in Terengganu. By Clifford's account, the sultan was a mere 'boy' – a hostage to his advisers and Shaykh Tokku Paloh. In fact, he was about to turn 28, exactly Clifford's age, and both were effectively rulers of Peninsular polities. Yet the sultan was the *sayyid*'s disciple, and derived significant authority from his association with him, continuing a practice begun by his predecessor, Terengganu's Baginda Omar (r. 1839–76), who first installed a Shaykh al-Islām.[54] The Baginda had centralised royal authority, except over the Besut and Kemaman districts,[55] and yet could not claim divine authority – via Melaka – to legitimise his position. This weakness, compounded by Siamese pressure, existed despite the Terengganu sultanate's historical cultivation of relationships that connected Terengganu with Islam's sacred geography, centred on Mecca, including by marrying into the al-Baghdādī line of Hadrami *sayyids*. In addition, to further augment this 'precious gift of genealogy' through marriage,[56] Baginda Omar formally appointed a scion of the al-Baghdādī line as a court scholar, and further cultivated a connection with the al-ʿAydarūs *sayyid* family from which Tokku Paloh was descended. The first member of the al-ʿAydarūs was thought to have arrived in Terengganu in the eighteenth century, based on an old grave in Kuala Terengganu belonging to Sayyid Muḥammad b. Aḥmad al-ʿAydarūs, known locally as Tokku Makam Lama. Against competition from at least one other Hadrami family, the *sayyid*'s sons enjoyed close relationships with the royal family. One of these sons, the scholar and Naqshbandī Sufi, Sayyid Muḥammad b. Zayn al-ʿAbidin al-ʿAydarūs (Tokku Tuan Besar), returned from Mecca to become Terengganu's first Shaykh al-Islām. Sultan Zayn al-ʿAbidin III personally appointed the shaykh's son, Tokku Paloh, to succeed him as Shaykh al-Islām, while another of his sons was ensconced in his court as the *Engku Sayid Seri Perdana*.

This appointment marked the high-point of Terengganu's *ʿulamā ʾ*–royal symbiosis, reflected in a flourishing of locally produced Islamic literature expounding the sharʿia at the centre of the Muslim experience, urging rigorous personal piety and hostility to *bidʿa* or local 'cultural accretions'. Tokku Paloh, too, studied in Mecca, under Sayyid Aḥmad Zaynī Daḥlān and Sayyid ʿAbdallāh al-Zawāwī, and joined the Naqshbandiyya whose scripturalist pietism he popularised in Terengganu on his return. He had a reputation for being *karāmāt* (thaumaturgic), and the main tract he authored, *Maʿarij al-Lahfan* or *Milestones for the Desirous*, carried a polarising polemic against practices he regarded as standing apart from Sunni orthodoxy. Against a backdrop of colonial competition on the Peninsula, the *sayyid*'s capacity to polarise, draw a crowd and connect Terengganu with the imagined Muslim World beyond placed him in an excellent position to sponsor a *perang sabil* against both of the polity's would-be colonisers. As Clifford noted, the *sayyid* was 'held in greater esteem by the people of Trengganu than anyone else', and, 'at a pinch', could even 'command a larger following' than the sultan himself.[57] In addition, this following was relatively knowledgeable – Terengganu locals both understood and abided by the tenets of their faith, and as a population possessed a high level of mastery of the Qurʾān. As a result, Clifford noted, 'the people of this state are both more religiously superstitious and more fanatical than are any other race of Peninsula Malays with whom I am acquainted'.[58]

As Clifford's diagnosis of the situation in Terengganu became more acute, the story he was telling revealed his presence in a regional hub for holy war, central to the fight the tributaries were putting up against both Siam and Britain. This fight, as it turned out, was supported by Terengganu's peculiar geopolitical position, the ways in which the sultanate appealed to Islam as a pillar of its legitimacy and the presence of a *sayyid* shaykh of great prestige capable of mobilising religion as an idiom for resistance. Tokku Paloh was also capable of deploying physical weapons

– the muskets which Britain had been exporting to the polity to encourage rebellion against Siam were in fact now being 'imported by the Trengganu authorities for use in the Holy War'.[59] Further, this war had Siamese support – insofar as it could be expected to keep Britain out of Kelantan and Terengganu.[60] For Clifford, this only proved precisely that Siam should be kept out of Terengganu, despite having increased its influence in Kelantan, where it gave the rebels money and sent them back to Besut after judging their uprising to be an opportunity 'for which [it] had long been waiting'.[61] Perhaps ironically, however, it was the difference between Terengganu and Kelantan that made it so fertile a ground for holy war – unlike Kelantan, Terengganu was not devastated by disease, disaster or famine, as the Perak Magistrate and Collector C. F. Bozzolo, then exploring Kelantan, reported in 1889.[62]

Bozzolo attributed Kelantan's miserable state to its treatment by Siam, along with contradictory elite responses to Siamese pressure, resulting in population flight.[63] Terengganu, on the other hand was, as Clifford noted, densely populated, with 40 per cent more inhabitants than Pahang, despite Pahang's much larger size,[64] also a result of population flight during its civil war.[65] It is highly likely that Terengganu became a refuge for many who fled Pahang, along with many refugees from further north (including Patani). Many who fled Patani had first streamed into Kelantan, followed by Terengganu as Kelantan's condition deteriorated, having left in successive waves from Patani following its incorporation by Siam in 1785.[66]

Taming the Benighted Lands

Clifford's experience in Kelantan and Terengganu demonstrates the nature of the political ferment then transforming Terengganu into an inter-state hub for holy war, whose idiom informed counter-colonial uprisings well beyond its geographical limits. Its continued existence as a 'wild' space allowed it to project alternative, cosmopolitan models of political community and political subjectivity to the Peninsula's Malay Muslim population, derived from its connectedness with developments in Arabia and across the Indian Ocean. As a result, it stood in distinct contrast to the colonial states of the Peninsula, in which British thinking on race was beginning to restructure human relationships and relationships with nature, labour and the economy. Clifford, an important broker of this race-thinking, mapped Terengganu within a British tradition of narrative cartography, developed to sort the world's populations within both racial hierarchies and bounded, contiguous geo-bodies.[67] Creating such an ordering structure – part of the effort that established British colonialism's 'liberal geoculture'[68] – was essential for managing cosmopolitan populations and political movements such as those which Clifford found developing in Terengganu. On the Malay Peninsula, as elsewhere, this geo-culture was developed through a labour of representation, one modality of which was travel writing, long before the surveying teams entered to draw borders on the ground,[69] as they did in Pahang in 1902 after the uprising was quelled.

In 1895, 150 Siamese troops landed in Terengganu to capture the rebels,[70] five of whom they transported to Bangkok 'in chains', after a 'vigorous form of detention'.[71] Later, in 1896, the purported 'true story of the capture' emerged. Five rebel leaders – not including Imam Rasu (also known as Tok Gajah) – were tricked into attending a feast, unarmed except for Rasu's son Mat Kilau, with Siamese troops, all of whom were wearing concealed weapons. As the Siamese leader, 'Luang Swasti', uttered the signal word '*prak*', troops overpowered the rebels, including Dato' Bahaman, tied them up and tortured them with their weapons. Mat Kilau suffered most – he 'had his head split open with his own sword', and according to evidence 'that would not be received in a court of law on technical grounds', a Siamese official later 'twisted Mat Kilau's neck and broke it'.

In contrast to this 'truth', however, Siamese reports were believed to have told a different story. They were said to have stated that Mat Kilau 'died of wounds received while resisting arrest'. Such reports also asserted that Kelantan was now effectively a Siamese territory, due to its ruler being entirely dependent on Siamese support. With this ending the Pahang War was settled with Kelantan increasingly isolated from Terengganu, but the Peninsula's geopolitical contest nevertheless raged on, leaving 'no light, but rather darkness visible' in the Benighted Lands.[72]

Discussion immediately turned to measures for partitioning the Peninsula between British and Siamese spheres, including the possibility of determining a 'dividing line between the Malay and Siamese races [at] about the 7th degree'.[73] Clifford's writing and its narrative cartography had paved the way for this discussion by furnishing British officials in Malaya with a model of civilisational hierarchy in which British, Siamese and Malay Muslims could all be located. This model also involved geo-location – as the mooted latitudinal measure showed – helping to map this hierarchy of race onto the geography of the Peninsula. Wherever Malay Muslims were located, British colonisation should proceed without delay. Mat Kilau's treatment became proof that the Siamese were inappropriate colonisers for Malay Muslims, 'in spite of some newly-laid on varnish of superficial "civilisation" at Bangkok'.[74] The ensuing debate helped to seal the importance of racial and civilisational theory to the very structure of the Malayan geo-body, further enabling the emergence of race as a critical technology for establishing the liberal geo-culture across so much of the globe. Its logic, however, could not be acted on to its full extent, or up to the seventh degree, due to the refusal of Britain's Foreign Office to countenance dismembering Siam – a critical buffer state separating British Asia from French Indochina.

Conclusion

Examining the Pahang uprising and the official narratives surrounding it offers insight into political developments in the Siamese tributaries during the period of British forward movement. These developments cultivated a strong sense of trans-regional Muslim identity in the most independent of these tributaries, Terengganu, and this polity functioned as a channel between ideas originally produced in the Islamic cosmopolitan milieu of Mecca and peninsular struggles. Transported by the movements of shaykhs like Tokku Paloh, the elevation of holy war as the primary grammar for counter-colonial resistance transformed the Pahang uprising into a well-armed *perang sabil* aimed at keeping both Siam and Britain out of Terengganu. Due to the impact of colonial expansion on polities to the north and south, while Terengganu itself remained relatively unscathed, this polity was transformed into a dynamic, cosmopolitan destination for rebels and refugees from around the Siamese Malay world.

This dynamism dislocates dominant narratives in Malayan historiography. Many such narratives assert that multi-ethnic Penang and Singapore – both reconstructed as 'cosmopolitan' port cities by colonial power and labour migration – were the primary engines of 'reformist' Islamic transformation in Malaya.[75] Yet despite the public positioning of Muslim reformists against 'traditionalist' peninsular *'ulamā'*,[76] Tokku Paloh and his disciples delayed Terengganu's direct colonisation until 1919. Later, even under British rule, the shaykh's followers resisted colonial expansion, launching an uprising in the 1920s that kept Terengganu's hinterland both 'free' and 'wild' until 1930.[77] Indeed, the 1930s were a turning point in which Terengganu was reoriented as part of British Malaya, transforming political expression there into new forms of Malay nationalism, elaborated in terms that differed in significant ways from those of the wider Islamic cosmopolitan conceptions of a trans-regional *umma*.

Notes

1. For their great assistance in considering new directions and sources for this work, I thank the late Professor Jeffrey Hadler of the Center for Southeast Asia Studies and Ms Virginia Shih, Southeast Asia Librarian, at the University of California, Berkeley. I also thank R. Michael Feener of the University of Oxford and Joshua Gedacht of Rowan University for the opportunity to collaborate with them on the 'Wild Spaces and Islamic Cosmopolitanism' Conference at the Asia Research Institute of the National University of Singapore. The Social Science Research Council enabled my capacity to research this chapter through a Postdoctoral Fellowship in its InterAsia Program, with funds from the Andrew W. Mellon Foundation.
2. Lovat, Alice and Clifford, Hugh, *The Life of Sir Frederick Weld, G.C.M.G.: a Pioneer of Empire* (Cambridge: Cambridge University Press, 2011), p. 393.
3. Ibid., p. 393.
4. For a fuller treatment of the Pahang uprising, refer to Linehan, W., *A History of Pahang* (Kuala Lumpur: TMalaysian Branch of the Royal Asiatic Society, [1936] 1973), ch. 12; Thio, Eunice, 'Britain's Search for Security in North Malaya, 1886–1897', *Journal of Southeast Asian History* 10(2) (1969): 279–303; Gopinath, Aruna, *Pahang, 1880–1933: A Political History* (Kuala Lumpur: Council of the Malaysian Branch of the Royal Asiatic Society, 1991).
5. Clifford, Hugh, *Bush-Whacking and Other Asiatic Tales and Memories* (London: Heinemann, 1929), p. 6.
6. Colonial Office to Foreign Office, 23 June 1894, No. 114, FO422/39: Further Correspondence respecting the Affairs of Siam, Part IV.

7. See, for example, Andaya, Barbara Watson and Andaya, Leonard Y., *A History of Malaysia*, 3rd edn (London: Palgrave, 2017), esp. pp. 84–9. Note that the 'Pahang War' of 1891–5 is distinct from the 'Pahang Civil War' of 1857–63, which was a pre-colonial succession dispute that resulted in Wan Ahmad's ascension as Pahang's Raja Bendahara and his subsequent proclamation as sultan of Pahang in the early 1880s.
8. See Loos, Tamara Lynn, *Subject Siam: Family, Law, and Colonial Modernity in Thailand* (Ithaca, NY: Cornell University Press, 2006), pp. 80–8.
9. While activities related to such projects of world-making could include militant mobilisation, this was not necessarily the most common mode of participation in this Islamic cosmopolitan milieu. World-making could also involve constructing models more collaborative with, or simply at cross-purposes to, those preferred by European empires. For further discussion of such models, refer to Bang, Anne Katrine, *Islamic Sufi Networks in the Western Indian Ocean (c. 1880–1940): Ripples of Reform* (Leiden: Brill, 2014); Bradley, Francis R., *Forging Islamic Power and Place: the Legacy of Shaykh Daud bin Abd Allah al-Fatani in Mecca and Southeast Asia* (Honolulu, HI: University of Hawai'i Press, 2016); Laffan, Michael, *Islamic Nationhood and Colonial Indonesia: the Umma Below the Winds* (London: Routledge, 2003).
10. Feener, R. Michael, 'New Networks and New Knowledge: Migrations, Communications and the Refiguration of the Muslim Community in the Nineteenth and Early Twentieth Centuries', in Robert Hefner (ed.), *The New Cambridge History of Islam*, vol. 6 (Cambridge: Cambridge University Press, 2010), pp. 39–68.
11. For a general argument along these lines, see Aydin, Cemil, *The Idea of the Muslim World: a Global Intellectual History* (Cambridge, MA: Harvard University Press, 2017).
12. Linehan, *A History of Pahang*, p. 161. Refer also to Clifford, Hugh, 'Statement of Esah, Wife of Mat Kilau, Deserted by Him at Kuala Lebir, in Kelantan, on 20th May, Who Fell into Our Hands on 21st May', in *Report of an Expedition into Trengganu and Kelantan in 1895* (Kuala Lumpur: Malaysian Branch of the Royal Asiatic Society, [1895] 1992), Enclosure 9, pp. 154–60.
13. Linehan, *A History of Pahang* , pp. 163–4.
14. Clifford, Hugh, *Report of an Expedition into Trengganu and Kelantan in 1895*, pp. 3–4.
15. Clifford, *Bush-Whacking and Other Asiatic Tales and Memories*, p. 70; Linehan, *A History of Pahang*, p. 141.

16. See Suwannathat-Pian, Kobkua, *Thai–Malay Relations: Traditional Intra-Regional Relations from the Seventeenth to the Early Twentieth Centuries* (Singapore: Oxford University Press, 1988); Suwannathat-Pian, Kobkua, 'Special Thai–Malaysian Relations', *Journal of the Malayan Branch of the Royal Asiatic Society* 75(1) (2002): 1–22.
17. Governor Cecil Clementi Smith to Lord Knutsford, 6 October 1888, Inclosure 1; and 'Notes from Siamese Official Gazette "Raja Kitchambekoa"', 20 September 1888, Inclosure 3 in No. 4, Colonial Office to Foreign Office, 7 March 1889, FO422/21: Further Correspondence respecting British Influence and Policy in the Malay Peninsula, Part IV.
18. Refer to documents Nos 5–9 and their Inclosures in FO422/31: Further Correspondence respecting British Influence and Policy in the Malay Peninsula, Part VI.
19. King of Siam and Great Britain, 'Treaty Between Great Britain and Siam (20 June 1826)', in *Treaties and Engagements Affecting the Malay States and Borneo*, ed. William George Maxwell and William Sumner Gibson (London: J. A. S. Truscott & Son, 1924).
20. For a fuller discussion of this period, see Falarti, Maziar Mozaffari, *Malay Kingship in Kedah: Religion, Trade and Society* (Lanham: Rowman & Littlefield, 2013).
21. See Bradley, Francis R., 'Siam's Conquest of Patani and the End of Mandala Relations, 1786–1838', pp. 149–60; Suwannathat-Pian, Kobkua, 'Historical Identity, Nation, and History-Writing: the Malay Muslims of Southern Thailand, 1940s–1980s', pp. 228-55, both in Patrick Jory (ed.), *Ghosts of the Past in Southern Thailand: Essays on the History and Historiography of Patani* (Singapore: National University of Singapore Press, 2013).
22. Governor Cecil Clementi Smith to Lord Knutsford, 3 December 1888, Inclosure 10 in No. 4, FO422/21.
23. See Suwannathat-Pian, *Thai–Malay Relations* , pp. 66–79.
24. Consul-General Ernest Satow to the Earl of Granville, 23 January 1885, No. 1, FO422/12: Correspondence respecting British Influence and Policy in the Malay Peninsula, Part I. See also Tagliacozzo, Eric, 'Ambiguous Commodities, Unstable Frontiers: the Case of Burma, Siam, and Imperial Britain, 1800–1900', *Comparative Studies in Society and History* 46 (2) (2004): 354–77.
25. Satow to Granville, 23 January 1885, No. 1, FO422/12.
26. Tagliacozzo, 'Ambiguous Commodities, Unstable Frontiers', p. 361.

27. Refer to the papers in FO 422/10: Further Correspondence respecting the Rectification of the Boundary between Perak and Siam, 1886.
28. Consul-General Ernest Satow to the Marquis of Salisbury, 18 March 1899, No. 5, FO422/21.
29. Gullick, J. M., *Rulers and Residents: Influence and Power in the Malay States, 1870–1920* (Singapore: Oxford University Press, 1992), p. 150.
30. Malhi, Amrita, 'Forests of Islam: Territory, Environment and Holy War in Trengganu, Malaya, 1928' (PhD dissertation, Australian National University, 2010), pp. 60–1.
31. Prinz, Janosch, *The Conversation*, 17 October, 2015, available at: https://theconversation.com/ungoverned-space-the-concept-that-puts-humanitarian-aid-in-the-firing-line-of-the-war-on-terror-49010; Angel Rabasa et al., *Ungoverned Territories: Understanding and Reducing Terrorism Risks* (Santa Monica, CA: Rand Corporation, 2007).
32. Clifford, *Bush-Whacking and Other Asiatic Tales and Memories*, p. 79. Over the course of his nearly fifty-year career, which he began in Perak at the age of 17, Clifford went on to serve as a high-ranking colonial official in Trinidad, Ceylon and the Gold Coast, where he became governor. He later served as governor of Nigeria and Ceylon before returning to Malaya as governor of the Straits Settlements. For further details, refer to Gailey, Harry A., *Clifford: Imperial Proconsul* (London: Rex Collings, 1982).
33. Clifford, *Bush-Whacking and Other Asiatic Tales and Memories*, pp. 70–2. On British paramountcy in the Indian Ocean, refer to Bose, Sugata, *A Hundred Horizons: the Indian Ocean in the Age of Global Empire* (Cambridge, MA: Harvard University Press, 2009); Metcalf, Thomas R., *Imperial Connections: India in the Indian Ocean Arena, 1860–1920* (Berkeley, CA: University of California Press, 2008). For a brief, discursive analysis of Clifford's writing, refer to Noor, Farish A., *From Inderapura to Darul Makmur: a Deconstructive History of Pahang* (Kuala Lumpur: Silverfish Books, 2011), ch. 2.
34. Clunan, Anne L. and Trinkunas, Harold A., 'Conceptualising Ungoverned Spaces: Territorial Statehood, Contested Authority, and Softened Sovereignty', in Anne L. Clunan and Harold A. Trinkunas (eds), *Ungoverned Spaces: Alternatives to State Authority in an Era of Softened Sovereignty* (Palo Alto, CA: Stanford University Press, 2010), p. 17.
35. Winichakul, Thongchai, *Siam Mapped: a History of the Geo-Body of the Nation* (Honolulu, HI: University of Hawai'i Press, 1994), p. 16.
36. Work on the Kenyir hydroelectric dam, which produced Kenyir Lake, com-

menced in 1974 under the Malaysian Government's Third Malaysia Plan and was completed in 1985. For more details, see Malaysian Government, *Third Malaysia Plan, 1976–1980* (Kuala Lumpur: Malaysian Government Press, 1976), pp. 370–3.

37. The Limau route appears on a map published by the Royal Asiatic Society in 1891, which shows a portage or pedestrian route connecting Pahang's Tembeling River watershed with that of the Limau River that flowed into Kelantan. This same map represents Terengganu as a largely blank space, and posits only an 'approximate' boundary between Pahang and Terengganu. See Royal Asiatic Society of Great Britain and Ireland, Straits Branch, *Map of the Malay Peninsula* (London: Edward Stanford, 1891). For details of the Lebir route, see Clifford, Hugh, 'Statement of Marepin, Brother-in-Law of the Late Mamat Kelubi, Who was Killed at Kuala Tembeling by the Pulau Tawar Chiefs in June, 1894', in *Report of an Expedition into Trengganu and Kelantan in 1895*, Encloure 10, p. 161.
38. Clifford, *Report of an Expedition into Trengganu and Kelantan in 1895*, p. 119.
39. Scott, James C., *Seeing Like a State: How Certain Schemes to Improve the Human Condition have Failed* (New Haven, CT: Yale University Press, 1998).
40. Clifford, *Report of an Expedition into Trengganu and Kelantan in 1895*, p. 47.
41. Clifford, *Bush-Whacking and Other Asiatic Tales and Memories*, p. 15.
42. Ibid., p. 16.
43. Ibid., p. 19.
44. Ibid., p. 20.
45. Ibid., pp. 3, 28, 30, 51.
46. Clifford, *Report of an Expedition into Trengganu and Kelantan in 1895*, p. 47.
47. 'Mr. Duff's Report on Expedition to Besut', in *An Expedition to Trengganu and Kelantan in 1895*, Encloure 6, pp. 131–47.
48. 'Copy of Chap Granted by Sultan of Trengganu', in *Report of an Expedition into Trengganu and Kelantan in 1895*, Enclosure 4, p. 128; 'Translation of Chap Granted by Sultan of Trengganu', in *Report of an Expedition into Trengganu and Kelantan in 1895*, Enclosure 5, pp. 129–30.
49. Clifford, *Report of an Expedition into Trengganu and Kelantan in 1895*, p. 47.
50. Ibid., pp. 44–5.
51. Ibid., p. 45.
52. Ibid., pp. 45–6.

53. Ibid., p. 46.
54. Gullick, *Rulers and Residents*, p. 148.
55. Ibid., p. 149.
56. Ho, Engseng, *The Graves of Tarim: Genealogy and Mobility across the Indian Ocean* (Berkeley, CA: University of California Press, 2006), p. 168.
57. Hugh Clifford to Colonial Secretary, Straits Settlements, 5 September 1895, Inclosure 2 in No. 76, Colonial Office to Foreign Office, 10 October 1895, FO422/43: Further Correspondence respecting the Affairs of Siam Part VII.
58. Clifford, *Report of an Expedition into Trengganu and Kelantan in 1895*, p. 100.
59. Ibid., p. 46.
60. Ibid., p. 17.
61. Ibid., pp. 111–13.
62. 'Extracts from Abstract of Journal Kept by Mr C. F. Bozzolo, Magistrate and Collector, Upper Perak, during his Exploration of the Pass into Kelantan by the Plus Valley', Inclosure 12 in No. 4, Colonial Office to Foreign Office, 7 March 1889, FO422/21.
63. Ibid.
64. Clifford, Hugh, 'A Journey through the Malay States of Trengganu and Kelantan', *Geographical Journal* 9(1) (1897): 88. Terengganu was so densely populated that its authorities collected poll taxes triennially from 40,000 adult men, while supporting a diverse economy consisting of agricultural, fishing and manufacturing sectors, producing boats, textiles, weapons, and metal and wooden goods. See also Clifford, *Report of an Expedition into Trengganu and Kelantan in 1895*, pp. 88–95.
65. For the process by which Clifford delivered Britain's colonisation of Pahang in 1888, refer to Clifford, Hugh, *Journal of a Mission to Pahang, January 15 to April 11, 1887* (Honolulu, HI: Southeast Asian Studies Program, 1978).
66. Malhi, *Forests of Islam*, pp. 155–64.
67. For a full discussion of the production of the Siamese geo-body, refer to Winichakul, *Siam Mapped.*
68. On the consolidation of the liberal geo-culture and Britain's entry in the First World War, refer to Wallerstein, Immanuel, *The Modern World System, vol. 4: Centrist Liberalism Triumphant, 1789–1914* (Berkeley, CA: University of California Press, 2011).
69. For fuller discussions on the modalities of colonial knowledge, including travel writing, refer to Cohn, Bernard S., *Colonialism and its Forms of Knowledge: the British in India* (Princeton, NJ: Princeton University Press, 1996); Pratt, Mary

Louise, *Imperial Eyes: Travel Writing and Transculturation* (London: Routledge, [1992] 2008).

70. Lieutenant Commander May to Captain Fawkes, 31 August 1895, Inclosure in No. 73, Admiralty to Foreign Office, 3 October 1895, FO 422/43.
71. Refer to Nos 96, 102, 107 and 124 in FO422/43.
72. Mr Duff to the Acting British Resident, Pahang, 24 April 1896, Inclosure 2 in No. 100, Colonial Office to Foreign Office, 22 July 1896, FO422/45: Further Correspondence respecting the Affairs of Siam Part VIII. Note that many Malaysians believe that Mat Kilau returned to Pahang under the alias of 'Mat Siam', only revealing his true identity in 1969 after Friday prayers in a mosque in Jerantut. The tomb of this Mat Kilau lies in his birthplace, Pulau Tawar, Pahang, decorated by the state as a site of national importance, and is a tourist destination. For more details, refer to Sharani, Tuan Sharifah and Ishak, Mohd Shukri, 'Mat Kilau, the Malay Warrior', *The Star Online*, 29 January 2007, available at: https://www.thestar.com.my/news/community/2007/01/29/mat-kilau-the-malay-warrior/.
73. 'Memorandum', Inclosure 1 in No. 51, Colonial Office to Foreign Office, 25 February 1896, FO422/45.
74. Governor Sir F. Weld to the Earl of Derby, 12 March 1885, Inclosure to No. 1, Mr Meade to Mr Currie, 19 March 1885 in FO422/9: Correspondence respecting the Rectification of the Boundary between Perak and Siam. For a fuller discussion of this campaign, refer to Jackson, Peter A., 'The Ambiguities of Semicolonial Power in Thailand', in Rachel V. Harrison and Peter A. Jackson (eds), *The Ambiguous Allure of the West: Traces of the Colonial in Thailand* (Hong Kong: Hong Kong University Press, 2010), pp. 37–56.
75. For arguments along these lines, refer to Milner, Anthony, *The Invention of Politics in Colonial Malaya* (Cambridge: Cambridge University Press, [1995] 2002); Roff, William R.. *The Origins of Malay Nationalism* (New Haven, CT: Yale University Press, 1967).
76. One such reformist was Syed Shaykh al-Hadi, whose work is discussed in Milner, *The Invention of Politics in Colonial Malaya*, ch. 6. Al-Hadi used to rail against the *'ulamā'* of Terengganu, where he spent a portion of his childhood studying Islamic texts.
77. For discussions of the Terengganu uprising, refer to Malhi, *Forests of Islam*; Shaharil, Talib, *After its Own Image: the Trengganu Experience, 1881–1941* (Singapore: Oxford University Press, 1984); Shahridan Faiez bin Mohideen Abdul Kader, 'Mapping Modernities in Trengganu: Nature, Islam and the

Colonial State, 1850–1930', PhD dissertation, University of Cambridge, 2001; Timah, Hamzah, *Pemberontakan Tani 1928 Di Trengganu: Satu Kajian Ketokohan Dan Kepimpinan Haji Abdul Rahman Limbong* (Kuala Lumpur: Dewan Bahasa dan Pustaka, 1981).

9

Afghanistan's Cosmopolitan Trading Networks: A View from Yiwu, China

Magnus Marsden and Diana Ibañez-Tirado

Ḥaji Nazar had been living in the city of Yiwu in China's Zhejiang Province for about two years when we first met him in March 2016.[1] Ḥaji Nazar ran a trading office that arranged the procurement and shipment of merchandise from Yiwu's Futian market and the factories with which it is linked to the port of Rotterdam in the Netherlands. Ḥaji Nazar is a Farsi-speaking Sunni Muslim originally from a rural region of northeastern Afghanistan, but resident for many years in the northern Afghan city of Kunduz. His life has been characterised by mobility. In the mid-1970s he left Afghanistan to study in Saudi Arabia, where he also worked for a time as the cashier of a restaurateur from northern Afghanistan who ran a business in Jeddah, Saudi Arabia's principal port city. At the end of the decade, Ḥaji Nazar was awarded a scholarship to study in the United States, but he was told by officials in the Embassy of Afghanistan in Saudi Arabia that due to a change of regime in his country he would now have to return home to get a new passport to travel to the United States. Ḥaji Nazar returned to Kabul but was immediately arrested by the country's much-feared intelligence agency (KhAd). Having spent some time in jail, Ḥaji Nazar was released and thereafter played an active role in the resistance movement fighting against the pro-Soviet government of Afghanistan; more specifically, he became a member of the Islamist Hizb-i Islami party, led by Gulbuddin Hekmatyar. After some years of fighting with Hizb-i Islami *mujāhidīn*, Ḥaji Nazar began to have doubts about the sincerity of the leader of the regional wing of the party (for whom he also deputised) having seen the commander enter into truces with Soviet officers. Eventually, Ḥaji Nazar decided to leave the resistance and return to Saudi Arabia, a country in which he decided he would be safer than if he moved to Iran or Pakistan. Ḥaji Nazar resettled in the city of Jeddah, where he looked up his prior employer, only to discover that the restaurateur had left the city for Istanbul having had much of his savings 'eaten' by his local sponsor (*kafil*). Ḥaji Nazar secured work elsewhere in Jeddah, only returning permanently to Afghanistan after the defeat of the Taliban by US forces in 2001, at which point he secured employment as a clerk in one of the many NGOs active in development work in the country. By 2014, however, the scope for employment in such organisations was dwindling in the wake of the withdrawal of foreign forces and a subsequent decline in international development funds being ploughed into 'reconstructing' the country. In the wake of the difficulties in securing employment and therefore also raising his young family, Ḥaji Nazar was approached by one of his relatives – based in the Netherlands having moved there as a refugee – to ask if he would be interested in running an office in China that would be responsible for arranging the export of the goods in which his wholesale business dealt in Europe: souvenirs such as key rings and pens, as well as hashish leaf grinders that are principally sold in Amsterdam to tourists.

Having experience in both travel and working for trading companies, as well as needing money to support his family and his children through higher education, Ḥaji Nazar agreed, and established himself in Yiwu, where we met him in 2016. Ḥaji Nazar's gentle mannerisms and deep knowledge of Afghan trade and mobility ensured that we soon struck up a friendship; his formal education in the Islamic sciences also convinced us that he would be an excellent source of information on the role played by Islam in shaping the commercial activities of Afghan traders (*tojiron*) in Yiwu and China more generally. We thus asked him how the traders from Afghanistan managed to live according to *sharīʿa* conventions in Yiwu, especially in such areas of everyday life that saw repeated interactions between Afghan men and Chinese women working alongside one another in trading offices. Ḥaji Nazar politely replied that according to *sharīʿa* there was an argument to be made for treating such interactions as permissible because traders were 'compelled' to hire Chinese women to work for them as a result of their need for staff with expert language skills. Yet, he went on, we might well also have noticed that a clear majority of the traders of Afghan background in Yiwu were not especially 'bothered in issues relating to *sharīʿa*' (*dār qissa-i sharīʿa nistand*); he thought such calculations rarely formed part of their thinking.

Ḥaji Nazar's mobile lifestyle distils some of the key concerns with which this book opened: the distinction between the deep forms of Islamic cosmopolitanism traditionally held to be available to travellers to Islamic centres (in the Ḥaji's case, Jeddah) with forms of travel to 'wild spaces' where the Muslim faith is deemed to be at risk from un-Islamic influences. Likewise, Ḥaji Nazar's trajectory also brings attention to the coercive nature of the forms of cosmopolitan-inducing mobility in which he has been involved: his decision to leave Afghanistan has on each occasion arisen in a context of instability, international intervention and violent conflict. And yet the Ḥaji's experiences of life in the centres and peripheries of Islamic Asia cannot be simply defined either in terms of discourses that would treat him either as an Islamist militant or a hapless refugee. There is, rather, the conscious display of irony in the way in which the Ḥaji narrates his life to us: a former *mujahidin* fighter shows his ability to practically adapt to life in China and also to ship containers of hashish leaf grinders to the shores of Europe. Ḥaji Nazar's mobile life provides a glimpse into a wider world of Afghan mobility, circulation, adaption and exchange.

Yiwu: International Trading City in China

The ethnographic focus of this chapter is on transnational networks of Afghan commodity traders that criss-cross much of Asia and also the world beyond. An increasingly important node for these networks is the Chinese city of Yiwu.[2] For Afghan trading networks, the city has become a 'commercial and affective centre'[3] that is connected to multiple nodes salient for these people's trading activities elsewhere, especially Moscow and St Petersburg in Russia, Odessa and Kharkov in Ukraine, and London, Hamburg and Rotterdam in Western Europe.[4] Afghan traders are also active in a plethora of settings across Muslim Asia, especially in Saudi Arabia, Turkey, Pakistan and Iran.[5]

Located 280 km from Shanghai, Yiwu is an international hub for the provision of commodities for everyday use and has come to play a central role over the past decade in the worldwide trade in Chinese-made 'small commodities'.[6] The International Trade City, popularly known in Yiwu as Futian, attracts over 210,000 buyers every day[7]; in addition to the buyers in Yiwu's Huangyuen Market (specialising in clothes), there are other smaller commercial centres dedicated to the sale of auto parts and furniture. Yiwu is also known for its industrial area with factories mainly producing jewellery, hair accessories, socks and haberdashery products. Purposely designed to be an inland Chinese port, 650,000 cargo containers are exported from Yiwu to 219 different countries each year.[8]

With approximately 2 million inhabitants, the city is also a base for merchants from around the world. There are over 14,000 foreign traders who own and/or work in trading and cargo companies involved in purchase and export. In addition, every year Yiwu receives around 400,000 foreign visitors for trading purposes.[9] Travelling to and being physically present in Yiwu is central to the practices of global commodity traders, who must contend with the risks of being sold faulty goods or seeing the arrival of these in their home ports delayed by the production process, customs officials and port closures.[10] Traders from all over the world, including overseas Chinese, arrive from Latin America, Asia, the Middle East and Africa to Yiwu in order to provision goods and export these to the markets in which they work.

While Yiwu does attract many business people who do not belong to organised trading groups or networks,[11] many trading networks of world historic significance are present in Yiwu, including traders of Levantine background from Mexico and Brazil[12]; Yemeni Hadrami traders who hold Thai citizenship[13]; Armenian merchants hailing from Armenia and Iran[14]; Afghans who are citizens of the Ukraine, Russia, the United Kingdom, Holland and Sweden, and who ship goods to all of these countries[15]; and Indians who are active in the trade between Yiwu and many countries in Africa and Latin America.[16] Not all, but many, of the traders who operate from Yiwu work within and identify with extensively scattered trading communities that bear comparison with trading networks,[17] such as the Sindhi networks studied by Claude Markovits and Mark-Anthony Falzon,[18] and the West African Muslim Murids whose activities in Africa, Europe and the United States have been documented by scholars including Beth Buggenhagen and Mamadou Diouf.[19] Of all these foreign traders, those arriving from West Asia constitute the majority in Yiwu.[20] Especially visible in the city are traders from Syria, Egypt, Algeria, Palestine, Iraq (both Arabs and Kurds) and Iran (Persian, Azeri and Kurds). Yiwu thus is an important meeting point for long-distance trading networks, and a city that has come to be thought of by the city's inhabitants and its international visitors as especially attractive to Muslim traders.[21]

Islamic Cosmopolitanism: Analytical Starting Points?

It is impossible to understand the nature of the Muslim networks and connected forms of cosmopolitanism described and analysed in this chapter without considering these in relationship to modern forms of economic globalisation. Anthropologists are now making considerable headway in documenting and understanding such forms of global connectedness. On the one hand, there is a growing body of literature that analyses such forms of trade as being a distinctively 'bottom-up' form of globalisation.[22] On the other hand, those involved in such processes are widely depicted as adapting to the global economy or having become traders as part of a survival strategy developed to deal with hard times that reflect the legacy of structural readjustment and neo-liberal forms of capitalism.[23] These studies have brought a great deal to the understanding of the types of networks and connections upon which the global trade in low-grade goods depends.

Scholars have also increasingly recognised that globalisation from below and globalisation from above are interpenetrated. For example, Keith Hart suggests this distinction, and that between formal and informal forms of economic phenomena, can lead to the assumption that 'informal' economic practices, concepts and institutions are of significance only in the world's 'peripheral spaces'. In turn, this obfuscates the ways in which 'the global economy' at large has undergone 'informalisation' over the past two decades.[24] It is also commonly acknowledged that the success of trading cities such as Yiwu, and consequentially its connected outposts around the world, depends on the policies of nation-states and local authorities, their willingness to turn a blind eye to practices such as the import and export of counterfeit goods, and, indeed, the participation of their personnel in such processes.[25]

In this chapter we reflect upon a network made up predominantly, though not exclusively, of people of Muslim background that has come to fill important niches in the forms of economic activity identified analytically as 'globalisation from below'. In light of this volume's overall concerns, we are interested in reflecting on the extent to which the Afghan traders who are the focus of the chapter are helpfully conceptualised as being 'Muslim cosmopolitans' or, indeed, the creator-participants of expansive forms of 'Islamic cosmopolitanism'. Before proceeding to the ethnographic sections of the chapter, which explore the nature of the networks formed by traders from Afghanistan, as well as the modes in which such traders inhabit the city of Yiwu, we wish to make two general points about the relevance of the notion of 'Islamic cosmopolitanism' to this case study.

First, early anthropological work on globalisation argued that a range of mobile actors – including preachers, working-class labour migrants and even 'refugees' – were fashioning hybrid and cosmopolitan identities. By crossing the boundaries of nation, ethnicity, culture and religion, migrants and the flows of finance, technology and culture they engendered, invigorated and forged open-ended, or 'cosmopolitan', forms of self and subjectivity. More recently, however, scholars have tempered their emphasis on the opening if not liberating effects of globalisation. Mobility does not inevitably result in the fashioning of open-ended forms of self and society or the apparently effortless achievement of unqualified human openness: it often leads to the production, rather, of heightened forms of attachment to locality.[26] 'Mobility, flows and the transgression of boundaries' according to Ulrike Freitag and Achim Oppen (p. 4),[27] are leading to the production of ideas about globality, yet people in the midst of experiencing such processes often attempt to 'cope with transgression' by localising 'some kind of order', rather than celebrating their having come to inhabit a 'global space'. The term 'global' itself, moreover, is often deployed in a 'complacent' manner that suggests an ever-expanding scale of progressive possibility, connected, in recent times, to forms of humanitarianism that justify political intervention in 'failed states' on the grounds that their inhabitants have not lived up to the standards of 'global civilisation': Paul Gilroy captures the paradoxes implicit in a such processes by referring to the forms of humanitarianism practised in Iraq and Afghanistan over the past decade and more as reflecting an ideology of 'armoured cosmopolitanism', a concept that bears some similarity to the notion of coercive cosmopolitanism introduced by the editors in the opening pages of this book.[28] In the context of both these analytical debates, as well as Afghanistan's history as a testing ground for modern ideologies over the past century and more,[29] the notion of Islamic cosmopolitanism needs to be applied to the ethnographic material on which this chapter is based with caution. The mobile and highly flexible actors (including Ḥaji Nazar) explored below have both witnessed the 'armoured cosmopolitanism' visited upon their home country as well as come to lead mobile lives as a result of the coercive policies of the foreign powers active there.

Secondly, we have come to see how important it is not to take the Islamic aspect of the worlds created and inhabited by Afghan traders for granted. Afghan traders' self-understandings, social relationships and ties with host communities and state officials, as well as the tactics that such people deploy to cross international boundaries, reveal them as being highly flexible social actors. This flexibility is evident at varying intersections of everyday life. One of the themes that we focus on in this chapter, for example, is the traders' understandings of what being Muslim and 'Afghan' means and how this affects their modes of forging relations with one another and the people in whose midst they live. People who are part of trading networks often showcase their capacity to be versatile and adaptable in their religious lives and the ways in which doing so allows them to 'span religious and cultural divides as well as continents and oceans' (p. 79).[30] We suggest in what follows that Afghan traders are people whose lives are not one-dimensionally geared towards making a homogeneous 'Islamic space' or a globally oriented form of 'Muslim network'. It is more helpful to think of our informants, rather, as being men who value their capacity to diplomatically mediate between and profit from arbitrages between different types of spaces.[31] They are individuals who embody connections to one another that are as much about trade and pragmatism as about being Muslim.[32] If in the Kantian tradition the notion of cosmopolitanism arose as a requirement to temper the nationalist extremes of the modern nation-state, many traders from Afghanistan emphasise their capacity to achieve prestige and repute by moving across transregional spaces that transcend, yet not in a manner that contests the boundaries of such nation-states. The ways in which they do so challenges the notion that being Muslim in a global and cosmopolitan way inevitably results in hostility towards the idea of the nation-state.[33]

Beyond Diasporas: Poly-stranded and Multimodal Trading Networks

The traders from Afghanistan with whom we have been working do not form a homogeneous 'diaspora' in the conventional sense of collectively defining themselves as belonging to a group from a shared geographical locale that is able to trace its origins back to a single moment of dispersal. The traders are better thought of, rather, as forming poly-stranded and multimodal trading networks.[34] The traders' networks are poly-stranded in that while they are made up by individuals willing to describe themselves as being 'from Afghanistan', they are simultaneously organised in relationship to specific regional identities; the specific nature of the networks play a critical role in shaping the particular commodities in which individual traders deal, as well as the geographical contexts in which they operate. The networks are multimodal in that the collective trading activities of merchants from Afghanistan do not rely on a single, central node in which information is shared and capital distributed but, rather, on multiple and interlinked nodes, none of which is significantly more influential than the others.

The different networks that people from Afghanistan form collaborate with one another, but more often specialise in either different merchandise or in the distribution of commodities to distinct geographical regions. Traders in Yiwu who freight goods from China to Afghanistan are especially numerous. Such traders belong to various ethnic groups (though many are Pashto-speaking Pashtuns from Afghanistan's eastern provinces and Farsi-speaking Tajiks from provinces to the north of Kabul). Such traders are mostly Sunni, but there are also several and well-established Shiʿī traders involved in the trade in commodities of daily use between China and Afghanistan. In Yiwu, these traders have forged high degrees of commercial organisation. They have established committees that seek to define and delimit the price of shipping containers to Afghanistan. As we shall see below, the traders organise weekly meetings in Yiwu at which information about business and the activities of traders is shared. Their ties and obligations to one another are repeatedly established and sustained in relationship to shared Islamic rituals, especially those performed during Ramadan (the organisation of *tarawih* prayers and *iftar* feasts), as well as charitable feasts (*khayrat*) that mark the death of relatives back home in Afghanistan (*faitiha*). These merchants also forge close ties with the state of Afghanistan, most especially the Kabul-based Chamber of Commerce.

A second network comprises traders working across the former Soviet Union, though especially in Russia and Ukraine. These traders are ethnically mixed (being both Persian and Pashto speakers, as well as including a much smaller number of Uzbek speakers). Nevertheless, despite differences in language and ethnicity, such traders do tend to share an ideological commitment to 'being Afghan' (partly derived out of past membership of the People's Democratic Party of Afghanistan) as well as shared educational experiences – most studied in higher education institutes in the Soviet Union during the late 1980s. Indeed, the long-term workings of coercive cosmopolitanism are especially visible in the membership of this trading network. Amongst traders working in the former Soviet Republics are individuals who initially travelled to the region as part of Soviet programmes that placed Afghan orphans in Soviet boarding schools (*internat*) in the 1980s with the aim of creating a cadre of loyal pro-Soviet government servants.[35] At the same time, however, that commitment to Afghanistan reflects the country's modern history and its relationship to the Soviet Union, the specific niche activities of traders tends to be organised in relationship to their regional backgrounds. For example, in the Ukrainian port city of Odessa, home to the Seventh-Kilometre market, the import of children's scooters and roller blades from Yiwu is carried out largely by traders from Afghanistan's northeastern Badakhshan Province; by contrast, the import of umbrellas from China as well as their sale in the Ukraine is dominated by traders from Panjshir; the business in hardware items is largely handled by traders from the eastern provinces of Khost and Paktika, both Hindu and Muslim in terms of religious affiliation (see below). Importantly, though, not all of the sub-networks are formed in relationship to regional identity – shared professional experience can also be important in defining their nature. For example, during fieldwork in Yiwu we encountered a trading company that was involved in the export of goods to Russia and Ukraine, the partners of which included Pashto and Farsi speakers from different regions of the country who had all served as pilots during the 1980s in Afghanistan's air force.

Traders able to import goods from Yiwu to the former Soviet Union tend to be well established in Russia and Ukraine and lead stable lives. Many traders live with their families in the cities in which they work (St Petersburg, Moscow, Odessa and Khakov being key nodes); they hold the passports of Russia or Ukraine and also own property there in the form of shops, warehouses and homes. We have explored elsewhere the role played by marriages and informal relationships between Afghan traders and local women to the activities of traders in the former Soviet Union.[36] Such marriages root mobile merchants in particular contexts and therefore also ensure the durability of such settlements as nodes for commercial activities over time. Local wives also bring critical skills to the trading activities of Afghan traders in this region of the world: they offer insights into the changing fashions of the populations they serve. For this reason, many traders travel with their wives to China at least once a year to ensure they get valuable input in terms of the orders they place with their Chinese suppliers. Importantly, while some women married to Afghans in Russia and Ukraine do convert to Islam, this is by no means the norm or even something that is expected by individual traders or the wider networks they form. Several traders have remarked to us that if they had wished to marry a Muslim there was no shortage of women in Afghanistan to choose from: they were interested, rather, in women they could trust and build a relationship with based on sincerity (*ikhlas*).

In recent years, these networks have increasingly demonstrated their dynamism and responsiveness to changing geopolitical circumstances. A significant market for goods sent from Yiwu to Odessa, for example, was Crimea. The annexation of Crimea by Russia in 2014 made this trade route increasingly complex for Ukraine-based Afghans. Nevertheless, within months of Crimea's annexation several Odessa-based Afghan traders had moved to Sevastopol in Crimea, either bringing their goods from Ukraine using illicit routes or exporting directly from China to Crimea via Russia. In recent years, traders based in the former Soviet Union have increasingly penetrated the markets of Western Europe: traders have migrated from the former Soviet Union to countries in the European Union and gradually established trading activities in the cities to which they have moved; others have supplied goods sourced in China to relatives who have migrated from Afghanistan to Europe (often as refugees). Indeed, traders based in the former Soviet Union are developing increasingly complex business models. A trader yet to receive identity documents in the country in which he is based, for example, might appoint his UK-based brother to an office in Yiwu thereby ensuring a steady flow of goods from China to Russia or Ukraine. Similarly, a trader based in Ukraine who has relatives in Afghanistan in need of work might arrange for someone to move to Yiwu in order to open a trading office that supplies him with the goods he requires. It goes without saying that such responsiveness to changing geopolitical contexts requires globally-oriented forms of knowledge and skill: the ability to interact with Russian officials in Crimea, for example, or the willingness to learn Chinese.

A third network that we have identified in Yiwu is made up of traders who work between China and the Gulf states, most especially Saudi Arabia but also the UAE and Oman. Most traders working in Saudi Arabia identify themselves as being Uzbek- and Turkmen-speaking people who are the descendants of migrants who came to Afghanistan from Central Asia after the Bolshevik Revolution began to affect the organisation of their societies in the 1920s. These traders – who mostly procure clothing and machine-made carpets in Yiwu – are helpfully conceptualised as forming a 'mobile community'[37]: having left Central Asia in the 1920s they lived first in Afghanistan and then Pakistan; today they regularly divide their lives between Saudi Arabia (where they own wholesale businesses) and Turkey (a country in which they own homes, carpet and clothing factories, and frequently educate their children).[38] Traders operating in the UAE and Oman also include Central Asian émigrés active in the sale of machine-made carpets, though in numerical terms merchants who identify themselves as belonging to Pashtun tribes from the eastern region of Paktika are most visible. These Pashtun traders are active in the sale of cloth, including silks and chiffons, from Yiwu and the nearby town of Keqiao to the Naif market in Dubai: from there, the cloth is distributed to a range of markets across the Gulf.[39] These traders, however, are considerably more involved in the economy of Khost than the more mobile Central Asian émigrés. Gulf-based merchants have played an active role in the property market of eastern Afghanistan, as well as the opening of various higher education institutes.

There is a third type of more complex and multimodal network that criss-cross different geographies. Traders from regions of Afghanistan that are known for having reserves of precious and semi-precious stones (such as Panjshir, Badakhshan and Ghazni) often lead highly itinerant lives taking stones mined in Afghanistan for polishing in Jaipur and for sale in cities across China. Such traders also procure stones in Bangkok and sometimes in Congo and Zambia; their travels are often facilitated by them holding passports of the countries that have become their home and that are also key nodes for their business activities (including Germany, South Korea, Japan, the United States and Hong Kong). Indeed, Marsden has spoken with several traders from Afghanistan who hold US passports and are involved in the gemstone trade between various Latin American countries (especially Peru and Mexico) and Hong Kong. Although these types of gemstones are traded by merchants of diverse nationalities from Yiwu's Futian Market District 5 (a section of the market that is devoted to the sale of goods imported to China), the city itself is not an influential node in the global gemstone trade. Nevertheless, these Afghan traders are present in Yiwu as a result of the city's relatively streamlined administrative procedures, which makes Yiwu a good place to open a trading office and apply for the relevant category of Chinese visa.

Finally, while the networks introduced above are made up either of people who would identify themselves as being Muslim in one respect or another (though of course holding very different attitudes towards Islam and what its practice entails), Afghanistan's international trading networks also include substantial communities of non-Muslims. In particular, Afghanistan's Hindu and Sikh communities are especially active in long-distance trade. Historians have demonstrated the historic importance of such groups to Afghanistan's commercial relations with both South Asia and Eurasia.[40] Since the civil war of the 1990s, however, most of Afghanistan's Hindu and Sikh families have left the country, migrating primarily to India, Russia or Europe (especially London and Hamburg). In these contexts, Afghan Hindu and Sikh traders import commodities from China (especially Yiwu) and sell these on cash (*pull-e narkh*) or on a credit (*qarz*) basis to Muslim traders from Afghanistan working in the same settings. We are often told during the course of fieldwork how the majority of Afghan businesses run by Muslims in Russia rely on traders who identify themselves as Hindu and import commodities to Moscow from China. Indeed, Hindu and Sikh traders from Afghanistan are a visible feature of life in Yiwu: they regularly hold evening parties for their guests coming from one or other of the contexts in which the community is located. Afghan Muslim traders are open about the important role that Hindu and Sikhs have played in their business activities, often saying that it would have been impossible to commence trading abroad if the country's 'Hindus' had not been willing to provide them with goods on credit.[41]

Geographically, therefore, the traders are active globally, though, as noted above, particular networks specialise in the trade in commodities between relatively well-defined regions. In terms of ethnicity and regional identity, some networks are more homogeneous and cohesive (e.g., Central Asian émigrés) than others (Yiwu–Afghanistan traders). Yet given that they operate in nodes like Yiwu where multiple networks coalesce, all the networks ultimately establish relationships with people from Afghanistan who identify with different groups than their own. Indeed, whether traders based in Yiwu from Afghanistan are working in the markets of Russia, Afghanistan or Saudi Arabia, they are often strongly encouraged by the community to attend a weekly Thursday evening social gathering (*majlis ijtimoye*) that is held in an Afghan-owned shisha parlour. During the gathering, traders share information about the conditions in the settings in which they are working, including legal and policy changes in Yiwu that affect their practices and everyday lives in the city. Far from being either the one-dimensional victims of the instability of their home country or the type of persons that are easily lured by the cosmopolitan visions of global Islamic community or a re-imagined caliphate, these traders and their networks are increasingly successful, well established and able to profit from the many different settings and countries over which they operate.

A Walking Tour through Yiwu

Yiwu has been widely represented in the media and more scholarly accounts as being the supermarket of the Arab world: not only is the mix of traders that travel to the city far more diverse than this image suggests, but so too do traders from many more parts of the world than the Middle East and Africa visit the city as commodity traders.[42] Over a period of seven months in 2016, we conducted several fieldwork exercises in order to map the trading communities that are a relatively stable and established feature of Yiwu's landscape. Surveys concerning the backgrounds of the foreign traders were conducted on a daily basis in the Five Districts of Futian Market, weekly visits were made to the Wu Ai stock market and Huanyuen Garment Market, and we also undertook a detailed spatial analysis of Chouzhou Lu – the main artery connecting the city to Futian Market. We also spent time exploring the Bingwan Night Market (there are several retail shops in the market that are frequented by foreign visitors keen to buy presents to take home or seek inspiration for new products to purchase at a wholesale level) and interviewing the owners of numerous international restaurants in the city. Finally, we also conducted participant observation with owners of foreign companies and their staff, as well as with foreign traders who had enrolled into schools that offered Chinese-language lessons tailored to the needs of business people. We were invited on occasions to accompany foreign traders to place orders in Futian and nearby factories, to receive merchandise from suppliers in warehouses, and to fill containers in Yiwu's inland port.

Let us take the reader on a brief walking tour of Yiwu in order to give a sense of the many communities present in and their distribution through space in the city. We will treat the city's main artery (Chouzhou Lu) as the basis for our tour. The neighbourhoods of Futian Second District and Changchun are located in the part of Chouzhou Lu closest to the Futian Market. These areas of five-storey apartment buildings, which include the Futian Tower, are used for both living and commercial purposes. This zone is popular amongst Russian, Iranian, Azeri, Ukrainian, Uzbek, Kazakh, Turkmen, Tajik and Afghan trading companies. While diverse, in this part of the city the main international languages of trade and sociality are Russian, multiple Turkic languages (especially Uyghur, Uzbek, Azeri, Turkmen and Kazakh), and Persian (Farsi, Dari and Tajik).[43] The area is also the site of many wholesale shops selling jewellery and beads, as well as Uyghur, Central Asian and Afghan restaurants catering for foreign visitors and, on occasion, their Chinese guests. This area is not homogeneously made up of traders from post-Soviet Central Asia and neighbouring regions; Changchun is also an attractive space for Latin American traders and companies, especially those from Colombia and Bolivia.

Further down Chouzhou Lu in the direction of the city centre the walker will come to a crossroads at which two landmarks famous amongst Yiwu's foreign traders are located: the Jimao and Jimei Towers. Numerous Afghan companies run offices in these buildings, as well as two rooms popularly called 'mosques' that are mostly used by worshippers from Afghanistan to conduct their daily prayers. On a street perpendicular to Jimao Tower lies a zone that is noticeable for a preponderance of Indian restaurants, hotels and trading companies. Between these Indian-characterised streets and Zongze Road, there are several buildings dedicated mainly to the wholesale of Christmas decorations, LED-lights, beads, supermarket trolleys, shelves and mannequins, along with the odd Nepali eatery. As the walker proceeds closer to the city centre, she or he will begin to encounter clusters of Afghan and Iranian companies – the latter mainly being run by Kurds who ship goods from Yiwu to the Iraqi sectors of Kurdistan and from there, by road, to the many commercial border cities in the Iranian provinces of Kurdistan and Azerbaijan. Unsurprisingly, the restaurants in this area of Yiwu included the now closed 'Tehran' and the unambiguously named 'Kurdistan'.

Another important intersection in Yiwu is the crossroads of Chouzhou Lu and Zongze Road. This intersection is home to a restaurant that has become a well-known geographical reference point in Yiwu: 'Ariana', an Afghan-owned eatery that, with over ten years of service, has come to be thought of by traders as being a high-end establishment, and is said to have captured a significant portion of the city's culinary market. Afghans often remark that the establishment's owner (a Farsi-speaker from northeastern Afghanistan) was clever to choose this particular location: a 'crossroads' (*chahrahi*) on the route taken by traders between the market and the city, it captures the attention of everyone in the city. Even Chinese taxi drivers unmistakably know the location of 'Ariana' – meaning that the corner where the restaurant stands is now also a popular meeting point. On the opposite side of the road, an Afghan competitor opened another restaurant to the public a couple of years back, although its cheap buffet finds Ariana and its hard-won clientele a tough act to follow. There are further Afghan establishments in this part of town: a café ('Qasr-e-Shirin', or Palace of Sweets), and 'Kabul Darbar'– an eatery popular with some Afghans but mostly with Arabs and Pakistanis.

About 10 minutes further down the street the walker will encounter the central office of the Bank of China (noticeable for the throngs of Hui foreign currency dealers standing outside): this building marks the first signs of the influence of 'the Middle East' on Yiwu's urban space. An Egyptian restaurant and a joint Turkish–Syrian venture are popular for food and shisha amongst traders from the Middle East, although Afghanistan's Central Asian émigrés also organise their *iftar* feasts here, saying they have come to appreciate Turkish food during their many visits to Istanbul. There are also retail shops owned by Syrian traders that sell clothing (especially veils, *ʿabayas* and dresses aimed at Muslim women), as well as retail shops (also owned by well-established Arab traders from the Middle East) selling electronics and lights.[44] On the corner of Chouzhou Lu and Bingwan Road, the famous 'Sultan' restaurant can be found, which offers Turkish cuisine and is frequented by traders of all nationalities. From 'Sultan' further down the street there are a string of Middle Eastern establishments, including a Syrian-owned supermarket, a Syrian butcher, as well as another Turkish restaurant. This Turkish establishment is often frequented by Russian-speaking traders as the restaurant staff speak Russian because the Turkish businessman who owns it is married to a woman from Belorussia. Nearby, there is the bar-restaurant 'Moscow' offering Russian and European cuisine as well as live music performed on occasion by a Mongolian student married to a Russian woman. At the frontiers of this Turkish–Russian area can be found an Iranian restaurant (*Shirin*): Shirin's sober and typically Iranian interior (including a small fountain and traditional raised wooden benches, or *takht*, on which diners may recline and relax while drinking tea and taking a *qailoon*) is in contrast to the nightclub below 'Empire', which is renowned for its attractive Russian female entertainers or 'party girls'. As the walker continues her or his stroll down Chouzhou Lu she or he will come across several Arab establishments and also an increasingly lively street scene: MC Café, for example, is usually full of traders from Algeria, Mauritania and Morocco, seeking good coffee and a chair on the kerb. Nearby is Bubus Café, owned by a trader from Bosnia, and next to Bubus, are two restaurants owned by Coptic Egyptians – a good escape for traders (and fieldworkers) attempting to find something to eat in the day during Ramadan.

In this zone, McDonald's is typically full of Chinese and foreign traders seeking a fast and cheap meal and a good view of the road towards the park that lies opposite and the popular Bingwan Night Market. Between the night market and the area officially called Bingwan, but popularly known as Maedha (after a famous Egyptian-owned restaurant), there are dozens of establishments owned by Arabs, including the Syrian restaurants 'Aleppo' and

'Damascus', the Kurdish-Iraqi-owned 'Shakhawan', the Chinese-owned but Iraqi established 'Erbil', and the Yemeni 'Sabah', which is especially popular amongst traders from East Africa (Ethiopia, Kenya, Somalia and Tanzania). An Afghan restaurant was also established in this area, though it was unsuccessful because, as one trader told us, everybody already has their 'own line' in this part of the city and an Afghan eatery did not fit in. In this otherwise distinctly Middle Eastern space, the Bingwan night market is a context in which Chinese shopkeepers and foreign visitors meet on a daily basis for shopping, strolling and relaxing in the evenings. The area around the night market is thus home to numerous Uyghur-run restaurants, mini-markets and stalls selling barbecued meat, as well as vendors of Chinese street food, the smell of which is a constant source of complaint by our Afghan informants. A short ride by taxi from this night market is to be found in the Wu Ai area, home to numerous trading companies owned by Arabs, as well as restaurants from the Middle East, including the Yemeni 'Shibam'. Wu Ai is one of several neighbourhoods in which foreign traders with families prefer to live.

Living the City

If the above description covers the areas running along Chouzhou Lu from Futian market to the night market, elsewhere in the city mixed and multinational forms of sociality are more pronounced. For the children of traders who run established companies in the city, there are several foreign schools that have been opened and are managed by foreigners, including the Chinese–Egyptian Modern School and the Rainbow Kids preschool near Yiwu's central mosque. The latter preschool is staffed by female teachers from Muslim backgrounds, including both foreigners, Chinese Han who have converted to Islam, as well as Uyghurs and Hui. The owner of the school has also popularised electronic books that help Muslims seeking to memorise the Qur'ān. Yiwu is indeed home to growing communities of people of Muslim background from elsewhere in China, especially Hui Chinese-speaking Muslims who migrate to the city from the provinces of Yunnan, Nagxi and Gansu, and Uyghurs from various locales across Xinjiang.[45] Yiwu's Muslims – foreigners and Chinese citizens – tend to gather on Fridays at the city's mosque (a former silk factory) that was completed in 2012, thanks to donations made by local and foreign Muslims, including one donation in the form of several tonnes of Iranian marble. It is calculated that every week 7,000 people attend the mosque.[46] Yet, in addition to this busy mosque, Yiwu also hosts several officially registered and non-registered places of worship; many of the Muslim restaurants mentioned above also house prayer rooms for Muslims. There is also a Hindu temple inside the Futian market, several Catholic churches with services in Spanish, English, Korean and Chinese, as well as a Protestant and a Coptic church – the latter being frequented by Egyptian, Syrian and Sudanese Christian merchants, as well as converted Han Chinese.

It is in the field of religious practice that the traders from Afghanistan with whom we are acquainted are most circumspect about their daily behaviour in Yiwu. Few of the traders in the city are especially public or ostentatious about their religiosity, except in terms of their having undertaken the *ḥajj* pilgrimage, a ritual that even Afghans in their thirties based in Yiwu have performed on several occasions. Indeed, traders often remarked to us that in China the local police are less concerned about Muslim foreigners if they knew they drink and attend nightclubs than if they are perceived to be particularly pious and God-fearing. During Ramadan, however, tensions between traders from Afghanistan willing to organise religious events and the local authorities who are suspicious of such activities do arise. In June 2016, for example, traders from Afghanistan owning hotels that in previous years had been used as venues for prayer gatherings, Qur'ānic recitations and *ifṭar* feasts were told by the local authorities that such gatherings could be held only in rooms especially designated for such purposes. This change in state attention was believed to have been caused by security concerns arising from the G20 meeting scheduled to be held in Hangzhou around that time.

To what extent are forms of mixing across ethnic, regional, national and regional groupings an aspect of the everyday sociality of foreign traders based in Yiwu? Islamic cosmopolitanism (or the promise of it) requires Muslims and non-Muslims from very different backgrounds to jointly participate in establishing open-ended relationships. At first glance, the spatial organisation of Yiwu reveals above all else the importance of the nation-state and the ethno-linguistically defined region as being the salient markers of the identities of the traders. As we have seen above, particular city districts have been shaped as distinctively 'post-Soviet', 'Indian', 'Arab' or 'Afghan' by the day-to-day activities of foreign traders. Importantly, however, if Yiwu appears at first sight to be organised in relationship to ethnicity or nationality, then the spaces delimited above correspond more to trans-regional borderlands than to nation-states per se. Traders from Afghanistan and Iranian Kurdistan own businesses cheek by jowl, for example; at times, Kurdish Iranians find in some Afghan traders the ideal companionship to discuss their common Sunni identity or the politics and tensions between Sunni and Shiʿī in their respective nation-states. While the Iraqi Kurdish restaurants in the 'Arab quarter' are visited by Iranian Kurds (who are often also cross-border business partners), Russian-speaking Afghans frequently gather in a Tajik restaurant to talk to their Central Asian peers and their Russian-speaking Han Chinese associates hailing from cities along the China–Russia border. Similarly, the Arab area of the city is a complex mixture of traders who are not only Arab but also from settings across East Africa. The preponderance of spaces catering to Muslims from distinct borderlands reflects, more generally, the role that such types of geopolitical spaces and their populations are playing in processes defined as collectively forming 'globalisation from below'.

But whilst ethnicity and regional identity have contributed in significant ways to the distribution of businesses and the organisation of public space in Yiwu, how do Muslims living in the city inhabit the city on a daily basis? Many of the Afghan traders with whom we have spent time, for example, confessed to preferring to spend their evening leisure time in parts of the city that were not clearly marked out by their businesses or clientele as being particularly 'Afghan'. This reflected multiple concerns on the part of traders. Traders of Afghan background visiting Yiwu from the former Soviet Union often remarked to us that their attitudes were distinct from those of their countrymen based in Afghanistan: as a result, they preferred to spend their time in parts of the city that were Russian or 'international' rather than in the cafes and restaurants run by their compatriots. Only by doing so, they admitted, could they enjoy a drink in a street-side cafe owned by an African and soak up Yiwu's distinctive atmosphere. Thus, a group of traders with whom Marsden spent several nights at shisha parlours preferred to visit establishments owned by Arabs and Iranians rather than members of the Afghan community. Other Afghan traders who have been based in Yiwu for years and spoke fluent Chinese told Ibañez-Tirado that they preferred to spend their day off at barbecues organised by their Chinese friends at which litres of beer were available, and that would usually end up at raucous KTV's karaoke bars where other Afghan visitors, or indeed, Muslim traders, would rarely venture. Further informants – often those based permanently in Yiwu rather than men visiting the city on short-time procurement sorties from the settings in which they owned businesses – also remarked that they could talk more openly to one another about their business activities in parts of the city where there were less likely to be other Afghans. In terms of the choices that traders from Afghanistan make about leisure and sociality, then, the willingness to experience spaces other than those simply designated as 'Afghan' or 'Muslim' is an important part of their modes of experiencing and inhabiting the city.

Importantly, there are a range of activities undertaken by traders in Yiwu that are premised upon establishing relationships with people from backgrounds different from their own, including those that traverse the boundary between Muslim and non-Muslim. For many of the traders, Saturday night is the evening of the week in which it is normal to relax and spend time with friends, mostly in one of the two nightclubs that are frequented by the city's foreign traders. With a distinctively Latin atmosphere, as salsa music and similar rhythms are usually played in these disco-bars, such venues are preferred sites of relaxation for the numerous women from countries such as Ethiopia, Italy, Russia, Brazil, Bolivia and Mexico who work and live in Yiwu as traders, commodity designers and company managers. On one Saturday, for example, Marsden was invited to join a group of traders from northeast Afghanistan on a trip to one of these nightclubs. The traders (including one who was referred to by his friends as Ḥaji having undertaken the pilgrimage to Mecca) told Marsden that they hoped that he would be able to use his limited Spanish to help them meet women from Colombia who also attended the nightclub. The evening did not progress according to the traders' expectations, however: the men had anticipated being able to find a table around which they could sit and survey the dance floor, yet because it was a busy evening in the club, they were forced to stand awkwardly, and to their minds demandingly, at the edge of the bar. It was collectively decided – after they had ruefully remarked to Marsden that at least he could enjoy a beer, something they were unable to do – that there was no point spending further time in the nightclub. Having bid goodbye to the traders, Marsden spent the remainder of the evening with a small group of traders from Kabul and their Chinese girlfriends.

Conclusion

The focus of this chapter has been the city of Yiwu and the nature of Afghan networks present in the city. By inserting such networks both in the context of the wider global settings and in terms of the traders' experience of space in Yiwu, we have sought to contribute to an emerging body of literature on Muslim cosmopolitanism in two ways. First, we have brought attention to the ways in which the expressions of Muslim cosmopolitanism visible in Yiwu are premised on violent histories of international conflict and interference that have led to massive displacements of the country's people, as well the bleaching out of the country's own religious diversity.[47] Secondly, it is also important to recognise, as others have,[48] that if the traders with whom we work are cosmopolitan in some aspects of their lives, then in others they reinforce and sustain collective commitment to national, regional, ideological and confessional identities, identities that are also of critical significance to their activities as traders.

Besides, the Afghan traders whose lives are presented in the chapter bring attention to forms of mobility that are very different from those associated with commonplace understandings of Afghanistan. Whereas much scholarship and popular writing on Afghanistan points to the centrality of the flight by refugees and labour migrants to the West to contemporary forms of Afghan mobility, the people with whom we work travel across a wide range of Asian and Eurasian settings, most often in connection with their activities as commodity traders and transporters. The extensive, cyclical and repetitive nature of such journeys and connections reveal the role that these traders have played in forging long-distance trading routes and establishing durable nodes for their activities. Conventional treatments of Afghanistan would no doubt link such forms of movement to one or another form of illegality, be it money laundering or heroin trafficking. We have brought attention rather to the many skills and capacities that these mobile traders bring to their work, be they in terms of the ability and willingness to speak multiple languages, engage with and respond to geopolitical transformations, establish relationships with local authorities, and enter into long-term and mutually reinforcing relationships with women of diverse ethno-national and religious backgrounds. In these respects, the everyday lives of these traders suggest the possibility of the promise of open-ended forms of cosmopolitan Muslim identity, forms of cosmopolitanism moreover that are premised on relationships with Muslims and non-Muslims.

Notes

1. This work was supported by the European Research Council (ERC) under the European Union's Horizon 2020 research and innovation programme 669 132 – TRODITIES, 'Yiwu Trust, Global Traders and Commodities in a Chinese International City'. It has also benefited from a grant from the British Academy Small Grant scheme, 'Global Traders in a Chinese International City'.
2. Marsden, Magnus, 'Crossing Eurasia: Trans-Regional Afghan Trading Networks in China and Beyond', *Central Asian Survey* 35(1) (2016): 1–15.
3. Arsan, Andrew, *Interlopers of Empire: the Lebanese Diaspora in Colonial French West Africa* (London: Hurst, 2014).
4. Marsden, Magnus, *Trading Worlds: Afghan Merchants across Modern Frontiers* (London: Hurst, 2016); Marsden, 'Crossing Eurasia'; Marsden, M. and Ibañez-Tirado, D., 'Repertoires of Family Life and the Anchoring of Afghan Trading Networks in Ukraine', *History and Anthropology* 26(2) (2015): 145–64.
5. Marsden, Magnus, 'Islamic Cosmopolitanism beyond Muslim Asia: the Case of Odessa and Yiwu's Trading Relationship', *History & Anthropology* 29(1) (2018): 121–39.
6. Bodomo, Adam, 'The African Trading Community in Guangzhou: An Emerging Bridge for Africa–China Relations', *China Quarterly* 203 (2010): 693–707; Bodomo, Adam, *Africans in China: a Socio-Cultural Study and its Implications for Africa–China Relations* (New York: Cambria Press, 2012); Pliez, Olivier, 'Following the New Silk Road between Yiwu and Cairo', in G. Mathews, G. Lins Ribeiro and C. Alba Vega (eds), *Globalization from Below: the World's Other Economy* (London: Routledge, 2012) pp. 19–35.
7. Jacob, Mark. D., *Yiwu, China: a Study of the World's Largest Commodity Market* (Paramus, NJ: Homer & Sekey, 2016).
8. Jacob, *Yiwu, China*.
9. Marsden, 'Crossing Eurasia'; Ibañez-Tirado, D., 'Hierarchies of Trade in Yiwu and Dushanbe: the Case of an Uzbek Merchant Family from Tajikistan', *History & Anthropology* (forthcoming).

10. See, for example, Haugen, H. O., 'Chinese Exports to Africa: Competition, Complementarity and Cooperation between Micro-Level Actors', *Forum for Development Studies* 38(2) (2011): 157–76; Li Zhang, 'Ethnic Congregation in a Globalizing City', *Cities* 25 (2008): 383–95; Yang Yang, 'African Traders in Guangzhou: Routes, Reasons, Profits and Dreams', in G. Mathews, G. Lins Ribeiro and C. Alba Vega (eds), *Globalization from Below: the World's Other Economy* (London: Routledge, 2012), pp. 154–70.
11. Skrviskaja, Vera, '"The Russian Merchant" Innovation in Contemporary China: Culture(s) of Mistrust, Moral Economy and Economic Success', *History & Anthropology* (forthcoming).
12. Alfaro-Velcamp, Theresa, *So Far from Allah, So Close to Mexico: Middle Eastern Immigrants in Modern Mexico* (Austin, TX: University of Texas Press, 2007).
13. See, for example, Clarence-Smith, W. G., 'Hadhrami Entrepreneurs in the Malay World, c. 1750–c.1940', in Ulrike Freitag and W. Clarence-Smith (eds), *Hadhrami Traders, Scholars and Statesmen in the Indian Ocean, 1750s–1960s* (Leiden: Brill, 1997), pp. 297–314.
14. Aslanian, Sebouh David, *From the Indian Ocean to the Mediterranean: the Global Trade Networks of Armenian Merchants from New Julfa* (Berkeley, CA: University of California Press, 2014).
15. See, for example, Marsden, Magnus, 'Actually Existing Silk Roads', *Journal of Eurasian Studies* 8(1) (2017): 22–30.
16. Markovits, Claude, *Merchants, Traders, Entrepreneurs: Indian Business in the Colonial Era* (Ranikhet: Permanent Black, 2008).
17. Cohen, Abner, 'Cultural Strategies in the Organisation of Trading Diasporas', in Clause Meillassoux (ed.), *The Development of Indigenous Trade and Markets in West Africa* (London/Oxford: International African Institute/Oxford University Press, 1971), pp. 266–84.
18. Markovits, Claude, *The Global World of Indian Merchants, 1750–1947* (Cambridge: Cambridge University Press, 2000); Falzon, Mark-Anthony, *Cosmopolitan Connections: the Sindhi Diaspora, 1860–2000* (Leiden: Brill, 2004).
19. Buggenhagen, Beth, *Muslim Families in Senegal: Money takes Care of Shame* (Bloomington, IN: Indiana University Press, 2012); Diouf, M., 'The Senegalese Murid Trade Diaspora and the Making of Vernacular Cosmopolitanism', *Public Culture* 12(3) (2000): 679–702.
20. Belguidoum, S. and Pliez, O., 'Inconspicuous Globalization Yiwu: the Creation of a Global Market Town in China', *Articulo: Journal of Urban Research*, online, 2016.

21. Cf. Amrith, Sunil, 'Tamil Diasporas Across the Bay of Bengal', *American Historical Review* 114(3) (2009): 547–72; Amrith, Sunil, *Crossing the Bay of Bengal: the Furies of Nature and the Fortunes of Migrants* (Cambridge, MA: Harvard University Press, 2013).
22. Mathews, G., Lins Ribeiro, G. and C. Alba Vega (eds), *Globalization from Below: the World's Other Economy* (London: Routledge, 2012), pp. 203–20.
23. See, for example, Buggenhagen, Beth, 'Domestic Object(ion)s: the Senegalese Murid Trade Diaspora and the Politics of Marriage Payments, Love, and State privatization', in Brad Weiss (ed.), *Producing African Futures: Ritual and Reproduction in a Neoliberal Age* (Leiden: Brill, 2005), pp. 21–53; Buggenhagen, Beth, 'Killer Bargains: Global Networks of Senegalese Muslims and the Policing of Unofficial Economies in the War on Terror', in Anne-Maria Makhulu, Beth Buggenhagen and Stephen Jackson (eds), *Hard Work, Hard Times: Global Volatility and African Subjectivities* (Berkeley, CA: University of California Press, 2010), pp. 131–49; Sahadeo, Jeff, 'The Accidental Traders: Marginalization and Opportunity from the Southern Republics to late Soviet Moscow', *Central Asian Survey* 30(3/4) (2011): 521–40; Ferguson, James, *Global Shadows: Africa in the Neoliberal World Order* (Durham, NC: Duke University Press, 2006); Ong, Aihwa, *Flexible Citizenship: the Cultural Logics of Transnationality* (Durham, NC: Duke University Press, 1999); Piot, Charles, 'Border Practices', in Anne-Maria Makhulu, Beth Buggenhagen and Stephen Jackson (eds), *Hard Work, Hard Times: Global Volatility and African Subjectivities* (Berkeley, CA: University of California Press, 2010), pp. 150–64.
24. Hart, K., 'Informal Economy', in K. Hart, J. Laville and A. D. Cattani (eds), *The Human Economy: a Citizen's Guide* (Cambridge: Polity, 2010), pp. 142–54.
25. See, for example, McAlly, Christopher, 'Sino-Capitalism: China's Re-emergence and the International Political Economy', *World Politics* 64(4) (2012): 741–76; Belguidoum and Pliez, 'Inconspicuous Globalization Yiwu'; Polese, A. and Rekhviashvili, 'Introduction: Informality and Power in the South', *Caucasus. Caucasus Survey* 5(1) (2017): 1–10.
26. For example, Ho, E., *The Graves of Tarim* (Berkeley, CA: University of California Press, 2006),
27. Freitag, Ulrike and von Oppen, Achim, '"Translocality": An Approach to Connection and Transfer in Area Studies', in Ulrike Freitag and Achim von Oppen (eds), *Translocality* (Leiden: Brill, 2010), pp. 1–24.
28. Gilroy, Paul, *After Empire: Melancholia or Convivial Culture? Multiculture or Postcolonial Melancholia?* (London: Routledge, 2004).

29. Nunan, Timothy, *Humanitarian Invasion: Global Development in Cold War Afghanistan* (Cambridge: Cambridge University Press, 2016).
30. Israel, Jonathan, 'Diasporas Jewish and non-Jewish and the World Maritime Empires', in I. B. McCabe et al. (eds), *Diaspora Entrepreneurial Networks: Four Centuries of History* (Oxford: Berg, 2005), pp. 3–26.
31. Marsden, Magnus, Ibañez-Tirado, Diana and Henig, David, 'Everyday Diplomacy: Introduction to Special Issue', *Cambridge Journal of Anthropology* 34(2) (2016): 2–22; Marsden, Magnus, 'We are Both Diplomats and Traders: Afghan Transregional Traders across the Former Soviet Union', *Cambridge Journal of Anthropology* 34(2) (2016): 59–75.
32. Cf. Alavi, Seema, *Muslim Cosmopolitanism in the Age of Empire* (Cambridge, MA: Harvard University Press, 2015).
33. Cf. Aydin. Cemil, *The Making of the Muslim World: a Global Intellectual History* (Cambridge, MA: Harvard University Press, 2017).
34. Cf. Aslanian, *From the Indian Ocean to the Mediterranean.*
35. Nunan, *Humanitarian Invasion.*
36. Marsden and Ibañez-Tirado, 'Repertoires of Family Life'.
37. Ho, E., 'Inter-Asia Concepts for Mobile Societies', *Journal of Asian Studies* 76(4) (2017): 907–28.
38. Marsden, 'Islamic Cosmopolitanism beyond Muslim Asia'.
39. Cf. Cheuk, Ka-Kin, 'Everyday Diplomacy among the Indian Traders in a Chinese Fabric Market', *Cambridge Anthropology* 35(2) (2016): 42–58.
40. Dale, S. F., *The Garden of the Eight Paradises: Bābur and the Culture of Empire in Central Asia, Afghanistan and India, 1483–1530* (Leiden: Brill, 2004); Levi, S., *Caravans: Punjabi Khatri Merchants on the Silk Road* (London: Penguin, 2016); Markovits, *The Global World of Indian Merchants.*
41. Marsden, Magnus, 'Mobile Societies and Partial Neighbourhoods: Afghanistan's Central Asian Emigres between Saudi Arabia and Yiwu', *History & Anthropology* (forthcoming).
42. Pliez, 'Following the New Silk Road between Yiwu and Cairo'.
43. Ibañez-Tirado, 'Hierarchies of Trade in Yiwu and Dushanbe'.
44. Ibañez-Tirado, 'Hierarchies of Trade in Yiwu and Dushanbe'.
45. See, for example, Erie, Matthew, *China and Islam: the Prophet, the Party, and Law* (Cambridge: Cambridge University Press, 2016).
46. Bodomo, A. and Ma, G., 'From Guangzhou to Yiwu: Emerging Facets of the African Diaspora in China', *International Journal of African Renaissance Studies: Multi-, Inter- and Transdisciplinarity* 5 (2010): 283–9.

47. Cf. Marsden, 'Mobile Societies and Partial Neighbourhoods'; Green, Nile, 'The Demographics of Dystopia: the Muslim City in Asia's Future', *History and Anthropology* 27(3) (2016): 273–95.
48. See, for example, Ho, *The Graves of Tarim*; Osella, F. and Osella, Caroline, '"I am Gulf": the Production of Cosmopolitanism in Kozhikode, Kerala, India', in K. Kresse and E. Simpson (eds), *Struggling with History: Islam and Cosmopolitanism in the Western Indian Ocean* (London: Hurst, 2007), pp. 323–56.

Notes on the Contributors

J. Lilu Chen is Visiting Scholar at the Graduate Theological Union, Center for Islamic Studies. She received her PhD in Religious Studies from Stanford University, with a dissertation titled 'Chinese Heirs to Muhammad: Writing Islamic History in Early Modern China'. The project uses family genealogies, biographies of Muhammad and epitaph collections to reveal a rich literary tradition of historical discourse among Chinese Muslims. She points to three major modes of authority present in the creation of a Sino-Islamic past: imperial, mystical and genealogical. Currently, she is working on a comparative project exploring racial authority in American Islam and American Buddhism.

R. Michael Feener is the Sultan of Oman Fellow at the Oxford Centre for Islamic Studies, and Islamic Centre Lecturer in the History Faculty at the University of Oxford. He was formerly Research Leader of the Religion and Globalisation Research Cluster at the Asia Research Institute, and Associate Professor in the Department of History at the National University of Singapore. He has published extensively in the fields of Islamic studies and southeast Asian history, as well as on post-disaster reconstruction, religion and development.

Joshua Gedacht is currently Visiting Assistant Professor in Islamic World History at Rowan University, New Jersey. Before arriving at Rowan, he worked for several years in Asia as a Postdoctoral Fellow at the Asia Research Institute, National University of Singapore, and as Assistant Professor at the Institute of Asian Studies, Universiti Brunei Darussalam. His research examines colonial era war-making, Muslim networks and the reconfiguration of religious connections extending from southeast Asia through the Indian Ocean world. He is working on a variety of articles, chapters and his book project, *Islam, Colonial Warfare, and Coercive Cosmopolitanism in Island Southeast Asia.*

Diana Ibañez-Tirado is a social anthropologist trained at SOAS, University of London. Currently, she is a postgraduate researcher in the Department of Anthropology at the University of Sussex and works on the project 'Yiwu: Trust, Global Traders and Commodities in a Chinese International City' (TRODITIES) funded by an ERC-Advanced Grant. In 2016, she was awarded the Irene Hilgers Memorial Prize for her article titled '"How Can I Be post-Soviet if I was Never Soviet?" Rethinking Categories of Time and Social Change: a Perspective from Kulob, Southern Tajikistan', published in the journal *Central Asian Survey.*

Simon C. Kemper is currently enrolled as a PhD candidate at Leiden University for the programme 'The Making of Religious Traditions in Indonesia: History and Heritage in Global Perspective (1600–1940)'. As a result of the recent contracts drawn between Leiden University and Gadjah Mada University, he conducts his PhD research at not one but two universities. Since moving to Indonesia halfway through 2014, he has combined studies of warfare, language and religion to reconsider the importance of military mobility during early modern encounters between European trade companies and Javanese realms. He thereby collected new material in Malay, Javanese and Dutch in an attempt to trace interconnected narratives on the Mataram (1675–80) and Banten (1682–3) Wars. In addition, he participated in the digitisation and content analysis of the Dutch East India Company's (VOC) archives in Jakarta (see https://sejarah-nusantara.anri.go.id/) between 2014 and 2015, and has worked as a digital archivist of early modern Dutch cartography for the Rijksmuseum since early 2017 (see www.atlasofmutualheritage.nl/en).

Bruce B. Lawrence taught at Duke for forty years until he retired in 2011 as Marcus Family Humanities Professor of Religion. He is also Professor of Islamic Studies Emeritus, specialising in pre-modern Islam, South Asian Sufism and Islamicate cosmopolitans. He is currently Adjunct Professor at the Alliance of Civilizations Institute, Istanbul. Among his nineteen books are two recent monographs: *Who is Allah?* (2015) and *The Koran in English* (2017). With Vincent J. Cornell (Emory), he is co-editing *The Wiley-Blackwell Companion to Islamic Spirituality* (forthcoming, 2019).

Amrita Malhi is a historian based in the Department of Political and Social Change at the Australian National University. Her research focuses on environmental enclosure, colonial state and boundary formation, and the politics of Holy War and the caliphate in colonial Malaya, especially the Siamese tributaries of the northern Peninsula. She has published work in the *Journal of Peasant Studies, The Muslim World* and the 2015 volume *From Anatolia to Aceh: Ottomans, Turks and Southeast Asia*, edited by Andrew Peacock and Annabel Teh Gallop. She is also Development Economics Adviser at the Australian Council for International Development (ACFID).

Magnus Marsden is Professor of Social Anthropology and Director of the Sussex Asia Centre at the University of Sussex. He is the author of *Living Islam: Muslim Religious Experience in Pakistan's North-West Frontier* (2005), *Fragments of the Afghan Frontier* (with Benjamin Hopkins, 2012) and *Trading Worlds: Afghan Merchants across Modern Frontiers* (2016). He is currently the Principal Investigator of a project funded by an ERC Advanced grant titled, 'Yiwu Trust, Global Traders and Commodities in a Chinese International City'.

Tatsuya Nakanishi is an Associate Professor in the Institute for Research in Humanities, Kyoto University, Japan. He has studied the intellectual history of Islam in China, especially focusing on how Chinese Muslims harmonised Islam with Chinese traditional thoughts and social realities. He published a Japanese monograph, *Chūka to taiwa suru isurāmu: 17–19 seiki chūgoku musurimu no sisōteki eii* (*Islām in Dialogue with Chinese Civilization: Intellectual Activities of Chinese Muslims during the 17th–19th Centuries*)

(2013), that examined the above issue by investigating Chinese, Arabic and Persian historical sources.

A. C. S. Peacock is Professor of Middle Eastern and Islamic History at the University of St Andrews. His research focuses on the medieval and early modern history of the Middle East and the Indian Ocean. Major publications include *The Great Seljuk Empire* (Edinburgh University Press, 2015), and as editor, *Islamisation: Comparative Perspectives from History* (Edinburgh University Press, 2017).

Index

CPSIA information can be obtained
at www.ICGtesting.com
Printed in the USA
BVHW061554300620
582685BV00002B/16

9 781474 435109